SHAKESPE...

Laurence Lerner has published many volumes of poetry, including *Selected Poems* (1984) and *Rembrandt's Mirror* (198...). He has also written four novels and eight books of literary criticism, of which the most recent is *The Frontiers of Literature* (198...). He was for many years Professor of English at the University of Sussex and is now Edwin Mims Professor at Vanderbilt University in Tennessee. He divides his time between America and his home in Brighton.

SHAKESPEARE'S TRAGEDIES

An Anthology of Modern Criticism

EDITED BY
LAURENCE LERNER

*

PENGUIN BOOKS

PENGUIN BOOKS

Published by the Penguin Group
Penguin Books Ltd, 27 Wrights Lane, London W8 5TZ, England
Penguin Books USA Inc., 375 Hudson Street, New York, New York 10014, USA
Penguin Books Australia Ltd, Ringwood, Victoria, Australia
Penguin Books Canada Ltd, 10 Alcorn Avenue, Toronto, Ontario, Canada M4V 3B2
Penguin Books (NZ) Ltd, 182–190 Wairau Road, Auckland 10, New Zealand

Penguin Books Ltd, Registered Offices: Harmondsworth, Middlesex, England

This selection first published 1963
Reprinted in the Penguin Shakespeare Library 1968
Reprinted in Pelican Books 1982
Reprinted in Penguin Books 1992
1 3 5 7 9 10 8 6 4 2

Printed in England by Clays Ltd, St Ives plc
Set in Monotype Fournier

CONTENTS

Acknowledgements   7

Introduction   9

ROMEO AND JULIET

1. Wordplay in *Romeo and Juliet*   M. M. Mahood   17
2. *Romeo and Juliet* in the Cycle of Shakespeare
                                           Charles Williams   33

JULIUS CAESAR

3. Guilt and Innocence in *Julius Caesar*   David Daiches   39
4. The Ides of March   Roy Fuller   42

HAMLET

5. Hamlet Psychoanalysed   Ernest Jones   47
6. Hamlet: The Prince or the Poem?   C. S. Lewis   65
7. *Hamlet:* A Study in Critical Method   A. J. A. Waldock   78
8. A Letter to John Barrymore   Bernard Shaw   86

OTHELLO

9. Iago   A. C. Bradley   93
10. The Hero and the Devil   Maud Bodkin   99
11. Honest in *Othello*   William Empson   106
12. Modes of Irony in *Othello*   R. B. Heilman   120

KING LEAR

13. On Sitting Down to Read *King Lear* Once Again
                                            John Keats   127
14. The Moral of *King Lear*   George Orwell   128
15. *King Lear* and the Comedy of the Grotesque
                                           G. Wilson Knight   130
16. The Catharsis of *King Lear*   J. Stampfer   147
17. Shakespeare's Rituals and the Opening Scene of *King Lear*
                                           William Frost   161

CONTENTS

MACBETH

18. The Atmosphere of *Macbeth*   A. C. Bradley   173
19. The Capital Difficulty of *Macbeth*
                 Sir Arthur Quiller-Couch   174
20. Shakespeare's Tragic Villain   Wayne Booth   180
21. *Macbeth* as a Dramatic Poem   L. C. Knights   191
22. Tragic Structure   R. S. Crane   208
23. The 'Language of Props' in *Macbeth*   Alan S. Downer   213
24. Macbeth and Oedipus   W. H. Auden   217

ANTONY AND CLEOPATRA

25. The Construction of *Antony and Cleopatra*
                 Harley Granville-Barker   227
26. The Style of *Antony and Cleopatra*   J. Middleton Murry   232
27. The Morality of *Antony and Cleopatra*   W. K. Wimsatt   237

CORIOLANUS

28. Coriolanus as Political Character   John Palmer   249
29. Shakespeare's Politics   Eric Bentley   258

TIMON OF ATHENS

30. Introduction to *Timon of Athens*   J. C. Maxwell   265

ON TRAGEDY:
AND ON SHAKESPEARIAN TRAGEDY

31. The Dionysiac Greek   Friedrich Nietzsche   279
32. The Implications of Tragedy   Clifford Leech   285
33. The Elizabethan View of Tragedy   Evanthius   299
34. Shakespeare and the Stoicism of Seneca   T. S. Eliot   301
35. Gold Morning, Sweet Prince   Delmore Schwartz   314

ACKNOWLEDGEMENTS

THANKS are due to the following for permission to reprint the contents of this anthology:

The Clarendon Press, Oxford, for the extract from *The English Poetic Mind*, by Charles Williams.

Methuen and Co., Ltd, for the extract from *Shakespeare's Wordplay*, by M. M. Mahood.

Oliver & Boyd, Ltd, for the extract from *Literary Essays*, by David Daiches.

André Deutsch, Ltd, for 'The Ides of March', by Roy Fuller.

Geoffrey Bles, Ltd, for 'Hamlet: the Prince or the Poem?', from *They Asked for a Paper*, by C. S. Lewis.

The Cambridge University Press for the extracts from *Hamlet: A Study in Critical Method*, by A. J. A. Waldock.

Victor Gollancz, Ltd, and W. W. Norton and Co., Inc., for the extracts from *Hamlet and Oedipus*, by Ernest Jones.

The Public Trustee and the Society of Authors for the letter to John Barrymore by Bernard Shaw.

Macmillan and Co. and the St Martin's Press, Inc., for the extracts from *Shakespearean Tragedy*, by A. C. Bradley.

Chatto and Windus, Ltd, and New Directions for the extract from *The Structure of Complex Words*, by William Empson.

The Oxford University Press for the extract from *Archetypal Patterns in Poetry*, by Maud Bodkin.

The University of Kentucky Press for the extract from *Magic in the Web*, by R. B. Heilman.

Martin Secker & Warburg, Ltd, and Harcourt Brace and World, Inc., for the extract from 'Lear, Tolstoy and the Fool', from *Shooting an Elephant*, by George Orwell.

Methuen & Co., Ltd, for the extract from *The Wheel of Fire*, by G. Wilson Knight.

The Cambridge University Press for 'The Catharsis of King Lear', by J. Stampfer.

The Hudson Review for the extract from 'Shakespeare's Rituals and the Opening Scene of King Lear', by William Frost (*Hudson Review*, Vol. X, No. 4, Winter 1957–8).

ACKNOWLEDGEMENTS

Ernest Benn, Ltd, and Holt, Rinehart and Winston, Inc., for the extracts from *Shakespeare's Workmanship*, by Sir Arthur Quiller-Couch.

Chatto and Windus, Ltd, and George W. Stewart, Inc., for the extract from *Explorations*, by L. C. Knights.

The Hudson Review for the extract from 'The Life of our Design', by Alan S. Downer (*Hudson Review*, Vol. II, No. 2, Summer 1949).

The Journal of General Education for 'Shakespeare's Tragic Villain', by Wayne Booth.

The University of Toronto Press for the extract from *The Languages of Criticism and the Structure of Poetry*, by R. S. Crane.

Random House, Inc., for the extract from *The Dyer's Hand*, by W. H. Auden.

Field Roscoe and Co., and the Princeton University Press for the extract from Harley Granville-Barker's *Preface to Antony and Cleopatra*.

The Oxford University Press for the extract from *The Problem of Style*, by J. Middleton Murry.

The University of Kentucky Press for the extract from *The Verbal Icon*, by W. K. Wimsatt.

Macmillan and Co., for the extract from *Political Characters of Shakespeare*, by John Palmer.

Horizon Press, Inc., for the extract from 'Shakespeare's Politics', in *The Dramatic Event*, by Eric Bentley.

The Cambridge University Press for the extract from J. C. Maxwell's Introduction to the New Shakespeare edition of *Timon of Athens*.

Doubleday and Co., Inc., for the extract from *The Birth of Tragedy*, by Friedrich Nietzsche, translated by Francis Golffing.

Chatto and Windus, Ltd, and the Oxford University Press of New York for the opening chapter of *Shakespeare's Tragedies*, by Clifford Leech.

Faber and Faber, Ltd, and Harcourt Brace and World, Inc., for 'Shakespeare and the Stoicism of Seneca', by T. S. Eliot.

Doubleday and Co, Inc., for 'Gold Morning, Sweet Prince', from *Summer Knowledge*, by Delmore Schwartz.

INTRODUCTION

MAINLY, this is a book about Shakespeare's tragedies; secondarily, it is about Shakespearian Tragedy. Its aim is, first of all, to illuminate a number of particular plays; and I have not chosen any essay that doesn't seem to me to do this. But the best way to understand the particular is often to measure it against the general. It is valuable to discuss the tragic pattern of *Hamlet*, the imagery of *Macbeth*, the moral scheme of *Antony and Cleopatra*; it is even more valuable to ask, when doing this, what tragedy is, what sort of functions imagery can have in poetic drama, how far literature can have a moral purpose. So I have shown an occasional preference for essays that raise general questions, or at least encourage us to raise them; and I have concluded the book with a section on Shakespearian tragedy, including some discussions of tragedy itself. The reader who is a misologist – who dislikes theory and general reasoning – can ignore this section.

I have shown other preferences too. One is stylistic; the essays are all chosen primarily for their content, but I have not ignored their manner, and have put a veto on profound obscurity or over-exquisite subtlety. I think there is more danger, at the moment, of criticism being blinded by ingenuity than of being blunted by crudity. Those critics I have included who like subtlety (Empson, Heilman, Mahood) are controlled, I believe, by a sense of purpose and a conception of the whole play. My test for clarity has been simple: I have not included anything I don't understand. That eliminated a great deal of contemporary criticism, some of it famous. I think, and hope, that the resulting selection gives a sounder view of the plays than otherwise; I am quite sure it gives more entertaining reading.

Then too I have tried to spread my selection over all the main schools of Shakespeare criticism. This means that there is a pluralistic assumption running underneath this book: the assumption that

9

there is more than one way to talk about a play, and that the kind of help the critic can give depends on the questions he begins by asking. On the whole, I believe this. But even if I did not, I might still have done the book this way. The critic who is not a pluralist – who believes, really, in asking only one kind of question – ought surely to be able to recognize other questions, and other critical schools, in order to be able to draw the boundary beyond which he loses interest in what they are saying. I hope that some readers will react to these selections by saying, Yes, they all have a point; others by choosing the critic they wish to follow, detaching him triumphantly from the others.

Is it possible to say what are the kinds of question you can put to a Shakespeare play? A rough and ready answer can be pillaged from Aristotle. In the *Poetics*, Aristotle recognizes six elements in tragedy, which he called Plot, Character, Diction, Thought, Music, and Spectacle. I do not know – and I gather that Greek scholars do not always know either – how far the Aristotelian meanings of these terms are the same as ours. Let us, then, pretend that they are quite the same. In particular, let us attach to the most puzzling term of all – thought – the meaning that would link it with *theme*: that would say that the theme of *Macbeth* was ambition, of *Othello* jealousy, of *Julius Caesar* fellow-travelling. We can drop music from the list, since that has gone over to opera; and we are then left with five main headings to represent five main schools of Shakespeare criticism, asking five main kinds of question of a play.

Those who stress character were dominant in the later nineteenth century, and their culmination was A. C. Bradley. Bradley is the most celebrated of 'character-critics'. He writes as if the play gives us only *some* of the information we want about its characters, and we can deduce more; he treats the plays as if they were novels – even (sometimes) as if they were the biographies of real people. There is no example of Bradley's method at his most typical in this book, for his most typical is not usually his best: the brilliant study of Iago which I have included is free of many of his usual assumptions. There has, of course, been a school of Bradley in the twentieth century – unsubtle, commonsensical, old fashioned. It is seen at its best in John Palmer's study of Coriolanus.

Most modern Shakespearian criticism, however, has reacted against Bradley, in one of several possible directions. One of these does not concern us here: the back-to-the-Elizabethans reaction of the scholars (Bradley never thinks much about the Elizabethan theatre). I must say now that this anthology is only concerned with criticism, and not with scholarship. To tell us about the Globe playhouse, the establishing of the true text of the plays, the life of Shakespeare, the social and intellectual climate of Elizabethan England, would require an anthology in itself – and there is one already in Penguins, Dover Wilson's excellent *Life in Shakespeare's England*. To insist on historical knowledge does not, of course, imply any particular view of what a play is: theatrical critics, 'theme-critics', and indeed any of our five schools, could approach the plays either historically or as if they had been written yesterday.

The most famous of the reactions against 'character', known as the New Criticism, is that which stresses diction – or rather, since that term now has (and indeed had in Aristotle) too limited a meaning to be very interesting, let us say language. This is the school that sees a spatial unity in a play, resulting from the imagery, rather than a temporal unity, resulting from the action. They see a Shakespeare play as an expanded metaphor, a tissue of verbal echoes, and express their contempt for Bradley's painstaking inquiries in the question 'How many children had Lady Macbeth?' I don't suppose this approach is any more valuable, in itself, than any of the others; but because it has been fashionable lately, it has absorbed the energies of many of the best modern critics, and is therefore quite well represented here. G. Wilson Knight and J. Middleton Murry are both, in their ways, founding fathers of the New Criticism, and R. B. Heilman and Alan S. Downer, in theirs, are adherents.

It tells us a lot about the New Criticism that after imagery and language it has often put theme, or thought. We must make a distinction here, between a critic like Wilson Knight, who explicitly rejects what he considers a falsely moralistic approach, and regards the spatial theme as something that exists only within the world of the play; and the *Scrutiny* group, which loves to step from imagery and rhythm to moral implication, to Shakespeare's political wisdom, to maturity and responsibility and other stern non-literary qualities, and see in them the play's ultimate value. F. R. Leavis, the leading figure of this group, would not consent to appear in this anthology; his influence can be seen in both L. C. Knights and J. C. Maxwell – perhaps, in their different ways, finer Shakespearian critics than their master. Beyond the Scrutineers lie the even more nakedly moralizing Christians, who often see Shakespeare's plays as if they were sermons, and who are not represented in this book.

Aristotle thought the most important element was the plot, which he called the soul of tragedy; and to find plot seriously discussed today we turn to the neo-Aristotelians of Chicago. They are Aristotelians in more than one sense: because they are not Platonists, and prefer to stress the distinguishing qualities of literature, rather than those which make it like other activities; and because they are not New Critics, but find that structure is the most important element in a work. Also because they believe in *genres*, and will make great efforts to distinguish comic from tragic structure, and then different kinds of tragic structure from one another. I have chosen to represent them by the work of R. S. Crane and Wayne Booth on *Macbeth*: their fondness for this play is no doubt in itself a comment on it.

As for spectacle, there is the crude way of considering it, which insults Shakespeare by assuming that each of his plays is meant to be seen only once, and that great drama is nothing more than good theatre: such critics too are not represented in this book. A more intelligent version of this approach remembers that great drama will probably *include* being good theatre, that a play can be seen *and* read, that certain effects can be perceived in the study but fully experienced only on the stage, and that the theatre is, after all, a very good place for concentrating on the words. The most famous of theatre-minded critics in our century is Granville-Barker, whose *Prefaces* always show a keen sense of stagecraft, and often a good deal more. I'd have liked to have more criticism from this school, but there are difficulties: such critics are often at their best in notices of actual productions, and these are ephemeral. One of these essays, Eric Bentley's on *Coriolanus*, was originally a notice, and I have had to trim it heavily in order to keep only what was of permanent interest. It has stood up well to this, because Bentley's interest is never merely in the immediate theatrical impact.

The reader with a taste for critical theory can, as he reads, devise other methods of classifying Shakespeare criticism, or can amuse himself by breaking mine down – not a difficult task: William Empson, for example, the most brilliant (though not the most judicious) of them all, has a touch of every school about him. But I hope nobody will spend too long on this. Mainly, this book is a guide to the plays. I expect – and hope – that many readers will take it section by section, rather than reading straight through; will get most from the sections that deal with the plays they know best; and will tackle others as they grow interested in, or happen to see, a particular play. And I would like to think that every reader, after finishing the commentaries (but not too soon after: they must settle down first) went back and read the play again – and again and again.

*

I thought at first of interspersing the sections with a commentary, but I have decided against this: not because I had nothing to say, but because it would have looked too pontifical – as if, after giving a sampling of everyone else's view, I added my own to clear matters up. When two of my critics disagree, I have left them to fight their battle in the reader's mind. I will add that they disagree, in my opinion, much less often than the hasty reader might suppose: what look like two quite different interpretations of the same play may often turn out to be perfectly compatible answers to different questions about it.

I have, however, when an essay is seriously abridged, added a note indicating the gist of what is omitted. Quite a lot of the pieces are slightly abridged, and this has always been indicated. I hereby apologize to all the authors collectively (I have already apologized to them individually) for the sad necessity of making cuts; and if any of them still feels offended, I can only beg him to tell himself that *he* would have been the person left out if I had printed everything in full.

Some readers will be interested in the chronology of changing opinions about Shakespeare, and I have therefore given the date when each piece was first published: this may not always be the date of the edition cited, which is the most easily available. I have suggested some further reading on each play, and a few general books in the last section. These reading lists are short, and therefore highly personal; but there is no shortage of longer, and more authoritative, lists, such as (in rising order of length and seriousness) those in Vol. II of *The Pelican Guide to English Literature*, in *The English Renaissance* by V. de Sola Pinto (Cresset Press), and in the *Cambridge Bibliography of English Literature* and its even more valuable *Supplement*.

Quotations are given, where possible, in the text of the New Penguin Shakespeare.

LAURENCE LERNER

1963

ROMEO AND JULIET

ONE

Wordplay in Romeo and Juliet

M. M. MAHOOD

I

ROMEO AND JULIET is one of Shakespeare's most punning plays; even a really conservative count yields a hundred and seventy-five quibbles. Critics who find this levity unseemly excuse it by murmuring, with the Bad Quarto Capulet, that 'youth's a jolly thing' even in a tragedy. Yet Shakespeare was over thirty, with a good deal of dramatic writing already to his credit, when *Romeo and Juliet* was first performed. He knew what he was about in his wordplay, which is as functional here as in any of his later tragedies. It holds together the play's imagery in a rich design and gives an outlet to the tumultuous feelings of the central characters. By its proleptic second and third meanings it serves to sharpen the play's dramatic irony. Above all, it clarifies the conflict of incompatible truths, and helps to establish their final equipoise.

Shakespeare's sonnet-prologue offers us a tale of star-crossed lovers and 'The fearful passage of their death-marked loue'.* *Death-marked* can mean 'marked out for (or by) death; foredoomed'. If, however, we take *passage* in the sense of a voyage (and this sub-meaning prompts traffic in the twelfth line) as well as a course of events, *death-marked* recalls the 'ever fixed mark' of Sonnet 116 and the sea-mark of Othello's utmost sail, and suggests the meaning 'With death as their objective'. The two meanings of *fearful* increase the line's oscillation; the meaning 'frightened' makes the lovers helpless, but they are not necessarily so if the word means 'fearsome' and so suggests that we, the audience, are awe-struck by their undertaking. These ambiguities pose the play's fundamental question at the outset: is its ending frustration or fulfilment? Does death choose the lovers or do they elect to die? This question emerges from the language of the play itself and thus differs from the conventional, superimposed problem: is *Romeo and Juliet* a

* l. 9. The prologue is not given in the Folio, but is found in the second, third and fourth Quartos.

tragedy of character or of fate? which can be answered only by a neglect or distortion of the play as a dramatic experience. To blame or excuse the lovers' impetuosity and the connivance of others is to return to Arthur Broke's disapproval of unhonest desire, stolen contracts, drunken gossips and auricular confession. Recent critics have, I believe, come nearer to defining the play's experience when they have stressed the *Liebestod* of the ending and suggested that the love of Romeo and Juliet is the tragic passion that seeks its own destruction. Certainly nearly all the elements of the *amour-passion* myth as it has been defined by Denis de Rougemont* are present in the play. The love of Romeo and Juliet is immediate, violent, and final. In the voyage imagery of the play† they abandon themselves to a rudderless course that must end in shipwreck:

> Thou desperate pilot, now at once run on
> The dashing rocks thy seasick weary bark!
> Here's to my love!   v. 3. 117

The obstacle which is a feature of the *amour-passion* legend is partly external, the family feud; but it is partly a sword of the lovers' own tempering since, unlike earlier tellers of the story, Shakespeare leaves us with no explanation of why Romeo did not put Juliet on his horse and make for Mantua. A *leitmotiv* of the play is death as Juliet's bridegroom; it first appears when Juliet sends to find Romeo's name: 'If he be married, My grave is like to be my wedding bed.' At the news of Romeo's banishment Juliet cries 'And death, not Romeo, take my maiden head', and she begs her mother, rather than compel her to marry Paris, to 'make the bridal bed In that dim monument where Tybalt lies.' The theme grows too persistent to be mere dramatic irony:

> O son the night before thy wedding day
> Hath death lain with thy wife. There she lies,
> Flower as she was, deflowered by him.
> Death is my son-in-law, Death is my heir,
> My daughter he hath wedded.   IV. 5. 35

Romeo, gazing at the supposedly dead Juliet, could well believe

---

* *L'Amour et l'Occident* (Paris, 1939).

† See Kenneth Muir and Sean O'Loughlin, *The Voyage to Illyria* (1937), p. 72.

> That unsubstantial death is amorous,
> And that the lean abhorrèd monster keeps
> Thee here in dark to be his paramour.   v. 3. 103

Most significant of all, there is Juliet's final cry:

> O happy dagger!
> This is thy sheath; there rust, and let me die.   v. 3. 169

where *happy* implies not only 'fortunate to me in being ready to my hand' but also 'successful, fortunate in itself' and so suggests a further quibble on *die*. Death has long been Romeo's rival and enjoys Juliet at the last.

In all these aspects *Romeo and Juliet* appears the classic literary statement of the *Liebestod* myth in which (we are told) we seek the satisfaction of our forbidden desires; forbidden, according to Freud, because *amour-passion* is inimical to the Race, according to de Rougemont because it is contrary to the Faith. Shakespeare's story conflicts, however, with the traditional myth at several points. Tragic love is always adulterous. Romeo and Juliet marry, and Juliet's agony of mind at the prospect of being married to Paris is in part a concern for her marriage vow: 'My husband is on earth, my faith in heaven'. Again, Romeo faces capture and death, Juliet the horror of being entombed alive, not because they want to die but because they want to live together. These woes are to serve them for sweet discourses in their time to come. In contrast to this, the wish-fulfilment of the *Liebestod* is accomplished only by the story of a suicide pact. Drama has furnished many such plots since the middle of the last century. Deirdre and her lover deliberately return to Ireland and the wrath of Conchubar because it is 'a better thing to be following on to a near death, than to be bending the head down, and dragging with the feet, and seeing one day a blight showing upon love where it is sweet and tender'. What makes Synge's play a tragedy is that the blight does show before the lovers are killed. By itself, the suicide pact offers the audience wish-fulfilment and not *katharsis*.

The real objection to reading *Romeo and Juliet* as the *Liebestod* myth in dramatic form is that it is anachronistic to align the play with pure myths like that of Orpheus and Eurydice or with the modern restatement of such myths by Anouilh and Cocteau. Shakespeare's intention in writing the play was not that of the post-Freud playwright who finds in a high tale of love and death the objective correlative to his own emotions and those of his audience. We may guess that the story afforded Shakespeare an excited pleasure of recognition because it made explicit a psychological experience; but he did not, on the strength of that recognition, decide to write a play about the death wish. Shakespeare believed his lovers to be historical people. He read and retold their adventures with the detached judgement we accord history as well as with the implicated excitement we feel for myth. The story is both near and remote; it goes on all the time in ourselves, but its events belong also to distant Verona in the dog days when the mad blood is stirred to passion and violence. The resultant friction between history and myth, between the story and the fable, kindles the play into great drama. When we explore the language of *Romeo and Juliet* we find that both its wordplay and its imagery abound in those concepts of love as a war, a religion, a malady, which de Rougemont has suggested as the essence of *amour-passion*. If the play were pure myth, the fictionalizing of a psychological event, all these elements would combine in a single statement of our desire for a tragic love. But because the play is also an exciting story about people whose objective existence we accept during the two hours' traffic of the stage, these images and quibbles are dramatically 'placed'; to ascertain Shakespeare's intentions in using them we need to see which characters are made to speak them and how they are distributed over the course of the action.

2

Act I begins with some heavy-witted punning from Sampson and Gregory – a kind of verbal tuning-up which quickens our ear for the great music to come. The jests soon broaden. This is one of Shakespeare's most bawdy plays, but the bawdy has always a dramatic function. Here its purpose is to make explicit, at the beginning of this love tragedy, one possible relationship between man and woman: a brutal male dominance expressed in sadistic quibbles. After the brawl has been quelled, the mood of the scene alters 'like a change from woodwind, brass and tympani to an andante on the strings'* in Benvolio's tale of Romeo's melancholia; and Romeo himself appears and expresses, in the numbers that Petrarch flowed in, the contrary relationship of the sexes: man's courtly subjection to women's tyranny. Rosaline is a saint, and by his quibbles upon theological terms Romeo shows himself a devotee of the Religion of Love:

> She is too fair, too wise, wisely too fair,
> To merit bliss by making me despair.   I. I. 221

Love is a sickness as well as a cult, and Romeo twists Benvolio's request to tell in sadness (that is, seriously) whom he loves, to an expression of *amour-maladie*:

> Bid a sick man in sadness make his will.
> Ah, word ill urged to one that is so ill!   I. I. 202

It is characteristic of this love learnt by rote from the sonnet writers that Romeo should combine images and puns which suggest this slave-like devotion to his mistress with others that imply a masterful attack on her chastity. Love is a man of war in such phrases as 'th' incounter of assailing eyes' which, added to the aggressive wordplay of Sampson and Gregory and to the paradox of 'O brawling love, O loving hate', reinforce the theme of ambivalence, the *odi-et-amo* duality of passion.

All the Petrarchan and anti-Petrarchan conventions are thus presented to us in this first scene: love as malady, as worship, as war, as conquest. They are presented, however, with an exaggeration that suggests Romeo is already aware of his own absurdity and is 'posing at posing'. 'Where shall we dine?' is a most unlover-like question which gives the show away; and Benvolio's use of 'in sadnesse' implies that he knows Romeo's infatuation to be nine parts show. Romeo is in fact ready to be weaned from Rosaline, and the scene ends with a proleptic pun that threatens the overthrow of this textbook language of love. 'Examine other beauties' Benvolio urges, but for Romeo, 'Tis the way to call hers (exquisite) in question more.' By *question* he means, with a play upon the etymology of *exquisite*, 'consideration and conversation'; but we

---

* Harley Granville-Barker, *Prefaces to Shakespeare, Second Series* (1930), p. 6.

guess, if we do not know, that Rosaline's charms will be called into question in another sense when set beside the beauty of Juliet.

Love in Verona may be a cult, a quest, or a madness. Marriage is a business arrangement. Old Capulet's insistence to Paris, in the next scene, that Juliet must make her own choice, is belied by later events. Juliet is an heiress, and her father does not intend to enrich any but a husband of his own choosing:

> Earth hath swallowed all my hopes but she;
> She is the hopeful Lady of my earth.   I. 2. 14

This quibbling distinction between *earth* as the grave and *earth* as lands (as Steevens points out, *fille de terre* means an heiress) is confounded when Juliet's hopes of happiness end in the Capulets' tomb. We recall the dramatic irony of this pun when Old Capulet speaks his last, moving quibble:

> O brother Montague, give me thy hand.
> This is my daughter's jointure, for no more
> Can I demand.   v. 3. 296

The ball scene at Capulet's house is prologued by a revealing punning-match between Romeo and Mercutio. Romeo's lumbering puns are the wordplay of courtly love: the other masquers have nimble soles, he has a soul of lead: he is too bound to earth to bound, too sore from Cupid's darts to soar in the dance. Mercutio's levity, on the other hand, is heightened by his bawdy quibbles. Mercutio appears in early versions of the tale as what is significantly known as a ladykiller, and his dramatic purpose at this moment of the play is to oppose a cynical and aggressive idea of sex to Romeo's love-idolatry and so sharpen the contrast already made in the opening scene. Yet just as Romeo's touch of self-parody then showed him to be ready for a more adult love, so Mercutio's Queen Mab speech implies that his cynicism does not express the whole of his temperament. The falsity of both cynicism and idolatry, already felt to be inadequate by those who hold these concepts, is to be exposed by the love between Romeo and Juliet. Like Chaucer two centuries previously, Shakespeare weighed the ideas of the masterful man and the tyrannical mistress and wisely concluded that 'Love wol nat be constreyned by maistrie'.

For the ball scene, Shakespeare deploys his resources of stage-craft and poetry in a passage of brilliant dramatic counterpoint. Our attention is divided, during the dance, between the reminis-cences of the two old Capulets (sketches for Silence and Shallow) and the rapt figure of Romeo who is watching Juliet. Nothing is lost by this, since the talk of the two pantaloons is mere inanity. We are only aware that it has to do with the passage of years too uneventful to be numbered, so that twenty-five is confused with thirty; simultaneously we share with Romeo a timeless minute that cannot be reckoned by the clock. Yet the old men's presence is a threat as well as a dramatic contrast. They have masqued and loved in their day, but ' 'tis gone, 'tis gone, 'tis gone'.

Romeo's first appraisal of Juliet's beauty is rich not only in its unforgettable images but also in the subtlety of its wordplay. Hers is a 'Beauty too rich for use, for earth too dear!' When we recall that *use* means 'employment', 'interest', and 'wear and tear', that *earth* means both 'mortal life' and 'the grave', that *dear* can be either 'cherished' or 'costly' and that there is possibly a play upon *beauty* and *booty* (as there is in *I Henry IV* I. 2. 28), the line's range of meanings becomes very wide indeed. Over and above the contrast between her family's valuation of her as sound stock in the marriage market and Romeo's estimate that she is beyond all price, the words contain a self-contradictory dramatic irony. Juliet's beauty is too rich for use in the sense that it will be laid in the tomb after a brief enjoyment; but for that very reason it will never be faded and worn. And if she is *not* too dear for earth since Romeo's love is powerless to keep her out of the tomb, it is true that she is too rare a creature for mortal life. Not all these meanings are consciously present to the audience, but beneath the conscious level they connect with later images and quibbles and are thus brought into play before the tragedy is over.

The counterpoint of the scene is sustained as Romeo moves towards his new love against the discordant hate and rage of her cousin. Tybalt rushes from the room, threatening to convert seem-ing sweet to bitter gall, at the moment Romeo touches Juliet's hand. The lovers meet and salute each other in a sonnet full of conceits and quibbles on the Religion of Love – 'palm to palm is holy palmers' kiss'; 'grant thou, lest faith turn to despair'; 'Saints

23

do not move' – for the place is public and they must disguise their feelings beneath a social persiflage. The real strength of those feelings erupts in Romeo's pun – 'O dear account!' – and in Juliet's paradox – 'My only love, sprung from my only hate' – when each learns the other's identity, and the elements of youth and experience, love and hate, which have been kept apart throughout the scene, are abruptly juxtaposed. Then the torches are extinguished and the scene ends with a phrase of exquisite irony, when the Nurse speaks to Juliet as to a tired child after a party: 'Come, lets away; the strangers all are gone.' Romeo is no longer a stranger and Juliet no longer a child.

A quibbling sonnet on love between enemies and some of Mercutio's ribald jests separate this scene from that in Capulet's orchard. It is as if we must be reminded of the social and sexual strife before we hear Romeo and Juliet declare the perfect harmony of their feelings for each other. At first Romeo seems still to speak the language of idolatry, but the 'winged messenger of heaven' belongs to a different order of imagination from the faded conceits of his devotion to Rosaline. The worn commonplaces of courtship are swept aside by Juliet's frankness. One of the few quibbles in the scene is on *frank* in the meanings of 'generous' and 'candid', 'open', and it introduces Juliet's boldest and most beautiful avowal of her feelings:

ROMEO: O, wilt thou leave me so unsatisfied?
JULIET: What satisfaction canst thou have to-night?
ROMEO: Th'exchange of thy love's faithful vow for mine.
JULIET: I gave thee mine before thou didst request it.
        And yet I would it were to give again.
ROMEO: Wouldst thou withdraw it? For what purpose, love?
JULIET: But to be frank and give it thee again.
        And yet I wish but for the thing I have.
        My bounty is as boundless as the sea,
        My love as deep; the more I give to thee,
        The more I have, for both are infinite.   II. 2. 125

Thus the distribution of wordplay upon the concepts of love-war, love-idolatry, love-sickness, serves to show that the feelings of Romeo and Juliet for each other are something quite different from the *amour-passion* in which de Rougemont finds all these disorders. For Romeo doting upon Rosaline, love was a malady and a religion; for Mercutio it is sheer lunacy ('a great naturall that runs lolling up and downe') or a brutal conquest with no quarter given. All these notions are incomplete and immature compared to the reality. When Romeo meets Mercutio the next morning a second quibbling-match ensues in which the bawdy expressive of love-war and love-madness is all Mercutio's. Romeo's puns, if wild, are gay and spontaneous in comparison with his laboured conceits on the previous evening. Then, as he explained to Benvolio, he was not himself, not Romeo. Now Mercutio cries: 'Now art thou sociable, now art thou Romeo'. In fact Romeo and Juliet have experienced a self-discovery. Like Donne's happy lovers, they 'possess one world, each hath one and is one'; a world poles apart from the Nirvana quested by romantic love. The play is a tragedy, not because the love of Romeo for Juliet is in its nature tragic, but because the ending achieves the equilibrium of great tragedy. The final victory of time and society over the lovers is counterpoised by the knowledge that it is, in a sense, *their* victory; a victory not only over time and society which would have made them old and worldly in the end (whereas their deaths heal the social wound), but over the most insidious enemy of love, the inner hostility that 'builds a Hell in Heaven's despite' and which threatens in the broad jests of Mercutio. For we believe in the uniqueness of Romeo's and Juliet's experience at the same time as we know it to be, like other sublunary things, neither perfect nor permanent. If our distress and satisfaction are caught up in the fine balance of great tragedy at the end of the play, it is because, throughout, the wordplay and imagery, the conduct of the action and the grouping of characters contribute to that balance. The lovers' confidence is both heightened and menaced by a worldly wisdom, cynicism and resignation which, for the reason that candleholders see more of the game, we are not able to repudiate as easily as they can do.

3

The play's central paradox of love's strength and fragility is most clearly expressed in the short marriage scene (II. 6). On the one hand there is Romeo's triumphant boast:

> come what sorrow can,
> It cannot countervail the exchange of joy
> That one short minute gives me in her sight.
> Do thou but close our hands with holy words
> Then love-devouring death do what he dare –
> It is enough I may but call her mine.   l. 3

On the other hand there are the forebodings of Friar Laurence:

> These violent delights have violent ends
> And in their triumph die, like fire and powder,
> Which, as they kiss, consume.   l. 9

where *consume* means both 'reach a consummation' (*N.E.D.* v.²) and 'burn away, be destroyed'. These conflicting themes of satisfaction and frustration coalesce in the Friar's words on Juliet's entry:

> Here comes the lady. O, so light a foot
> Will ne'er wear out the everlasting flint.   l. 16

An ambiguity of pronunciation between 'near' and 'ne'er' and another of meaning in *wear out** enable us to distinguish four possible readings here before, with cormorant delight, we swallow the lot. Juliet's foot is so light that

> (i) it will never wear away the everlasting flint;
> (ii) it will never last it out;
> (iii) it will nearly outlast it;
> (iv) it will nearly wear it away.

The first of these is the obvious meaning, platitudinously suited to the speaker. The second anticipates our fear that the lovers are too beset with enemies on the hard road of life to be able to last the course, whereas the third contradicts this by saying that Juliet's love and beauty, because time will not have the chance to wear them away, will last in their fame nearly as long as the rocks of earth. And this contradiction is heightened by (iv) in which *light*

---

* As in the shoe polish advertisement: 'They're well-worn but they've worn well.' For discussion of the *Romeo and Juliet* passage see the correspondence in the *T.L.S.* for 3, 17, and 24 April and 1 May 1943.

has a suggestion of Juliet's luminous beauty,* and the flint is that of a flintlock; so that the line is connected with the sequence of paradoxical light images running through the play. Love is spoken of as a sudden spark or a flash of lightning. Juliet's forebodings in the balcony scene –

> I have no joy of this contract to-night.
> It is too rash, too unadvised, too sudden;
> Too like the lightning, which doth cease to be
> Ere one can say 'It lightens'.   II. 2. 117

– are deepened here by the friar's talk of fire and powder and again in the next act by his reproaches to Romeo:

> Thy wit, that ornament to shape and love,
> Misshapen in the conduct of them both
> Like powder in a skilless soldier's flask,
> Is set afire by thine own ignorance.   III. 3. 130

In sum, love is as easily extinguishable as it appears to Lysander in *A Midsummer Night's Dream*:

> Brief as the lightning in the collied night,
> That in a spleen, unfolds both heaven and earth,
> And ere a man hath power to say 'Behold!'
> The jaws of darkness do devour it up:
> So quick bright things come to confusion.   I. I. 145

But alongside the images of sparks, torches, lightning, are others which associate Romeo and Juliet with the unquenchable heavenly lights. Mercutio's 'We waste our lights in vain, light lights by day' is ironically apposite to Romeo's love of Rosaline, who is a mere candle before the sun that breaks from Juliet's window. Two passages which have been slighted as conceits are an essential part of this theme:

> Two of the fairest stars in all the heaven,
> Having some business, do† entreat her eyes

---

* There are previous puns on *light*:
   Away from light steals home my heavy son (I. I. 137); Being but
   heavy, I will bear the light (I. 4. 12); And not impute this yielding to
   light love, Which the dark night hath so discovered (II. 21.105–6).
† For the Second Quarto's *to*.

To twinkle in their spheres till they return.
What if her eyes were there, they in her head?
The brightness of her cheek would shame those stars
As daylight doth a lamp; her eyes in heaven,
Would through the airy region stream so bright
That birds would sing, and think it were not night. II. 2. 15

Give me my Romeo. And, when he shall die,
Take him and cut him out in little stars,
And he will make the face of heaven so fine
That all the world will be in love with night
And pay no worship to the garish sun.   III. 2. 21

Romeo and Juliet stellify each other; the love which appears to
be quenched as easily as a spark is extinguished is, in fact, made as
permanent as the sun and stars when it is set out of the range of
time.

The same paradox is sustained by the flower images which are
closely associated with those of light. The 'gather the rose' theme
was of course inevitable in a love tragedy of the High Renaissance.
Shakespeare's rose imagery, however, is more than rhetorical,
and serves to stress the central themes of the play.* The rose was
dramatically appropriate as a love symbol because it was so often a
prey to the invisible worm: 'Loathsome canker lives in sweetest
bud.' Romeo is devoured by his infatuation for Rosaline 'as is the
bud bit with an envious worm' and the friar, gathering herbs,
moralizes over the adulteration of the good in a life by its evil until
'the canker death eats up that plant'. Romeo and Juliet are spared
this. Death lies on Juliet just as its earlier semblance had done.

like an untimely frost
Upon the sweetest flower of all the field.   IV. 5. 28

This early frost forestalls the heat of the sun as well as the blight
in the bud, since a further fitness of the image consists in the speed
with which both roses and 'fresh female buds'† bloom and wither

* As the author of *II Henry VI*, Shakespeare must almost unconsciously
have connected rose images with the rivalry of two great houses. For the light-
flowers cluster see I. 1. 134–40 and 151–3; I. 2. 24–30; II. 2. 117–22.

† I borrow the phrase from the Bad Quarto. The accepted texts have 'fresh
fennell buds'.

in the south. Although Lady Capulet seems never to have been young she tells Juliet

> I was your mother much upon these years
> That you are now a maid.   I. 3. 73

and the cruelty of Verona's summer is implicit in Old Capulet's words:

> Let two more summers wither in their pride
> Ere we may think her ripe to be a bride.   I. 2. 10

The marriage scene, after its strong statement of love as the victor-victim of time, closes with a quibbling passage already discussed in which Romeo and Juliet defy time's most powerful allies. Romeo, in an image of music, challenges the notion that passion is discordant by nature, Juliet rejects the prudence of social considerations in her declaration of love's richness – 'I cannot sum up sum of half my wealth.' This last image is a foretaste of *Antony and Cleopatra*, and it would be interesting to compare the success of love's three enemies in Shakespeare's three double-titled tragedies. In *Troilus and Cressida* they win hands down. Society, in the shape of the Trojan War, again compels secrecy and again separates the lovers; the inner corruption of love itself makes Cressida unfaithful; and the burden of the play is that 'Love, friendship, charity, are subjects all To envious and calumniating time'. By contrast, *Antony and Cleopatra* is a clear victory for the lovers. Society, seen as the pomp of Rome, is a world well lost; the dismal drunken party we witness on Pompey's barge contrasts poorly with the revels of Antony and Cleopatra – which are left to our imagination. The lovers are old and wise enough to be reconciled to the ambivalence of their feelings, implicit in the play's imagery. Finally, time cannot harm them when they have eternity in their lips and eyes; at the end of the play Cleopatra is again for Cydnus to meet Mark Antony.

In *Romeo and Juliet* love's enemies have a Pyrrhic victory which begins with the slaying of Mercutio at the beginning of Act III. Like many of Shakespeare's characters, Mercutio dies with a quibble that asserts his vitality in the teeth of death. He jests as long as he has breath; only if we ask for him *tomorrow* shall we find him a grave man. But it is a grim joke, to accompany a dying curse. The Elizabethans, who believed in the power of curses, would have seen in the play's subsequent events the working out of Mercutio's cynical knowledge that love is inseparably commingled with hate in human affairs. Romeo kills Tybalt, the cousin whose name he now tenders as dearly as his own. Juliet responds to the news with an outburst – 'O serpent heart, hid with a flow'ring face! . . .' which, by recalling the loving hate of Romeo's infatuation with Rosaline, threatens the harmony and permanence of the love between Romeo and Juliet. She recovers her balance, but we have felt the tremor and know that even these lovers cannot sustain many such shocks.

Some of the most notorious puns in Shakespeare occur in this scene between Juliet and her nurse, when the nurse's confusion misleads Juliet into thinking Romeo has killed himself:

> Hath Romeo slain himself? say thou but 'Ay',
> And that bare vowel 'I' shall poison more
> Then the death-darting* eye of cockatrice.
> I am not I, if there be such an 'I'
> Or those eyes shut,* that makes thee answer 'Ay'.
> If he be slain, say 'Ay', or if not, 'no'.　　　III. 2. 45–51

Excuses might be made for this. It achieves a remarkable sound-effect by setting Juliet's high-pitched keening of 'I' against the Nurse's moans of 'O Romeo, Romeo'. It also sustains the eye imagery of Juliet's great speech at the opening of this scene: the runaways' eyes, the blindness of love, Juliet hooded like a hawk, Romeo as the eye of heaven. But excuses are scarcely needed since this is one of Shakespeare's first attempts to reveal a profound disturbance of mind by the use of quibbles.† Romeo's puns in the next scene at Friar Laurence's cell are of the same kind: flies may kiss Juliet, but he must fly from her; the friar, though a friend *professed*, will offer him no sudden mean of death, though ne'er so mean; he longs to know what his concealed lady says to their cancelled love. This is technically crude, and perhaps we do well to

---

* For the Second Quarto's *arting* and *shot*.

† He had already done so in *Two Gentlemen of Verona* but the device is less startling in a comedy.

omit it in modern productions; but it represents a psychological discovery that Shakespeare was to put to masterly use in later plays. Against this feverish language of Romeo's, Shakespeare sets the friar's sober knowledge that lovers have suffered and survived these calamities since the beginning of time. For the friar, 'the world is broad and wide', for Romeo, 'there is no world without Verona wall'. When the friar tries to dispute with him of his 'estate', the generalized, prayer-bookish word suggests that Romeo's distress is the common human lot, and we believe as much even while we join with Romeo in his protest: 'Thou canst not speak of that thou dost not feel.' Tragedy continually restates the paradox that 'all cases are unique and very similar to others'.

The lovers' parting at dawn sustains this contradiction. Lovers' hours may be full eternity, but the sun must still rise. Their happiness has placed them out of the reach of fate; but from now on, an accelerating series of misfortunes is to confound their triumph in disaster without making it any less of a triumph. With Lady Capulet's arrival to announce the match with Paris, love's enemies begin to close in. Juliet meets her mother with equivocations which suggest that Romeo's 'snowy Dove' has grown wise as serpents since the story began, and which prepare us for her resolution in feigning death to remain loyal to Romeo:

> Indeed I never shall be satisfied
> With Romeo till I behold him – dead –
> Is my poor heart so for a kinsman vexed.   III. 5. 94

This is a triple ambiguity, with one meaning for Juliet, another for her mother, and a third for us, the audience: Juliet will never in fact see Romeo again until she wakes and finds him dead beside her.

A pun which has escaped most editors is made by Paris at the beginning of Act IV. He tells the friar he has talked little of love with Juliet because 'Venus smiles not in a house of tears'. Here *house of tears* means, beside the bereaved Capulet household, an inauspicious section of the heavens – perhaps the eighth house or 'house of death'. Spenser's line 'When oblique Saturne sate in the house of agonyes'* shows that the image was familiar to the Elizabethans, and here it adds its weight to the lovers' yoke of

---

* *The Faerie Queen*, II. 9. 1. 52

inauspicious stars. But this is one of very few quibbles in the last two acts. The wordplay which, in the first part of the play, served to point up the meaning of the action is no longer required. What quibbles there are in the final scenes have, however, extraordinary force. Those spoken by Romeo after he has drunk the poison re-affirm the paradox of the play's experience at its most dramatic moment:

> O *true* apothecary!
> Thy drugs are *quick*. Thus with a kiss I die.   v. 3. 119

Like the friar's herbs, the apothecary's poison both heals and destroys. He is *true* not only because he has spoken the truth to Romeo in describing the poison's potency, but because he has been true to his calling in finding the salve for Romeo's ills. His drugs are not only speedy, but also *quick* in the sense of 'life-giving'. Romeo and Juliet 'cease to die, by dying'.

It is the prerogative of poetry to give effect and value to incompatible meanings. In *Romeo and Juliet*, several poetic means contribute to this end: the paradox, the recurrent image, the juxtaposition of old and young in such a way that we are both absorbed by and aloof from the lovers' feelings, and the sparkling wordplay. By such means Shakespeare ensures that our final emotion is neither the satisfaction we should feel in the lovers' death if the play were a simple expression of the *Liebestod* theme, nor the dismay of seeing two lives thwarted and destroyed by vicious fates, but a tragic equilibrium which includes and transcends both these feelings.

from *Shakespeare's Wordplay*, 1957

TWO

Romeo and Juliet *in the Cycle of Shakespeare*

CHARLES WILLIAMS

The aim of Charles Williams's long essay, 'The Cycle of Shakespeare', is 'to consider the changes in Shakespeare's way of dealing with things in his poetry'. In his early plays (*Love's Labour's Lost, Romeo and Juliet*), his verse 'indulges itself with a romantic idea, and with romantic laughter at the romantic idea'; but there is in them the shadow of a coming change, a seriousness that is mooted in Berowne's line, 'worthies away, the scene begins to cloud'. Williams then turns to examine this 'cloud' in a number of plays, beginning with *Romeo and Juliet*.

IN *Romeo* its name is accident; in *Richard II*, Bolingbroke; in the *Dream*, Puck or Oberon or, perhaps even more exactly, 'a little western flower'. It cannot be called Fate, but it is something incalculable and sometimes destructive. It is not enough to make the poetry seriously attend to it; or rather – at least in the two romantic plays – it only offers poetry an opportunity of dancing to new measures, of luxuriating in grief, or turning fairies into charming copies of men and women.

Yet poetry is still in the stage that Wordsworth described when he spoke of 'unknown modes of being'. Romeo's great speech is precisely that. Shakespeare is thoroughly enjoying himself in luxurious grief. There is no analysis of many emotions; it is all magniloquence and brave rhetoric of sorrow. We know nothing more about Romeo at the end than at the beginning, nor do we want. It is perfect – for Romeo. With it may be compared the chorus that laments in the Capulets' house over Juliet; in the midst of which Shakespeare does not in the least mind having his little bit of fun with the Nurse – 'Death is my son-in-law, Death is my heir', says Capulet, and the Nurse almost parodies him, and then Paris elegantly paraphrases her, and then Capulet comes back. It is, no doubt, partly the fashion of speech and behaviour of the time. Capulet might, in Elizabethan London, have said just that: 'Death

is my son-in-law, Death is my heir'. But Shakespeare did not risk
having any one like the Nurse about when he came to Constance –

> Grief fills the room up of my absent child,
> Lies in his bed, walks up and down with me,
> Puts on his pretty looks, repeats his words,
> Remembers me of all his gracious parts,
> Stuffs out his vacant garments with his form.

This is the banishment of Wordsworth's widow: the coming of 'a
grave unto a soul'. Much more like it in *Romeo* is Mercutio's dying
epigram, more incidental than Romeo's but more directly effective
– 'No, 'tis not so deep as a well, nor so wide as a church door; but
'tis enough, 'twill serve.' It is a sharper prophecy of the realism
that was to come than 'insubstantial death is amorous'. Or rather
the two speeches are two sides of a single thing; the greater poetry
was peeping out here and there through chinks and crevices, lines
and phrases. When it fully emerged all the irony and truth of
''twill serve' were found to be one with 'the palace of dim night'.
Romeo's speech and state of being is 'a palace of dim night', a
palace afterwards measured by phrases and meanings as exact as
'deep as a well ... wide as a church door'.

But this is an appearance of material tragedy; there exists also in
the play – I think the first – appearance of spiritual evil, in the unexpected and sudden apostasy of the Nurse, who has her moment
and becomes a premonition of horror. Juliet has defied her father
and mother, refusing to marry Paris, in a strenuous devotion to
romantic love. When they go, she turns to the Nurse with an
exquisite phrase –

> What say'st thou? Hast thou not a word of joy?
> Some comfort, Nurse.   III. 5. 212

The 'word of joy' which the Nurse offers is advice to marry Paris –
'Romeo's a dishclout to him', and

> is dead – or 'twere as good he were
> As living here and you no use of him.   III. 5. 225

'The use of him' that Juliet still has, the intense imagination and
sense of him that fills her, is understood at once, not merely now to

be, but through all the play to have been, entirely beyond the Nurse's apprehension. Her good humour, her harmless sensuality, is understood at once to be, in her case, a greedy and acquiescent sensuality – the enemy, not the ally, of 'true love's passion'. Love is to her but a use of him, a convenience, a pleasure. It is with the indignation of poetry itself that Juliet breathes after her (her back, as she hobbles away, turned on that high imagination which Juliet's love possesses), breathes after the denial of poetry itself –

> Ancient damnation! O most wicked fiend!   III. 5. 236

It is not merely that the Nurse is a realist; Falstaff is a realist. But if Falstaff had ever wanted to give similar advice, he would have done it by defeating imagination by imagination; he would have cast out one spirit by another. The Nurse is thinking of casting out spirit by flesh.

from *The English Poetic Mind* (1932), Chapter III, section 1

Suggestions for Further Reading

H. GRANVILLE-BARKER: *Prefaces to Shakespeare II*. Like all Granville-Barker's criticism, this is primarily the work of a man of the theatre, aware of Shakespeare as a practising craftsman.

E. C. PETTET: 'The Imagery of *Romeo and Juliet*' (in *English*, 1950). 'Shakespeare uses the poetry of the play to reinforce its themes and motives.' These are, in particular, Fate and the conflict between Eros and death.

The same author has another discussion of the play in his *Shakespeare and the Romance Tradition*, in which he asks how far Friar Lawrence is intended as a chorus, and whether we are meant to share his insistence on the value of prudence and restraint.

MARK VAN DOREN: '*Romeo and Juliet*' (in *Shakespeare*). '*Romeo and Juliet* is still a youthful play; its author, no less than its hero and heroine, is furiously literary.'

JULIUS CAESAR

THREE

Guilt and Innocence in Julius Caesar

DAVID DAICHES

LET me begin my inquiry by asking: What is guilt? If we assume that there are forces of good and of evil both at work in the world, then we might say that the guilty man is one who cooperates with the forces of evil to increase evil's effectiveness in human affairs. Innocence is on the side of the good, guilt on the side of evil. Or so it would be pleasant to believe. A closer look at life convinces us that innocence often achieves evil. If Brutus had been a less simply virtuous man, he would not have helped to kill one of his best friends and brought tyranny to Rome (the opposite of what he intended). If Othello had been less innocent, he would not have trusted Iago and so he would not have been brought to murder his wife. If Hamlet had been less of a sensitive idealist, he would not have destroyed his own house as well as the house of Polonius. A more worldly Brutus, a less morally sensitive Hamlet, a tougher and more cunning Othello, would have done less harm in the world. The first tragic problem faced by Shakespeare in his maturity concerns the ambiguity of innocence.

This problem goes far deeper than the relation between private and public virtue, which is in some degree the theme of *Julius Caesar*. It includes, among other problems, that of the relation between innocence and virtue, or at least between innocence of character and effectiveness of moral action. It is an old dilemma. Milton was to treat it, in his own way, in *Paradise Lost*, where 'our credulous mother, Eve' allowed herself to be fooled by Satan into tasting of the forbidden tree. If Satan, in the form of the serpent, had been telling the truth, then Eve would have done right to believe him and to eat of the fatal fruit. Eve's real fault was lack of sophistication; she was unsuspicious of what the serpent told her; she was, to use the American slang term, a 'sucker' and swallowed his story. But is it morally wrong to be a sucker – as Eve was with respect to the serpent, as Othello was with respect to Iago, as

Brutus was with respect to such political sophisticates as Antony, as Hamlet was, we might almost say, with respect to life?

Innocence plays into the hands of evil; only the tarnished and sophisticated mind can achieve that approximate good which alone lies within human reach. Is this one of the themes of Shakespearian tragedy? Perhaps; but before we conclude that it is we must inquire a little more closely. The case of Brutus is that of the liberal intellectual in a world of *Realpolitik* – a familiar enough case in the modern world. Cassius is the co-hero of the play, and, skilled politician though he is, with little scruple in playing on Brutus's finer feelings, he admires Brutus and cannot help allowing Brutus to achieve moral ascendancy over him, once the murder of Caesar is accomplished. The coarser nature is dominated by the finer, to the destruction of both of them and of the ideal to which they had sacrificed everything. In the quarrel scene it is Cassius who first gives way, and it is under the influence of this moral domination by Brutus that, against his better judgement, Cassius allows Brutus to have his way in the ill-advised plan of seeking immediate battle at Philippi. Nowhere is the Epicurean Cassius more like the Stoic Brutus than when he commits suicide because he is ashamed of having lived 'so long, to see my best friend ta'en before my face'. And that suicide, rather than military defeat, seals the doom of the republican cause. But Cassius is not as unlike Brutus as he thinks he is. Though he is the shrewder and the more practical, he is basically an idealist too, an intellectual, whom Caesar had come to suspect because 'he thinks too much'. If he appears as a cunning man of action beside Brutus, he is almost equally a babe in the wood when seen beside Antony, the man without innocence, the man who knows how to unite his personal affections with his political ambitions. (Though Shakespeare shows us in *Antony and Cleopatra* what happens when that unstable equilibrium collapses.) In *Julius Caesar* Antony's is the success story; he is the tarnished man who knows how to come to terms with life. He is not evil – he is generous, noble and kind-hearted – but he lacks innocence: he is post-lapsarian man, who has adapted himself to life after the Fall.

Wherein lies Antony's success? Is it not in his ability to manipulate people, to act the puppeteer and utilize the worthy emotions of innocent people for his own purposes? Cassius does this in a very mild way with Brutus, but Antony is the great puppeteer of the play, and his famous oration is the work of a supreme puppet master. He manipulates other people's innocence. So does Richard III, and Edmund in *King Lear*, and Iago. But we are not to conclude from this that Antony is intended to be a villain like these characters: that would be manifestly absurd. Richard III and Edmund and Iago are evil; Antony is sophisticated and cunning, but far from evil. All four manipulate the innocence of others for their own ends. Antony stands midway between innocence and evil, the tarnished sensual man, the man whose way of life is – to use a term the politicians are now so fond of – above all *viable*. 'Human nature being what it is', Antony's way is not to be rejected out of hand. But I have a friend who says that whenever he has had a guest at dinner who has begun a political conversation with the remark, 'human nature being what it is', he always counts the spoons. The argument is an excuse for being content with imperfection: one could not imagine Brutus or Hamlet using it.

Antony manipulates his self-interest and his ideals into a compromise that is above all practicable. He is too good to be a tragic villain, too bad to be a tragic hero. Are we to say, then, that he is Shakespeare's ideal practical man? Shakespeare answers that question for us in his *Antony and Cleopatra*, which shows us, as Granville-Barker has said, the nemesis of the sensual man. The unstable equilibrium cannot last; Antony in the end surrenders wholly to his passions and loses the political world to young Octavius Caesar, the man whose fortunes he had earlier saved. *There*, perhaps, is Shakespeare's ideal practical man, Octavius Caesar, shrewd, cool-headed, altogether a cold fish. Obviously it is not the ideal practical man who is the glory of the human species, and we do not need Octavius to tell us that practical success was not, for Shakespeare, the greatest thing in life.

from 'Guilt and Justice in Shakespeare', in *Literary Essays*, 1956

FOUR

The Ides of March

ROY FULLER

FIREBALLS and thunder augment the wailing wind:
A vulgar score, but not inappropriate
To my romantic, classic situation.
Within the house my wife is asleep and dreaming
That I, too, am cocooned inside the world
Of love whose fear is that the other world
Will end it. But I wait uneasy here
Under the creaking trees, the low dark sky,
For the conspirators. This is the place
Where I come, in better weather, with a book
Or pen and paper – for I must confess
To a little amateur scribbling. Love and letters:
One ought to be content – would, if the times
Were different; if state and man were free,
The slaves fed well, and wars hung over us
Not with death's certainty but with the odds
Merely of dying a not too painful death.
Yes, I have caught the times like a disease
Whose remedy is still experimental;
And felt the times as some enormous gaffe
I cannot forget. And now I am about
To cease being a fellow traveller, about
To select from several complex panaceas,
Like a shy man confronted with a box
Of chocolates, the plainest after all.
I am aware that in my conscious wish
To rid the empire of a tyrant there
Is something that will give me personal pleasure;
That usually one's father's death occurs
About the time one becomes oneself a father.
These subtleties are not, I think, important –

THE IDES OF MARCH

No more than that I shall become a traitor,
Technically, to my class, my friend, my country.
No, the important thing is to remove
Guilt from this orchard, which is why I have
Invited here those men of action with
Their simpler motives and their naked knives.
I hope my wife will walk out of the house
While I am in their compromising presence,
And know that what we built had no foundation
Other than luck and my false privileged role
In a society that I despised.
And then society itself, aghast,
Reeling against the statue also will
Be shocked to think I had a secret passion.
Though passion is, of course, not quite the word:
I merely choose what history foretells.
The dawn comes moonlike now between the trees
And silhouettes some rather muffled figures.
It is embarrassing to find oneself
Involved in this clumsy masquerade. There still
Is time to send a servant with a message:
'Brutus is not at home'; time to postpone
Relief and fear. Yet, plucking nervously
The pregnant twigs, I stay. Good morning, comrades.

from *Brutus' Orchard*, 1957

Suggestions for Further Reading

H. GRANVILLE-BARKER: *Prefaces to Shakespeare I*.

JOHN PALMER: 'Marcus Brutus' (in *Political Characters of Shakespeare*). 'Brutus has precisely the qualities which in every age have rendered the conscientious liberal ineffectual in public life.'

BRENTS STIRLING: 'Or Else this were a Savage Spectacle' (*Publications of the Modern Language Association of America*, 1951; reprinted in *Unity in Shakespearian Tragedy*, and in *Shakespeare: Modern Essays in Criticism*, ed. by Leonard F. Dean). Stresses the element of ritual in the play.

MARK VAN DOREN: '*Julius Caesar*' (in *Shakespeare*). Suggests that the concentration on public affairs is a limitation. 'The fatigue of Brutus is the noble tiredness of a great man, and we respect it; but our pity for the sufferer is not tinged with fear. This is the noblest Roman of them all, and even in distress he keeps his distance.'

LEO KIRSCHBAUM: 'Shakespeare's Stage Blood' (in *Publications of the Modern Language Association of America*, 1949). A more interesting essay than the title might suggest. Suggests that Shakespeare introduced scenes of blood and carnage (real blood, not just metaphors) into *Julius Caesar* and *Coriolanus* in order to make us realize what was going on. 'Blood is both factual and messy.'

HAMLET

FIVE

Hamlet Psychoanalysed

ERNEST JONES

Ernest Jones's study of *Hamlet* has appeared in several versions: it was first published in 1910, in the *American Journal of Psychology*, reprinted in 1923 in the author's *Essays in Applied Psycho-Analysis*, reprinted again in 1949 as the introduction to an edition of the play, and finally issued as a book, *Hamlet and Oedipus*, in 1949. The extract which follows is an abbreviated version of Chapters III and IV of the book – the heart of its argument, and indeed the only valuable part of it. It is certainly worth while reading these two chapters in full; but little is lost by omitting Jones's earlier discussion of *Hamlet* criticism, or his later speculations on Shakespeare's personal sex-life.

Jones has been attacked, even ridiculed, by those critics who are contemptuous of his lack of sophistication as a literary critic: certainly he does not write like someone who is used to discussing literary subtleties. But this attack can lead to a Pyrrhic victory at best. It is easy to insist on the self-contained nature of literature, and to make of criticism a professional, even an arcane activity; but the price you pay is to cease believing that it can tell us anything about life – and eventually, it will cease to be read by any save professionals and scholars. If we prefer to praise great writers for their insight, their wisdom, their understanding of the world, even their psychology, then we must be prepared to take seriously the comments of those who know about the world, and about people, and about psychology.

And the psycho-analytic view of *Hamlet* has one great strength, which Jones himself points out: it can explain why no one has solved the problem before. If the whole point of Hamlet's delay is that it has a compelling cause that he cannot discover, can we be surprised that so many others have failed to discover it too?

*

W E are compelled then to take the position that there is some cause for Hamlet's vacillation which has not yet been fathomed. If this lies neither in his incapacity for action in general, nor in the inordinate difficulty of the particular task in question, then it must of necessity lie in the third possibility – namely, in some special feature of the task that renders it repugnant to him. This conclusion, that Hamlet at heart does not want to carry out the task, seems so obvious that it is hard to see how any open-minded reader of the play could avoid making it. . . . .

Hamlet's hesitancy may have been due to an internal conflict between the impulse to fulfil his task on the one hand and some special cause of repugnance to it on the other; further, the explanation of his not disclosing this cause of repugnance may be that he was not conscious of its nature; and yet the cause may be one that doesn't happen to have been considered by any of the upholders of this hypothesis. . . . This is the view that will now be developed, but before dealing with the third stage of the argument, it is first necessary to establish the probability of the first two – namely, that Hamlet's hesitancy was due to some special cause of repugnance for his task and that he was unaware of the nature of this repugnance.

A preliminary obstruction to this line of thought, based on some common prejudices on the subject of mental dynamics, may first be considered. If Hamlet was not aware of the nature of his inhibition, doubt may be felt concerning the possibility of our penetrating to it. This pessimistic thought was expressed by Baumgart as follows: 'What hinders Hamlet in his revenge is for him himself a problem and *therefore* it must remain a problem for us all.' Fortunately for our investigation, however, psycho-analytic studies have demonstrated beyond doubt that mental trends hidden from the subject himself may come to external expression in ways that reveal their nature to a trained observer, so that the possibility of success is not to be thus excluded. Loening has further objected to this hypothesis that the poet himself has not disclosed this hidden mental trend, or even given any indication of it. The first part of his objection is certainly true – otherwise there would be no problem to discuss, but we shall presently see that the second is by no means true. It may be asked: why has the poet not put in a clearer light the mental trend we are trying to discover? Strange as it may appear, the answer is probably the same as with Hamlet himself – namely, he could not because he was unaware of its nature. We shall later deal with this question in connexion with the relation of the poet to the play.

As Trench well says: 'We find it hard, with Shakespeare's help, to understand Hamlet: even Shakespeare, perhaps, found it hard to understand him: Hamlet himself finds it impossible to understand himself. Better able than other men to read the hearts and motives of others, he is yet quite unable to read his own.' I know of no more authentic statement than this in the whole literature on the Hamlet problem. But, if the motive of the play is so obscure, to what can we attribute its powerful effect on the audience, since, as Kohler asks, 'Who has ever seen Hamlet and not felt the fearful conflict that moves the soul of the hero?' This can only be because the hero's conflict finds its echo in a similar inner conflict in the mind of the hearer, and the more intense is this already present conflict the greater is the effect of the drama. Again, it is certain that the hearer himself does not know the inner cause of the conflict in his own mind, but experiences only the outer manifestations of it. So we reach the apparent paradox that the hero, the poet, and the audience are all profoundly moved by feelings due to a conflict of the source of which they are unaware. . . .

That Hamlet is suffering from an internal conflict, the essential nature of which is inaccessible to his introspection, is evidenced by the following considerations. Throughout the play we have the clearest picture of a man who sees his duty plain before him, but who shirks it at every opportunity and suffers in consequence the most intense remorse. To paraphrase Sir James Paget's well-known description of hysterical paralysis: Hamlet's advocates say he cannot do his duty, his detractors say he will not, whereas the truth is that he cannot will. Further than this, the deficient will-power is localized to the one question of killing his uncle; it is what may be termed a *specific aboulia*. Now instances of such specific aboulias in real life invariably prove, when analysed, to be due to an unconscious repulsion against the act that cannot be performed (or else against something closely associated with the act, so that the idea of the act becomes also involved in the repulsion). In other words, whenever a person cannot bring himself to do something that every conscious consideration tells him he should do – and which he may have the strongest conscious desire to do – it is always because there is some hidden reason why a part of him doesn't want to do it; this reason he will not own to himself and is only dimly if at all aware of. That is exactly the case with Hamlet. Time

49

and again he works himself up, points out to himself his obvious duty, with the cruellist self-reproaches lashes himself to agonies of remorse – and once more falls away into inaction. He eagerly seizes at every excuse for occupying himself with any other matter than the performance of his duty – even in the last scene of the last act entering on the distraction of a quite irrelevant fencing-match with a man who he must know wants to kill him, an eventuality that would put an end to all hope of fulfilling his task: just as on a lesser plane a person faced with a distasteful task, e.g. writing a difficult letter, will whittle away his time in arranging, tidying, and fidgeting with any little occupation that may serve as a pretext for procrastination. Bradley even goes so far as to make out a case for the view that Hamlet's self-accusation of 'bestial oblivion' is to be taken in a literal sense, his unconscious detestation of his task being so intense as to enable him actually to forget it for periods.

Highly significant is the fact that the grounds Hamlet gives for his hesitancy are grounds none of which will stand any serious consideration, and which continually change from one time to another. One moment he pretends he is too cowardly to perform the deed, at another he questions the truthfulness of the ghost, at another – when the opportunity presents itself in its naked form – he thinks the time is unsuited, it would be better to wait till the King was at some evil act and then to kill him, and so on. They have each of them, it is true, a certain plausibility – so much so that some writers have accepted them at face value; but surely no pretext would be of any use if it were not plausible. As Madariaga truly says: 'The argument that the reasons given by Hamlet not to kill the king at prayers are cogent is irrelevant. For the man who wants to procrastinate cogent arguments are more valuable than mere pretexts'. Take, for instance, the matter of the credibility of the ghost. There exists an extensive and very interesting literature concerning Elizabethan beliefs in supernatural visitation. It was doubtless a burning topic, a focal point of the controversies about the conflicting theologies of the age, and moreover, affecting the practical question of how to treat witches. But there is no evidence of Hamlet (or Shakespeare!) being specially interested in theology, and from the moment when the ghost confirms the slumbering suspicion in his mind ('O my prophetic soul! My uncle?') his intuition must indubitably have convinced him of the ghost's veridical nature. He never really doubted the villainy of his uncle.

When a man gives at different times a different reason for his conduct it is safe to infer that, whether consciously or not, he is concealing the true reason. Wetz, discussing a similar problem in reference to Iago, truly observes: 'Nothing proves so well how false are the motives with which Iago tries to persuade himself as *the constant change in these motives.*' We can therefore safely dismiss all the alleged motives that Hamlet propounds, as being more or less successful attempts on his part to blind himself with self-deception. Loening's summing-up of them is not too emphatic when he says: 'They are all mutually contradictory; *they are one and all false pretexts*'. The alleged motives excellently illustrate the psychological mechanisms of evasion and rationalization I have elsewhere described. . . .

The whole picture presented by Hamlet, his deep depression, the hopeless note in his attitude towards the value of life, his dread of death, his repeated reference to bad dreams, his self-accusations, his desperate efforts to get away from the thoughts of his duty, and his vain attempts to find an excuse for his procrastination: all this unequivocally points to a *tortured conscience*, to some hidden ground for shirking his task, a ground which he dare not or cannot avow to himself. We have, therefore, to take up the argument again at this point, and to seek for some evidence that may serve to bring to light the hidden counter-motive.

The extensive experience of the psycho-analytic researches carried out by Freud and his school during the past half-century has amply demonstrated that certain kinds of mental processes show a greater tendency to be inaccessible to consciousness (put technically, to be 'repressed') than others. In other words, it is harder for a person to realize the existence in his mind of some mental trends than it is of others. In order therefore to gain a proper perspective it is necessary briefly to inquire into the relative frequency with which various sets of mental processes are 'repressed'. Experience shows that this can be correlated with the degree of compatibility of these various sets with the ideals and standards accepted by the conscious ego; the less compatible they are with these the more likely they are to be 'repressed'. As the standards acceptable to consciousness are in considerable measure derived from the immediate environment, one may formulate the following generalization: those processes are most likely to be 'repressed' by the individual which are most disapproved of by the particular circle of society to whose influence he has chiefly been subjected during the period when his character was being formed. Biologically stated, this law would run: 'That which is unacceptable to the herd becomes unacceptable to the individual member', it being understood that the term herd is intended here in the sense of the particular circle defined above, which is by no means necessarily the community at large. It is for this reason that moral, social, ethical, or religious tendencies are seldom 'repressed', for, since the individual originally received them from his herd, they can hardly ever come into conflict with the dicta of the latter. This merely says that a man cannot be ashamed of that which he respects; the apparent exceptions to this rule need not be here explained.

The language used in the previous paragraph will have indicated that by the term 'repression' we denote an active dynamic process. Thoughts that are 'repressed' are actively kept from consciousness by a definite force and with the expenditure of more or less mental effort, though the person concerned is rarely aware of this. Further, what is thus kept from consciousness typically possesses an energy of its own; hence our frequent use of such expressions as 'trend', 'tendency', etc. A little consideration of the genetic aspects of the matter will make it comprehensible that the trends most likely to be 'repressed' are those belonging to what are called the innate impulses, as contrasted with secondarily acquired ones. . . . It only remains to add the obvious corollary that, as the herd unquestionably selects from the 'natural' instincts the sexual one on which to lay its heaviest ban, so it is the various psycho-sexual trends that are most often 'repressed' by the individual. We have here the explanation of the clinical experience that the more intense and the more obscure is a given case of deep mental conflict the more certainly will it be found on adequate analysis to centre about a sexual problem. On the surface, of course, this does not appear so, for, by means of various psychological defensive mechanisms, the depression, doubt, despair, and other manifestations of the conflict are transferred on to more tolerable and permissible topics, such as anxiety about worldly success or failure, about immortality and the salvation of the soul, philosophical considerations about the value of life, the future of the world, and so on.

Bearing these considerations in mind, let us return to Hamlet. It should now be evident that the conflict hypotheses discussed above, which see Hamlet's conscious impulse towards revenge inhibited by an unconscious misgiving of a highly ethical kind, are based on ignorance of what actually happens in real life, since misgivings of this order belong in fact to the more conscious layers of the mind rather than to the deeper, unconscious ones. Hamlet's intense self-study would speedily have made him aware of any such misgivings and, although he might subsequently have ignored them, it would almost certainly have been by the aid of some process of rationalization which would have enabled him to deceive himself into believing that they were ill-founded; he would in any case have remained conscious of the nature of them. We have therefore to invert these hypotheses and realize – as his words so often indicate – that the positive striving for vengeance, the pious task laid on him by his father, was to him the moral and social one, the one approved of by his consciousness, and that the 'repressed' inhibiting striving against the act of vengeance arose in some hidden source connected with his more personal, natural instincts. The former striving has already been considered, and indeed is manifest in every speech in which Hamlet debates the matter; the second is, from its nature, more obscure and has next to be investigated.

This is perhaps most easily done by inquiring more intently into Hamlet's precise attitude towards the object of his vengeance, Claudius, and towards the crimes that have to be avenged. These are two: Claudius's incest with the Queen, and his murder of his brother. Now it is of great importance to note the profound difference in Hamlet's attitude towards these two crimes. Intellectually of course he abhors both, but there can be no question as to which arouses in him the deeper loathing. Whereas the murder of his father evokes in him indignation and a plain recognition of his obvious duty to avenge it, his mother's guilty conduct awakes in him the intensest horror. . . .

Now, in trying to define Hamlet's attitude towards his uncle we have to guard against assuming off-hand that this is a simple one of mere execration, for there is a possibility of complexity arising in the following way: The uncle has not merely committed *each* crime, he has committed *both* crimes, a distinction of considerable importance, since the combination of crimes allows the admittance of a new factor, produced by the possible inter-relation of the two, which may prevent the result from being simply one of summation. In addition, it has to be borne in mind that the perpetrator of the crimes is a relative, and an exceedingly near relative. The possible inter-relationship of the crimes, and the fact that the author of them is an actual member of the family, give scope for a confusion in their influence on Hamlet's mind which may be the cause of the very obscurity we are seeking to clarify.

Let us first pursue further the effect on Hamlet of his mother's misconduct. Before he even knows with any certitude, however much he may suspect it, that his father has been murdered, he is in the deepest depression, and evidently on account of this misconduct. The connexion between the two is unmistakable in the monologue in Act 1, Scene 2, in reference to which Furnivall writes: 'One must insist on this, that before any revelation of his father's murder is made to Hamlet, before any burden of revenging that murder is laid upon him, he thinks of suicide as a welcome means of escape from this fair world of God's, made abominable to his diseased and weak imagination by his mother's lust, and the dishonour done by her to his father's memory' . . . .

But we can rest satisfied with this seemingly adequate explanation of Hamlet's weariness of life only if we accept unquestioningly the conventional standards of the causes of deep emotion. Many years ago Connolly, a well-known psychiatrist, pointed out the disproportion here existing between cause and effect, and gave it as his opinion that Hamlet's reaction to his mother's marriage indicated in itself a mental instability, 'a predisposition to actual unsoundness'; he writes: 'The circumstances are not such as would at once turn a healthy mind to the contemplation of suicide, the last resource of those whose reason has been overwhelmed by calamity and despair.' In T. S. Eliot's opinion, also, Hamlet's emotion is in *excess* of the facts as they appear, and he specially contrasts it with Gertrude's negative and insignificant personality. Wihan attributes the exaggerated effect of his misfortunes to Hamlet's *Masslosig-keit* (lack of moderation) which is displayed in every direction. We have unveiled only the exciting cause, not the predisposing cause. The very fact that Hamlet is apparently content with the explanation arouses our misgiving, for, as will presently be expounded, from the very nature of the emotion he cannot be aware of the true cause of it. If we ask, not what ought to produce such soul-paralysing grief and distaste for life, but what in actual fact does produce it, we are compelled to go beyond this explanation and seek for some deeper cause. In real life speedy second marriages occur commonly enough without leading to any such result as is here depicted, and when we see them followed by this result we invariably find, if the opportunity for an analysis of the subject's mind presents itself, that there is some other and more hidden reason why the event is followed by this inordinately great effect. The reason always is that the event has awakened to increased activity mental processes that have been 'repressed' from the subject's consciousness. His mind has been specially prepared for the catastrophe by previous mental processes with which those directly resulting from the event have entered into association. This is perhaps what Furnivall means when he speaks of the world being made abominable to Hamlet's 'diseased imagination'. In short, the special nature of the reaction presupposes some special feature in the mental predisposition. . . .

Shakespeare's extraordinary powers of observation and penetration granted him a degree of insight that it has taken the world three subsequent centuries to reach. Until our generation (and even now in the juristic sphere) a dividing line separated the sane and responsible from the irresponsible insane. It is now becoming more and more widely recognized that much of mankind lives in an intermediate and unhappy state charged with what Dover Wilson well calls 'that sense of frustration, futility, and human inadequacy which is the burden of the whole symphony' and of which Hamlet is the supreme example in literature. This intermediate plight, in the toils of which perhaps the greater part of mankind struggles and suffers, is given the name of psychoneurosis, and long ago the genius of Shakespeare depicted it for us with faultless insight.

Extensive studies of the past half century, inspired by Freud, have taught us that a psychoneurosis means a state of mind where the person is unduly, and often painfully, driven or thwarted by the 'unconscious' part of his mind, that buried part that was once the infant's mind and still lives on side by side with the adult mentality that has developed out of it and should have taken its place. It signifies *internal* mental conflict. We have here the reason why it is impossible to discuss intelligently the state of mind of anyone suffering from a psychoneurosis, whether the description is of a living person or an imagined one, without correlating the manifestations with what must have operated in his infancy and is *still operating*. That is what I propose to attempt here.

For some deep-seated reason, which is to him unacceptable, Hamlet is plunged into anguish at the thought of his father being replaced in his mother's affections by someone else. It is as if his devotion to his mother had made him so jealous for her affection that he had found it hard enough to share this even with his father and could not endure to share it with still another man. Against this thought, however, suggestive as it is, may be urged three objections. First, if it were in itself a full statement of the matter, Hamlet would have been aware of the jealousy, whereas we have concluded that the mental process we are seeking is hidden from him. Secondly, we see in it no evidence of the arousing of an old and forgotten memory. And, thirdly, Hamlet is being deprived by Claudius of no greater share in the Queen's affection than he had been by his own father, for the two brothers made exactly similar claims in this respect – namely, those of a loved husband. The last-named objection, however, leads us to the heart of the situation. How if, in fact, Hamlet had in years gone by, as a child, bitterly resented having had to share his mother's affection even with his own father, had regarded him as a rival, and had secretly wished him out of the way so that he might enjoy undisputed and undisturbed the monopoly of that affection. If such thoughts had been present in his mind in childhood days they evidently would have been 'repressed', and all traces of them obliterated, by filial piety and other educative influences. The actual realization of his early wish in the death of his father at the hands of a jealous rival would then have stimulated into activity these 'repressed' memories, which would have produced, in the form of depression and other suffering, an obscure aftermath of his childhood's conflict. This is at all events the mechanism that is actually found in the real Hamlets who are investigated psychologically.

The explanation, therefore, of the delay and self-frustration exhibited in the endeavour to fulfil his father's demand for vengeance is that to Hamlet the thought of incest and parricide combined is too intolerable to be borne. One part of him tries to carry out the task, the other flinches inexorably from the thought of it. How fain would he blot it out in that 'bestial oblivion' which unfortunately for him his conscience condemns. He is torn and tortured in an insoluble inner conflict. . . .

We are now in a position to expand and complete the suggestions offered above in connexion with the Hamlet problem. The story thus interpreted would run somewhat as follows.

As a child Hamlet had experienced the warmest affection for his mother, and this, as is always so, had contained elements of a disguised erotic quality, still more so in infancy. The presence of two traits in the Queen's character accord with this assumption, namely her markedly sensual nature and her passionate fondness for her son. The former is indicated in too many places in the play to need specific reference, and is generally recognized. The latter is also manifest: Claudius says, for instance (Act IV, Scene 7), 'The Queen his mother lives almost by his looks.' Nevertheless Hamlet appears to have with more or less success weaned himself from her and to have fallen in love with Ophelia. The precise nature of his original feeling for Ophelia is a little obscure. We may assume that at least in part it was composed of a normal love for a prospective bride, though the extravagance of the language used (the passionate need for absolute certainty, etc.) suggests a somewhat morbid frame of mind. There are indications that even here the influence of the old attraction for the mother is still exerting itself. Although some writers, following Goethe, see in Ophelia many traits of resemblance to the Queen, perhaps just as striking are the traits contrasting with those of the Queen. Whatever truth there may be in the many German conceptions of Ophelia as a sensual wanton – misconceptions that have been questioned by Loening and others – still the very fact that it needed what Goethe happily called the 'innocence of insanity' to reveal the presence of any such libidinous thoughts demonstrates in itself the modesty and chasteness of her habitual demeanour. Her naïve piety, her obedient resignation, and her unreflecting simplicity sharply contrast with the Queen's character, and seem to indicate that Hamlet by a characteristic reaction towards the opposite extreme had unknowingly been impelled to choose a woman who should least remind him of his mother. A case might even be made out for the view that part of his courtship originated not so much in direct attraction for Ophelia as in an unconscious desire to play her off against his mother, just as a disappointed and piqued lover so often has resort to the arms of a more willing rival. It would not be easy otherwise to understand the readiness with which he later throws himself into this part. When, for instance, in the play scene he replies to his mother's request to sit by her with the words 'No good, mother. Here's metal more attractive' and proceeds to lie at Ophelia's feet, we seem to have a direct indication of this attitude; and his coarse familiarity and bandying of ambiguous jests with the woman he has recently so ruthlessly jilted are hardly intelligible unless we bear in mind that they were carried out under the heedful gaze of the Queen. It is as if his unconscious were trying to convey to her the following thought: 'You give yourself to other men whom you prefer to me. Let me assure you that I can dispense with your favours and even prefer those of a woman whom I no longer love.' His extraordinary outburst of bawdiness on this occasion, so unexpected in a man of obviously fine feeling, points unequivocally to the sexual nature of the underlying turmoil.

Now comes the father's death and the mother's second marriage. The association of the idea of sexuality with his mother, buried since infancy, can no longer be concealed from his consciousness. As Bradley well says: 'Her son was forced to see in her action not only an astounding shallowness of feeling, but an eruption of coarse sensuality, "rank and gross", speeding post-haste to its horrible delight.' Feelings which once, in the infancy of long ago, were pleasurable desires can now, because of his repressions, only fill him with repulsion. The long 'repressed' desire to take his father's place in his mother's affection is stimulated to unconscious activity by the sight of someone usurping this place exactly as he himself had once longed to do. More, this someone was a member of the same family, so that the actual usurpation further resembled the imaginary one in being incestuous. Without his being in the least aware of it these ancient desires are ringing in his mind, are once more struggling to find conscious expression, and need such an expenditure of energy again to 'repress' them that he is reduced to the deplorable mental state he himself so vividly depicts.

There follows the Ghost's announcement that the father's death was a willed one, was due to murder. Hamlet, having at the moment his mind filled with natural indignation at the news, answers normally enough with the cry (Act 1, Scene 5):

> Haste me to know't, that I, with wings as swift
> As meditation or the thoughts of love,
> May sweep to my revenge.

The momentous words follow revealing who was the guilty person, namely a relative who had committed the deed at the bidding of lust. Hamlet's second guilty wish had thus also been realized by his uncle, namely to procure the fulfilment of the first – the possession of the mother – by a personal deed, in fact by murder of the father. The two recent events, the father's death and the mother's second marriage, seemed to the world to have no inner causal relation to each other, but they represented ideas which in Hamlet's unconscious fantasy had always been closely associated. These ideas now in a moment forced their way to conscious recognition in spite of all 'repressing forces', and found immediate expression in his almost reflex cry: 'O my prophetic soul! My uncle?'. The frightful truth his unconscious had already intuitively divined, his consciousness had now to assimilate as best it could. For the rest of the interview Hamlet is stunned by the effect of the internal conflict thus reawakened, which from now on never ceases, and into the essential nature of which he never penetrates.

One of the first manifestations of the awakening of the old conflict in Hamlet's mind is his reaction against Ophelia. This is doubly conditioned by the two opposing attitudes in his own mind. In the first place, there is a complex reaction in regard to his mother. As was explained above, the being forced to connect the thought of his mother with sensuality leads to an intense sexual revulsion, one that is only temporarily broken down by the coarse outburst discussed above. Combined with this is a fierce jealousy, unconscious because of its forbidden origin, at the sight of her giving herself to another man, a man whom he had no reason whatever either to love or to respect. Consciously this is allowed to express itself, for instance after the prayer scene, only in the form of extreme resentment and bitter reproaches against her. His resentment against women is still further inflamed by the hypocritical prudishness with which Ophelia follows her father and brother in seeing evil in his natural affection, an attitude which poisons his love in exactly the same way that the love of his childhood, like that of all children, must have been poisoned. He can forgive a woman neither her rejection of his sexual advances nor, still less, her alliance with another man. Most intolerable of all to him, as Bradley well remarks, is the sight of sensuality in a quarter from which he had trained himself ever since infancy rigorously to exclude it. The total reaction culminates in the bitter misogyny of his outburst against Ophelia, who is devastated at having to bear a reaction so wholly out of proportion to her own offence and has no idea that in reviling her Hamlet is really expressing his bitter resentment against his mother. 'I have heard of your paintings too, well enough. God has given you one face, and you make yourselves another; you jig, you amble, and you lisp; you nickname God's creatures and make your wantonness your ignorance. Go to, I'll no more on 't; it hath made me mad' (Act III, Scene I). On only one occasion does he for a moment escape from the sordid implication with which his love has been impregnated and achieve a healthier attitude towards Ophelia, namely at the open grave when in remorse he breaks out at Laertes for presuming to pretend that his feeling for her could ever equal that of her lover. Even here, however, as Dover Wilson has suggested, the remorse behind his exaggerated behaviour springs not so much from grief at Ophelia's death as from his distress at his bad conscience that had killed his love – he acts the lover he fain would have been. . . .

The intensity of Hamlet's repulsion against woman in general, and Ophelia in particular, is a measure of the powerful 'repression' to which his sexual feelings are being subjected. The outlet for those feelings in the direction of his mother has always been firmly dammed, and now that the narrower channel in Ophelia's direction

has also been closed the increase in the original direction consequent on the awakening of early memories tasks all his energy to
maintain the 'repression'. His pent-up feelings find a partial vent in
other directions. The petulant irascibility and explosive outbursts
called forth by his vexation at the hands of Guildenstern and
Rosencrantz, and especially of Polonius, are evidently to be interpreted in this way, as also is in part the burning nature of his
reproaches to his mother. Indeed, towards the end of his interview
with his mother the thought of her misconduct expresses itself in
that almost physical disgust which is so characteristic a manifesta-
tion of intensely 'repressed' sexual feeling.

> Let the bloat king tempt you again to bed;
> Pinch wanton on your cheek, call you his mouse;
> And let him, for a pair of reechy kisses,
> Or paddling in your neck with his damn'd fingers,
> Make you to ravel all this matter out.   III. 4. 182

Hamlet's attitude towards Polonius is highly instructive. Here
the absence of family ties and of other similar influences enables
him to indulge to a relatively unrestrained extent his hostility
towards what he regards as a prating and sententious dotard. The
analogy he effects between Polonius and Jephthah is in this connexion especially pointed. It is here that we see his fundamental
attitude towards moralizing elders who use their power to thwart
the happiness of the young, and not in the over-drawn and melodramatic portrait in which he delineates his father: 'A combination
and a form indeed, Where every god did seem to set his seal To give
the world assurance of a man.'

It will be seen from the foregoing that Hamlet's attitude towards
his uncle-father is far more complex than is generally supposed. He
of course detests him, but it is the jealous detestation of one evil-
doer towards his successful fellow. Much as he hates him, he can
never denounce him with the ardent indignation that boils straight
from his blood when he reproaches his mother, for the more
vigorously he denounces his uncle the more powerfully does he
stimulate to activity his own unconscious and 'repressed' com-
plexes. He is therefore in a dilemma between on the one hand
allowing his natural detestation of his uncle to have free play, a

consummation which would stir still further his own horrible wishes, and on the other hand ignoring the imperative call for the vengeance that his obvious duty demands. His own 'evil' prevents him from completely denouncing his uncle's, and in continuing to 'repress' the former he must strive to ignore, to condone, and if possible even to forget the latter; *his moral fate is bound up with his uncle's for good or ill.* In reality his uncle incorporates the deepest and most buried part of his own personality, so that he cannot kill him without also killing himself. This solution, one closely akin to what Freud has shown to be the motive of suicide in melancholia, is actually the one that Hamlet finally adopts. The course of alternate action and inaction that he embarks on, and the provocations he gives to his suspicious uncle, can lead to no other end than to his own ruin and, incidentally, to that of his uncle. Only when he has made the final sacrifice and brought himself to the door of death is he free to fulfil his duty, to avenge his father, and to slay his other self – his uncle.

There are two moments in the play when he is nearest to murder, and it is noteworthy that in both the impulse has been dissociated from the unbearable idea of incest. The second is of course when he actually kills the King, when the Queen is already dead and lost to him for ever, so that his conscience is free of an ulterior motive for the murder. The first is more interesting. It is clear that Hamlet is a creature of highly charged imagination; Vischer, for instance, quite rightly termed him a '*Phantasiemensch*'. As is known, the danger then is that fantasy may on occasion replace reality. Now Otto Rank, who uses the same term, has plausibly suggested that the emotionally charged play scene, where a nephew kills his uncle (!), and when there is no talk of adultery or incest, is in Hamlet's imagination an equivalent for fulfilling his task. It is easier to kill the King when there is no ulterior motive behind it, no talk of mother or incest. When the play is over he is carried away in exultation as if he had really killed the King himself, whereas all he has actually done is to warn him and so impel him to sign a death warrant. That his pretext for arranging the play – to satisfy himself about Claudius's guilt and the Ghost's honesty – is specious is plain from the fact that *before* it he had been convinced of both and was reproaching himself for his neglect. When he then comes on the King praying and so to speak finds him surprisingly still alive, he realizes that his task is still in front of him, but can only say 'Now *might* I do it' (not 'will'). He then expresses openly the unconscious thoughts of his infancy – the wish to kill the man who is lying with his mother ('in th' incestuous pleasure of his bed') – but he knows only too well that his own guilty motive for doing so would always prevent him. So there is no way out of the dilemma, and he blunders on to destruction.

The call of duty to kill his stepfather cannot be obeyed because it links itself with the unconscious call of his nature to kill his mother's husband, whether this is the first or the second; the absolute 'repression' of the former impulse involves the inner prohibition of the latter also. It is no chance that Hamlet says of himself that he is prompted to his revenge 'by heaven and hell'.

In this discussion of the motives that move or restrain Hamlet we have purposely depreciated the subsidiary ones – such as his exclusion from the throne where Claudius has blocked the normal solution of the Oedipus complex (to succeed the father in due course) – which also play a part, so as to bring out in greater relief the deeper and effective ones that are of preponderant importance. These, as we have seen, spring from sources of which he is quite unaware, and we might summarize the internal conflict of which he is the victim as consisting in a struggle of the 'repressed' mental processes to become conscious. The call of duty, which automatically arouses to activity these unconscious processes, conflicts with the necessity of 'repressing' them still more strongly; for the more urgent is the need for external action the greater is the effort demanded of the 'repressing' forces. It is his moral duty, to which his father exhorts him, to put an end to the incestuous activities of his mother (by killing Claudius), but his unconscious does not want to put an end to them (he being identified with Claudius in the situation) and so he cannot. His lashings of self-reproach and remorse are ultimately because of this very failure, i.e. the refusal of his guilty wishes to undo the sin. By refusing to abandon his own incestuous wishes he perpetuates the sin and so must endure the stings of torturing conscience. And yet killing his mother's husband would be equivalent to committing the original sin itself, which would if anything be even more guilty. So of the two impossible alternatives he adopts the passive solution of letting the incest continue vicariously, but at the same time provoking destruction at the King's hand. Was ever a tragic figure so torn and tortured!

Action is paralysed at its very inception, and there is thus produced the picture of apparently causeless inhibition which is so inexplicable both to Hamlet and to readers of the play. This paralysis arises, however, not from physical or moral cowardice, but from that intellectual cowardice, that reluctance to dare the exploration of his inmost soul, which Hamlet shares with the rest of the human race. 'Thus conscience does make cowards of us all.'

from *Hamlet and Oedipus*, 1910

SIX

Hamlet: The Prince or the Poem?

C. S. LEWIS

A CRITIC who makes no claim to be a true Shakespearian scholar and who has been honoured by an invitation to speak about Shakespeare to such an audience as this, feels rather like a child brought in at dessert to recite his piece before the grown-ups. I have a temptation to furbish up all my meagre Shakespearian scholarship and to plunge into some textual or chronological problem in the hope of seeming, for this one hour, more of an expert than I am. But it really wouldn't do. I should not deceive you: I should not even deceive myself. I have therefore decided to bestow all my childishness upon you.

And first, a reassurance. I am not going to advance a new interpretation of the character of Hamlet. Where great critics have failed I could not hope to succeed; it is rather my ambition (a more moderate one, I trust) to understand their failure. The problem I want to consider today arises in fact not directly out of the Prince's character nor even directly out of the play, but out of the state of criticism about the play.

To give anything like a full history of this criticism would be beyond my powers and beyond the scope of a lecture; but, for my present purposes, I think we can very roughly divide it into three main schools or tendencies. The first is that which maintains simply that the actions of Hamlet have not been given adequate motives and that the play is so far bad. . . . In our own time Mr Eliot has taken this view: *Hamlet* is rather like a film on which two photographs have been taken – an unhappy superposition of Shakespeare's work 'upon much cruder material'. The play 'is most certainly an artistic failure'. If this school of critics is right, we shall be wasting our time in attempting to understand why Hamlet delayed. The second school, on the other hand, thinks that he did not delay at all but went to work as quickly as the circumstances permitted. . . . This position has been brilliantly defended in modern times. In the third school or group I include all those critics who admit that Hamlet procrastinates and who explain the procrastination by his psychology. Within this general agreement there are, no doubt, very great diversities. Some critics, such as Hallam, Sievers, Raleigh, and Clutton Brock, trace the weakness to the shock inflicted upon Hamlet by the events which precede, and immediately follow, the opening of the play; others regard it as a more permanent condition; some extend it to actual insanity, others reduce it to an almost amiable flaw in a noble nature. This third group, which boasts the names of Richardson, Goethe, Coleridge, Schlegel, and Hazlitt, can still, I take it, claim to represent the central and, as it were, orthodox line of *Hamlet* criticism.

Such is the state of affairs; and we are all so accustomed to it that we are inclined to ignore its oddity. In order to remove the veil of familiarity I am going to ask you to make the imaginative effort of looking at this mass of criticism as if you had no independent knowledge of the thing criticized. Let us suppose that a picture which you have not seen is being talked about. The first thing you gather from the vast majority of the speakers – and a majority which includes the best art critics – is that this picture is undoubtedly a very great work. The next thing you discover is that hardly any two people in the room agree as to what it is a picture of. Most of them find something curious about the pose, and perhaps even the anatomy, of the central figure. One explains it by saying that it is a picture of the raising of Lazarus, and that the painter has cleverly managed to represent the uncertain gait of a body just recovering from the stiffness of death. Another, taking the central figure to be Bacchus returning from the conquest of India, says that it reels because it is drunk. A third, to whom it is self-evident that he has seen a picture of the death of Nelson, asks with some temper whether you expect a man to look quite normal just after he has been mortally wounded. A fourth maintains that such crudely representational canons of criticism will never penetrate so profound a work, and that the peculiarities of the central figure really reflect the content of the painter's subconsciousness. Hardly have you had time to digest these opinions when you run into another group of critics who denounce as a pseudo-problem what the first group has been discussing. According to this second group there is nothing odd about the central figure. A more natural and self-explanatory pose they never saw and they cannot imagine what all the bother is about. At long last you discover – isolated in a corner of the room, somewhat frowned upon by the rest of the company, and including few reputable *connoisseurs* in its ranks – a little knot of men who are whispering that the picture is a villainous daub and that the mystery of the central figure merely results from the fact that it is out of drawing.

Now if all this had really happened to any one of us, I believe that our first reaction would be to accept, at least provisionally, the third view. Certainly I think we should consider it much more seriously than we usually consider those critics who solve the whole *Hamlet* problem by calling *Hamlet* a bad play. At the very least we should at once perceive that they have a very strong case against the critics who admire. 'Here is a picture,' they might say, 'on whose meaning no two of you are in agreement. Communication between the artist and the spectator has almost completely broken down, for each of you admits that it has broken down as regards every spectator except himself. There are only two possible explanations. Either the artist was a very bad artist, or you are very bad critics. In deference to your number and your reputation, we choose the first alternative; though, as you will observe, it would work out to the same result if we chose the second.' As to the next group – those who denied that there was anything odd about the central figure – I believe that in the circumstances I have imagined we should hardly attend to them. A natural and self-explanatory pose in the central figure would be rejected as wholly inconsistent with its observed effect on all the other critics, both those who thought the picture good and those who thought it bad.

If we now return to the real situation, the same reactions appear reasonable. There is, indeed, this difference, that the critics who admit no delay and no indecision in Hamlet have an opponent with whom the corresponding critics of the picture were not embarrassed. The picture did not answer back. But Hamlet does. He pronounces himself a procrastinator, an undecided man, even a coward: and the ghost in part agrees with him. This, coupled with the more general difficulties of their position, appears to me to be fatal to their view. If so, we are left with those who think the play bad and those who agree in thinking it good and in placing its goodness almost wholly in the character of the hero, while disagreeing as to what that character is. Surely the devil's advocates are in a very strong position. Here is a play so dominated by one character that 'Hamlet without the Prince' is a by-word. Here are critics justly famed, all of them for their sensibility, many of them for their skill in catching the finest shades of human passion and pursuing motives to their last hiding-places. Is it really credible that the greatest of dramatists, the most powerful painter of men, offering to such an audience his consummate portrait of a man should produce something which, if any one of them is right, all the rest have in some degree failed to recognize? Is this the sort of thing that happens? Does the meeting of supremely creative with supremely receptive imagination usually produce such results? Or is it not far easier to say that Homer nods, and Alexander's shoulder drooped, and Achilles' heel was vulnerable, and that Shakespeare, for once, either in haste, or over-reaching himself in unhappy ingenuity, has brought forth an abortion?

Yes. Of course it is far easier. 'Most certainly,' says Mr Eliot, 'an artistic failure.' But is it 'most certain'? Let me return for a moment to my analogy of the picture. In that dream there was one experiment we did not make. We didn't walk into the next room and look at it for ourselves. Supposing we had done so. Suppose that at the first glance all the cogent arguments of the unfavourable critics had dried on our lips, or echoed in our ears as idle babble. Suppose that looking on the picture we had found ourselves caught up into an unforgettable intensity of life and had come back from the room where it hung haunted for ever with the sense of vast dignities and strange sorrows and teased 'with thoughts beyond the reaches of our souls' – would not this have reversed our judgement and compelled us, in the teeth of *a priori* probability, to maintain that on one point at least the orthodox critics were in the right? 'Most certainly an artistic failure.' All argument is for that conclusion – until you read or see *Hamlet* again. And when you do, you are left saying that if this is failure, then failure is better than success. We want more of these 'bad' plays. From our first childish reading of the ghost scenes down to those golden minutes which we stole from marking examination papers on *Hamlet* to read a few pages of

Hamlet itself, have we ever known the day or the hour when its
enchantment failed? That castle is part of our own world. The
affection we feel for the Prince, and, through him, for Horatio, is
like a friendship in real life. The very turns of expression – half-
lines and odd connecting links – of this play are worked into the
language. It appears, said Shaftesbury in 1710, 'most to have affec-
ted English hearts and has perhaps been oftenest acted'. It has a
taste of its own, an all-pervading relish which we recognize even
in its smallest fragments, and which, once tasted, we recur to.
When we want that taste, no other book will do instead. It may
turn out in the end that the thing is not a complete success. This
compelling quality in it may coexist with some radical defect. But I
doubt if we shall ever be able to say, sad brow and true maid, that
it is 'most certainly' a failure. Even if the proposition that it has
failed were at last admitted for true, I can think of few critical
truths which most of us would utter with less certainty, and with
a more divided mind.

It seems, then, that we cannot escape from our problem by
pronouncing the play bad. On the other hand, the critics, mostly
agreeing to place the excellence of it in the delineation of the hero's
character, describe that character in a dozen different ways. If they
differ so much as to the kind of man whom Shakespeare meant to
portray, how can we explain their unanimous praise of the portrayal? I can imagine a sketch so bad that one man thought it was
an attempt at a horse and another thought it was an attempt at a
donkey. But what kind of sketch would it have to be which looked
like a *very good* horse to some, and like a *very good* donkey to
others? The only solution which occurs to me is that the critics'
delight in the play is not in fact due to the delineation of Hamlet's
character but to something else. If the picture which you take for a
horse and I for a donkey, delights us both, it is probable that what
we are both enjoying is the pure line, or the colouring, not the
delineation of an animal. If two men who have both been talking to
the same woman agree in proclaiming her conversation delightful,
though one praises it for its ingenuous innocence and the other for
its clever sophistication, I should be inclined to conclude that her
conversation had played very little part in the pleasure of either. I
should suspect that the lady was nice to look at. . . .

A good way of introducing you to my experience of *Hamlet* will be to tell you the exact point at which anyone else's criticism of it begins to lose my allegiance. It is a fairly definite point. As soon as I find anyone treating the ghost merely as the means whereby Hamlet learns of his father's murder – as soon as a critic leaves us with the impression that some other method of disclosure (the finding of a letter or a conversation with a servant) would have done very nearly as well – I part company with that critic. After that, he may be as learned and sensitive as you please; but his outlook on literature is so remote from mine that he can teach me nothing. Hamlet for me is no more separable from his ghost than Macbeth from his witches, Una from her lion, or Dick Whittington from his cat. The Hamlet formula, so to speak, is not 'a man who has to avenge his father' but 'a man who has been given a task by a ghost'. Everything else about him is less important than that. If the play did not begin with the cold and darkness and sickening suspense of the ghost scenes it would be a radically different play. If, on the other hand, only the first act had survived, we should have a very tolerable notion of the play's peculiar quality. I put it to you that everyone's imagination here confirms mine. What is against me is the abstract pattern of motives and characters which we build up as critics when the actual flavour or tint of the poetry is already fading from our minds.

This ghost is different from any other ghost in Elizabethan drama – for, to tell the truth, the Elizabethans in general do their ghosts very vilely. It is permanently ambiguous. Indeed the very word 'ghost', by putting it into the same class with the 'ghosts' of Kyd and Chapman, nay by classifying it at all, puts us on the wrong track. It is 'this thing', 'this dreaded sight', an 'illusion', a 'spirit of health or goblin damn'd', liable at any moment to assume 'some other horrible form' which reason could not survive the vision of. Critics have disputed whether Hamlet is sincere when he doubts whether the apparition is his father's ghost or not. I take him to be perfectly sincere. He believes while the thing is present: he doubts when it is away. Doubt, uncertainty, bewilderment to almost any degree, is what the ghost creates not only in Hamlet's mind but in the minds of the other characters. Shakespeare does not take the concept of 'ghost' for granted, as other dramatists had done. In his play the appearance of the spectre means a breaking down of the walls of the world and the germination of thoughts that cannot really be thought: chaos is come again.

This does not mean that I am going to make the ghost the hero, or the play a ghost story – though I might add that a very good ghost story would be, to me, a more interesting thing than a maze of motives. I have started with the ghost because the ghost appears at the beginning of the play not only to give Hamlet necessary information but also, and even more, to strike the note. From the platform we pass to the court scene and so to Hamlet's first long speech. There are ten lines of it before we reach what is necessary to the plot: lines about the melting of flesh into a dew and the divine prohibition of self-slaughter. We have a second ghost scene after which the play itself, rather than the hero, goes mad for some minutes. We have a second soliloquy on the theme 'to die . . . to sleep'; and a third on 'the witching time of night, when churchyards yawn'. We have the King's effort to pray and Hamlet's comment on it. We have the ghost's third appearance. Ophelia goes mad and is drowned. Then comes the comic relief, surely the strangest comic relief ever written – comic relief beside an open grave, with a further discussion of suicide, a detailed inquiry into the rate of decomposition, a few clutches of skulls, and then 'Alas, poor Yorick!' On top of this, the hideous fighting in the grave; and then, soon, the catastrophe. . . .

In a sense, the subject of *Hamlet* is death. I do not mean by this that most of the characters die, or even that life and death are the stakes they play for; that is true of all tragedies. I do not mean that we rise from the reading of the play with the feeling that we have been in cold, empty places, places 'outside', *nocte tacentia late*, though that is true. Before I go on to explain myself let me say that here, and throughout my lecture, I am most deeply indebted to my friend Mr Owen Barfield. I have to make these acknowledgements both to him and to other of my friends so often that I am afraid of their being taken for an affectation. But they are not. The next best thing to being wise oneself is to live in a circle of those who are: that good fortune I have enjoyed for nearly twenty years.

The sense in which death is the subject of *Hamlet* will become apparent if we compare it with other plays. Macbeth has commerce with Hell, but at the very outset of his career dismisses all thought of the life to come. For Brutus and Othello, suicide in the high tragic manner is escape and climax. For Lear death is deliverance. For Romeo and Antony, poignant loss. For all these, as for their author while he writes and the audience while they watch, death is the end: it is almost the frame of the picture. They think of dying: no one thinks, in these plays, of *being dead*. In Hamlet we are kept thinking about it all the time, whether in terms of the soul's destiny or of the body's. Purgatory, Hell, Heaven, the wounded name, the rights – or wrongs – of Ophelia's burial, and the staying-power of a tanner's corpse: and beyond this, beyond all Christian and all Pagan maps of the hereafter, comes a curious groping and tapping of thoughts, about 'what dreams may come'. It is this that gives to the whole play its quality of darkness and of misgiving. Of course there is much else in the play: but nearly always, the same groping. The characters are all watching one another, forming theories about one another, listening, contriving full of anxiety. The world of *Hamlet* is a world where one has lost one's way. The Prince also has no doubt lost his, and we can tell the precise moment at which he finds it again. 'Not a whit. We defy augury. There's a special providence in the fall of a sparrow. If it be now, 'tis not to come: if it be not to come, it will be now: if it be not now, yet it will come: the readiness is all: since no man has aught of what he leaves, what is't to leave betimes?'

If I wanted to make one more addition to the gallery of Hamlet's portraits I should trace his hesitation to the fear of death; not to a physical fear of dying, but a fear of being dead. And I think I should get on quite comfortably. Any serious attention to the state of being dead, unless it is limited by some definite religious or anti-religious doctrine, must, I suppose, paralyse the will by introducing infinite uncertainties and rendering all motives inadequate. Being dead is the unknown x in our sum. Unless you ignore it or else give it a value, you can get no answer. But this is not what I am going to do. Shakespeare has not left in the text clear lines of causation which would enable us to connect Hamlet's hesitations with this source. I do not believe he has given us data for any portrait of the kind critics have tried to draw. To that extent I agree with Hanmer,

Rümelin, and Mr Eliot. But I differ from them in thinking that it is a fault.

For what, after all, is happening to us when we read any of Hamlet's great speeches? We see visions of the flesh dissolving into a dew, of the world like an unweeded garden. We think of memory reeling in its 'distracted globe'. We watch him scampering hither and thither like a maniac to avoid the voices wherewith he is haunted. Someone says 'Walk out of the air', and we hear the word 'Into my grave' spontaneously respond to it. We think of being bounded in a nut-shell and king of infinite space: but for bad dreams. There's the trouble, for 'I am most dreadfully attended'. We see the picture of a dull and muddy-mettled rascal, a John-a-dreams, somehow unable to move while ultimate dishonour is done him. We listen to his fear lest the whole thing may be an illusion due to melancholy. We get the sense of sweet relief at the words 'shuffled off this mortal coil' but mixed with the bottomless doubt about what may follow then. We think of bones and skulls, of women breeding sinners, and of how some, to whom all this experience is a sealed book, can yet dare death and danger 'for an egg-shell'. But do we really enjoy these things, do we go back to them, because they show us Hamlet's character? Are they, from *that* point of view, so very interesting? Does the mere fact that a young man, literally haunted, dispossessed, and lacking friends, should feel thus, tell us anything remarkable? Let me put my question in another way. If instead of the speeches he actually utters about the firmament and man in his scene with Rosencrantz and Guildenstern Hamlet had merely said, 'I don't seem to enjoy things the way I used to,' and talked in that fashion throughout, should we find him interesting? I think the answer is 'Not very.' It may be replied that if he talked commonplace prose he would reveal his character less vividly. I am not so sure. He would certainly have revealed *something* less vividly; but would that something be himself? It seems to me that 'this majestical roof' and 'What a piece of work is a man' give me primarily an impression not of the sort of person he must be to lose the estimation of things but of the things themselves and their great value; and that I should be able to discern, though with very faint interest, the same condition of loss in a personage who was quite unable so to put before me what he was losing. And I do not think it true to reply that he would be a different character if he spoke less poetically. This point is often misunderstood. We sometimes speak as if the characters in whose mouths Shakespeare puts great poetry were poets: in the sense that Shakespeare was depicting men of poetical genius. But surely this is like thinking that Wagner's Wotan is the dramatic portrait of a baritone? In opera song is the medium by which the representation is made and not part of the thing represented. The actors sing; the dramatic personages are feigned to be speaking. The only character who sings dramatically in *Figaro* is Cherubino. Similarly in poetical drama poetry is the medium, not part of the delineated characters. While the actors speak poetry written for them by the poet, the dramatic personages are supposed to be merely talking. If ever there is occasion to *represent* poetry (as in the play scene from *Hamlet*), it is put into a different metre and strongly stylized so as to prevent confusion.

I trust that my conception is now becoming clear. I believe that we read Hamlet's speeches with interest chiefly because they describe so well a certain spiritual region through which most of us have passed and anyone in his circumstances might be expected to pass, rather than because of our concern to understand how and why this particular man entered it. I foresee an objection on the ground that I am thus really admitting his 'character' in the only sense that matters and that all characters whatever could be equally well talked away by the method I have adopted. But I do really find a distinction. When I read about Mrs Proudie I am not in the least interested in seeing the world from her point of view, for her point of view is not interesting; what does interest me is precisely the sort of person she was. In *Middlemarch* no reader wants to see Casaubon through Dorothea's eyes; the pathos, the comedy, the value of the whole thing is to understand Dorothea and see how such an illusion was inevitable for her. In Shakespeare himself I find Beatrice to be a character who could not be thus dissolved. We are interested not in some vision seen through her eyes, but precisely in the wonder of her being the girl she is. A comparison of the sayings we remember from her part with those we remember from Hamlet's brings out the contrast. On the one hand, 'I wonder that you will still be talking, Signior Benedick', 'There was a star danced and under that I was born', 'Kill Claudio'; on the other, 'The undiscovered country, from whose bourne no traveller returns', 'Use every man after his desert, and who should 'scape whipping?', 'The rest is silence.' Particularly noticeable is the passage where Hamlet professes to be describing his own character. 'I am myself indifferent honest, but yet I could accuse me of such things that it were better my mother had not borne me: I am very proud, revengeful, ambitious'. It is, of course, possible to devise some theory which explains these self-accusations in terms of character. But long before we have done so the real significance of the lines has taken possession of our imagination for ever. 'Such fellows as I' does not mean 'such fellows as Goethe's Hamlet, or Coleridge's Hamlet, or any Hamlet': it means *men* – creatures shapen in sin and conceived in iniquity – and the vast, empty visions of them 'crawling between earth and heaven' is what really counts and really carries the burden of the play.

It is often cast in the teeth of the great critics that each in painting *Hamlet* has drawn a portrait of himself. How if they were right? I would go a long way to meet Beatrice or Falstaff or Mr Jonathan Oldbuck or Disraeli's Lord Monmouth. I would not cross the room to meet Hamlet. It would never be necessary. He is always where I am. The method of the whole play is much nearer to Mr Eliot's own method in poetry than Mr Eliot suspects. Its true hero is man – haunted man – man with his mind on the frontier of two worlds, man unable either quite to reject or quite to admit the supernatural, man struggling to get something done as man has struggled from the beginning, yet incapable of achievement because of his inability to understand either himself or his fellows or the real quality of the universe which has produced him. To be sure, some hints of more particular motives for Hamlet's delay are every now and then fadged up to silence our questions, just as some show of motives is offered for the Duke's temporary abdication in *Measure for Measure*. In both cases it is only scaffolding or machinery. To mistake these mere *succedanea* for the real play and to try to work them up into a coherent psychology is the great error. I once had a whole batch of School Certificate answers on the 'Nun's Priest's Tale' by boys whose form-master was apparently a breeder of poultry. Everything that Chaucer had said in describing Chauntecleer and Pertelote was treated by them simply and solely as evidence about the precise breed of these two birds. And, I must admit, the result was very interesting. They proved beyond doubt that Chauntecleer was very different from our modern specialized strains and much closer to the Old English 'barn-door fowl'. But I couldn't help feeling that they had missed something. I believe our attention to Hamlet's 'character' in the usual sense misses almost as much.

Perhaps I should rather say that it *would* miss as much if our behaviour when we are actually reading were not wiser than our criticism in cold blood. The critics, or most of them, have at any rate kept constantly before us the knowledge that in this play there is greatness and mystery. They were never entirely wrong. Their error, in my view, was to put the mystery in the wrong place – in Hamlet's motives rather than in that darkness which enwraps Hamlet and the whole tragedy and all who read or watch it. It is a mysterious play in the sense of being a play about mystery. Mr Eliot suggests that 'more people have thought *Hamlet* a work of art because they found it interesting, than have found it interesting because it is a work of art'. When he wrote that sentence he must have been very near to what I believe to be the truth. This play is, above all else, *interesting*. But artistic failure is not in itself interesting, nor often interesting in any way: artistic success always is. To interest is the first duty of art; no other excellences will even begin to compensate for failure in this, and very serious faults will be covered by this, as by charity. The hypothesis that this play interests by being good and not by being bad has therefore the first claim on our consideration. The burden of proof rests on the other side. Is not the fascinated interest of the critics most naturally explained by supposing that this is the precise effect the play was written to produce? They may be finding the mystery in the wrong place; but the fact that they can never leave *Hamlet* alone, the continual groping, the sense, unextinguished by over a century of failures, that we have here something of inestimable importance, is surely the best evidence that the real and lasting mystery of our human situation has been greatly depicted.

The kind of criticism which I have attempted is always at a dis-advantage against either historical criticism or character criticism.

Their vocabulary has been perfected by long practice, and the truths with which they are concerned are those which we are accustomed to handle in the everyday business of life. But the things I want to talk about have no vocabulary and criticism has for centuries kept almost complete silence on them. I make no claim to be a pioneer. Professor Wilson Knight (though I disagree with nearly everything he says in detail), Miss Spurgeon, Miss Bodkin, and Mr Barfield are my leaders. But those who do not enjoy the honours of a pioneer may yet share his discomforts. One of them I feel acutely at the moment. I feel certain that to many of you the things I have been saying about *Hamlet* will appear intolerably sophisticated, abstract, and modern. And so they sound when we have to put them into words. But I shall have failed completely if I cannot persuade you that my view, for good or ill, has just the opposite characteristics – is naïve and concrete and archaic. I am trying to recall attention from the things an intellectual adult notices to the things a child or a peasant notices – night, ghosts, a castle, a lobby where a man can walk four hours together, a willow-fringed brook and a sad lady drowned, a graveyard and a terrible cliff above the sea, and amidst all these a pale man in black clothes (would that our producers would ever let him appear!) with his stockings coming down, a dishevelled man whose words make us at once think of loneliness and doubt and dread, of waste and dust and emptiness, and from whose hands, or from our own, we feel the richness of heaven and earth and the comfort of human affection slipping away.

from *Hamlet: The Prince or the Poem*
(British Academy Shakespeare Lecture, 1942)

Hamlet: *A Study in Critical Method*

A. J. A. WALDOCK

Waldock's little book on *Hamlet* examines the play by way of the critics. Beginning with a short history of *Hamlet* criticism (Richardson – Goethe – Coleridge – Bradley), he makes some of his main points almost incidentally. This has made it difficult to represent his argument fairly in a short extract; and eventually I decided to rearrange the order of the passages I had chosen. I begin with the opening of his discussion of the problem of delay, which shows the commonsense of his approach at its best; I then move back to his account of the central theme of the play, which follows his discussion of Ernest Jones; and finally I have put his description of the damage Shakespeare did by adding this new theme. The casual iconoclasm of this last is like a breath of fresh air in the awed and silent halls of modern adulation.

(i) HAMLET'S DELAY

IT must be emphasized that delay in real life is one thing, in a drama quite another. We know quite well that Hamlet delays two months or so before he kills the King. How do we find this out? We find it out by putting two and two together. We hear from one character in the drama that the old King has been dead not quite two months. Then another character, later, in an unguarded moment, lets slip the information that the King has now been dead 'twice two months'. We pounce on this. We subtract. Then we follow Laertes. We find that he has been in Paris some time and is now wanting supplies. We collect the evidence bit by bit, we calculate, we reach our conclusions. They are conclusions that, if *Hamlet* were a piece of real life actually occurring, could not be questioned. As it is, they cannot be questioned. Only, they may or may not be of use to us. Laertes could wander all over Europe and yet Hamlet, as far as our impressions go, could in that time have been living a mere two days. In some dramas such things perhaps do not happen; in Shakespearian dramas it is a mere fact that they do. We are here in an Einstein world, where time has strange oddities, where intervals are a delusion and durations a snare. What does it matter that a month or two have gone by between Acts I and II? They have gone by, but not noticeably where Hamlet is; somewhere in another plane of the drama they have gone by. Hamlet at the end of Act I has announced that he will presently put on an antic disposition; in the first scene of Act II we see the initial consequences: he has frightened Ophelia. What has he been doing with himself all the time? It is like asking for news from the fourth dimension. Of course we know that he did several things. He had time to disarrange his attire, and it was perhaps in this interval that he took Horatio into his confidence. But the point to be made is that the interval (apart from one or two such suggestions made about it) has really no dramatic existence. Delay does not exist in a drama simply because it is (as it were) embedded in it. The delay that exists in a drama is the delay that is displayed. Delay, in any case, does not here quite coincide with time duration, is not the same thing as a mere colourless lapse of days. It is not enough to say that Hamlet procrastinates because, as a matter of fact, and regarding the play somewhat as an historical document, we find that he did not act for two months or so. If he procrastinates, it is because he is shown procrastinating. To put it another way, it is not sufficient that delay should be negatively implicit in the play; it is necessary, for its dramatic existence, that it should be positively demonstrated. The delay, in a word, exists just inasmuch as and just to the degree in which it is conveyed.

It seems to me that if this principle is held in mind, the problem of *Hamlet* looms rather less large.

(ii) THE CENTRAL THEME OF HAMLET

What is the play of *Hamlet* really about? It is, of course, about many things; we understand how various are its appeals. But what is it most deeply about? Irresolution? Surely there is something in the play deeper than that. If we answer the question by asking ourselves another one, What is it that Hamlet himself is most deeply concerned about? – What is it that above all other things dominates his soul? – we can have no doubt what we must say. It would be too much to affirm that, compared with his horror at his mother, the shock of the murder is a trifle: yet it is nearly true. If the centre of the equilibrium of the play is the centre of the equilibrium of Hamlet's soul, then it is clear where it must lie. He forgets his vengeance; but he remembers this other thing. How he remembers it! It is strange that so vital a strain in the play should not have received more attention: it is impossible not to feel it. The first soliloquy beings it home to us; it is from then onwards the underlying theme. With Hamlet the feeling is an obsession and we are never left for long without an indication of its presence. We hear from Ophelia presently (II. I. 88) how he came to her, grasped her wrist, and, with his hand o'er his brow, fell to such perusal of her face as he would draw it; then, after the soul-searching scrutiny, raised a sigh that seemed

> to shatter all his bulk
> And end his being.   II. I. 95

It is as if already all womanhood has become suspect of the corruption he has discovered in his mother. A little later is the bitter gibing of the speech with Polonius (II. 2. 182): 'Have you a daughter? ... Let her not walk i' the sun. Conception is a blessing, but as your daughter may conceive . . .'. It is the same when next he meets Ophelia: the cruel harping on 'honesty' (III. I. 103), the savage cynicism of 'for wise men know well enough what monsters you make of them' (III. I. 138), that anguish that suddenly starts into his voice and makes us glimpse the abyss in his soul: 'Go to, I'll no more on't; it hath made me mad' (III. I. 146). Here too is that same spreading and deepening of the disgust to include all life: 'What should such fellows as I do crawling between earth and heaven?' (III. I. 128). We see him again soon in the play-scene. He and Horatio are supposed to be watching every movement of the King's features. How does he occupy himself? We remember how he lies down at Ophelia's feet and with what manner of jesting he passes the time. And then, the troubled Ophelia calling him 'merry', instantaneously, and, as it were, automatically, comes the sarcastic rejoinder: 'What should a man do but be merry? For look you how cheerfully my mother looks, and my father died within's two hours'. Presently, ''Tis brief, my lord,' comments

Ophelia, of the play; the response is inevitable: 'As woman's love.'
It is as if his experience has become woven into the very texture of
his mind; he thinks of nothing else. The very word 'mother' has
become an instrument of torture to him and he invents ways of
using it on himself: puns, innuendoes, cryptic jests (III. 2. 317):

ROSENCRANTZ: She desires to speak with you in her closet ere you
go to bed.
HAMLET: We shall obey, were she ten times our mother.

His good-bye to the King is a grotesque conundrum

Farewell, dear mother.
KING: Thy loving father, Hamlet.
HAMLET: My mother-father and mother is man and wife, man and wife
is one flesh, and so, my mother.   IV. 3. 48

The climax is reached in the scene in Gertrude's room, where his
tormented spirit relieves itself in those bitter upbraidings. But what
is most interesting to note is the quality of the dark thoughts and
images that now gush forth. The loathsome broodings that had
made his mind a hell now appear in all their hideousness in the light
of day. It is a terrible and wonderful scene and in figure after figure
('batten', 'compulsive ardour', 'frost that burns', 'rank sweat',
'stew'd in corruption', 'sty', 'compost') we are made to see with
what thoughts, what pictures, Hamlet had been living. We need
not wonder much further about what came to him in the bad
dreams. Perhaps most terrible, most touching of all, is that strangely
intimate, urgent pleading with the mother, that she should not
return to the marriage-bed. He can scarcely relinquish this subject;
it is as if it had fastened on his very soul.

It seems certain, too, that we must understand the mystery of his
relations with Ophelia (so far as we can understand it) in the light
of all this trouble. It is indeed rather a question of guessing than of
understanding. The whole matter is left, perhaps with some deliberation, enigmatic. We seem justified in assuming that Hamlet
loved Ophelia once, though even there we are given little chance
of doing more than speculate on the quality and intensity of his
love. It seems clear that the love, as we see it in the play, has been
poisoned by some strange resentment, suspicion, or hatred. The
rest is left undetermined. But we do seem warranted, at least, in

connecting this change with that other experience. All women fall under the ban. Perhaps we may go even farther. Those jeering allusions of Hamlet's to 'conception'; those pitiful songs of Ophelia in madness; do such hints amount to anything? Is it suggested that Hamlet savagely tried Ophelia, to see if she was of the selfsame metal as his mother? It would at least have been natural, in this wreckage of his world, to turn and experiment bitterly on this last piece of seeming innocence, testing, if it also were wreckable. If it were so, we can imagine what her death meant to him and gain, as Professor Allardyce Nicoll suggests, a new comprehension of the 'It is no matter' mood of Act v. But we cannot pursue this. We are left with the conclusion that Shakespeare did not trouble or did not wish to make the Hamlet-Ophelia story plainer, and in face of his refusal are helpless.

(iii) THE OLD PLAY AND THE NEW

What of the sources and of what can be gathered concerning the older *Hamlet*? It is clear at least that the story as it came to Shakespeare's hands was a story of comparatively crude build – of rather obvious motives and direct aims. In its oldest forms the narrative is one of revenge pure and simple. The murder is open and notorious; the madness of the avenger is assumed for cover; the avenger delays because he cannot help himself: there are serious difficulties – guards, courtiers about the King. In short, all is external and clear as day. It may be that in the lost play of *Hamlet* the clarity was already beginning to be obscured; but we may conjecture that the old lines were still followed and that the play was still one of downright and easily comprehensible revenge. Now, in Shakespeare, what has happened? We have, to begin with, the importation of almost a new central motive, for how we can deny centrality to the mother-son motive it is difficult to see. And what happens to *revenge*? Whether the task of welding the new motive to the old proved surprisingly irksome, whether it was that in the interest of his new ideas Shakespeare became absent-minded about the old groundwork, it is clear that the revenge theme in the final play has been considerably damaged: and this remains true apart from any theories we may cherish concerning the cause of the inaction. There are misfits. The old material seems here and there to bulge out awkwardly into the new play. Old consequences are retained, and sometimes do not have their proper causes. Episodes lose their *raison d'être* and inhere in the play like survivals.

We may note one or two of the most conspicuous examples. The madness is one. As we have seen, the madness in the original plot had point and logic. It was a shelter behind which the avenger would await his opportunity. Perhaps in the 'Ur-Hamlet' the madness had already lost some of its logic. If the murder by now had been made secret, such a device would at least not have been so obviously useful. In the Shakespearian play it has become really puzzling. For how much, after all, can we say about it? We know the famous explanation. It is an emotional safety-valve for Hamlet: he had some subtle feeling that he would need it. The explanation is exceedingly attractive and we wish we could be sure that Shakespeare so meant it. But we cannot, after all, be quite sure. Certainly the scene of the 'wild and whirling words' is wonderfully conceived. It is a scene that, apart from minor difficulties, is immediately convincing: the half-hysterical outburst after the Ghost's revelation, the drop from the tension to a buffoonery that strikes his companions as equally hysterical, his *silliness* as they question him –

> HORATIO: What news, my lord?
> HAMLET: O, wonderful! I. 5. 118

then the grotesque interlude with the subterranean Ghost, and, at the end, the returning melancholy. But it is doubtful whether the vivid impressions of this scene quite suffice to answer the question, why he put on the madness. There is that mysterious business of the swearing to secrecy; and then the instruction (I. 5. 168):

> But come.
> Here, as before, never, so help you mercy,
> How strange or odd some'er I bear myself –
> As I perchance hereafter shall think meet
> To put an antic disposition on –
> That you, at such times seeing me, never shall,
> With arms encumb'red thus, or this head-shake . . .

But why? we ask ourselves again. I think the conclusion is inescapable, that here is at all events a partial failure to assimilate, re-explain, original material. Nor can we help feeling that, compared with Shakespeare's own audiences, we are rather at a disadvantage. This swearing to secrecy, this assumption of the antic disposition, were familiar, time-honoured incidents. And though, in Shakespeare's new play, their old significances had almost disappeared, to the audiences, no doubt, they carried their old sanctions with them. They had become, as it were, institutional and could stand by their own prestige. It could not be detected, besides, until later in the play, that they had now become meaningless; at the moment they would seem natural enough. I feel that no other view is nearly so satisfactory. We *can* re-explain the antic disposition; but we do it without full warrant. Shakespeare has not proffered his assistance, and really in that case we have no business to help ourselves.

Then there is the voyage to England. Why does Hamlet sail for England? Apparently he does not know himself (there is a vague suggestion of compulsion – again a relic of the older play: he is 'without, guarded'; he 'must to England'); we do not know; and it seems doubtful if Shakespeare could have given an answer that would have been respectable. He could have given various inadmissible reasons. The actor playing the hero was badly in need of a rest hereabouts; in any case there seemed little else that Hamlet could be made to do just here except go to England; he always had, in the old play or plays, gone to England at this stage of the action and in short there seemed no just cause why he should not keep on going there. Professor Bradley has explained the difficulties attending a Fourth Act in the Shakespearian plan of drama. It comes after the climax and before the play has gathered its last momentum. There is almost compulsorily a lull, an interval not always easy to maintain at an interesting pitch. It is the 'delaying' act. Shakespeare surmounts the difficulties here with his customary dexterity. But the hero did present something of a problem. His absence from the action, already prescribed, was perhaps a dramatic convenience as well. He had already delayed; he must still delay; but perhaps better that he should seem vaguely occupied abroad than that he should embarrassingly loiter at home.

Such passages emphasize interestingly the distinction in our drama between dramatic and extra-dramatic causes. We can easily see the purposes which Hamlet's madness serves in the economy of the play. He realizes himself in and through it. And what a shield for his satiric comment! From its shelter, with the security of a jester, he launches his barbs. But the motivation of it is another question. So with the English voyage. The reasons for it may be surmised; we are still left to doubt whether these reasons are presentable dramatic reasons.

from *Hamlet: A Study in Critical Method*, 1931

EIGHT

A Letter to John Barrymore

from GEORGE BERNARD SHAW

22 February 1925

My dear Mr Barrymore:

I have to thank you for inviting me – and in such kind terms too – to your first performance of Hamlet in London; and I am glad you had no reason to complain of your reception, or, on the whole, of your press. Everyone felt that the occasion was one of extraordinary interest; and so far as your personality was concerned they were not disappointed.

I doubt, however, whether you have been able to follow the course of Shakespearian production in England during the last fifteen years or so enough to realize the audacity of your handling of the play. When I last saw it performed at Stratford-on-Avon, practically the entire play was given in three hours and three quarters, with one interval of ten minutes; and it made the time pass without the least tedium, though the cast was not in any way remarkable. On Thursday last you played five minutes longer with the play cut to ribbons, even to the breath-bereaving extremity of cutting out the recorders, which is rather like playing King John without little Arthur.

You saved, say, an hour and a half on Shakespear by the cutting, and filled it up with an interpolated drama of your own in dumb show. This was a pretty daring thing to do. In modern shop plays, without characters or anything but the commonest dialogue, the actor has to supply everything but the mere story, getting in the psychology between the lines, and presenting in his own person the fascinating hero whom the author has been unable to create. He is not substituting something of his own for something of the author's: he is filling up a void and doing the author's work for him. And the author ought to be extremely obliged to him.

But to try this method on Shakespear is to take on an appalling responsibility and put up a staggering pretension. Shakespear, with all his shortcomings, was a very great playwright; and the actor who undertakes to improve his plays undertakes thereby to excel to an extraordinary degree in two professions in both of which the highest success is extremely rare. Shakespear himself, though by no means a modest man, did not pretend to be able to play Hamlet as well as write it; he was content to do a recitation in the dark as the ghost. But you have ventured not only to act Hamlet, but to discard about a third of Shakespear's script and substitute stuff of your own, and that, too, without the help of dialogue. Instead of giving what is called a reading of Hamlet, you say, in effect, 'I am not going to read Hamlet at all: I am going to leave it out. But see what I give you in exchange!'

Such an enterprise must justify itself by its effect on the public. You discard the recorders as hackneyed back chat, and the scene with the king after the death of Polonius, with such speeches as 'How all occasions do inform against me!' as obsolete junk, and offer instead a demonstration of that very modern discovery called the Oedipus complex, thereby adding a really incestuous motive on Hamlet's part to the merely conventional incest of a marriage (now legal in England) with a deceased husband's brother. You change Hamlet and Ophelia into Romeo and Juliet. As producer, you allow Laertes and Ophelia to hug each other as lovers instead of lecturing and squabbling like hectoring big brother and little sister: another complex!

Now your success in this must depend on whether the play invented by Barrymore on the Shakespear foundation is as gripping as the Shakespear play, and whether your dumb show can hold an audience as a straightforward reading of Shakespear's rhetoric can. I await the decision with interest.

My own opinion is, of course, that of an author. I write plays that play for three hours and a half even with instantaneous changes and only one short interval. There is no time for silences or pauses: the actor must play on the line and not between the lines, and must do nine-tenths of his acting with his voice. Hamlet – Shakespear's Hamlet – can be done from end to end in four hours in that way; and it never flags nor bores. Done in any other way Shakespear is the worst of bores, because he has to be chopped into a mere cold stew. I prefer my way. I wish you would try it, and concentrate on acting rather than on authorship, at which, believe me, Shakespear can write your head off. But that may be vicarious professional jealousy on my part.

I did not dare to say all this to Mrs Barrymore on the night. It was chilly enough for her without a coat in the stalls without any cold water from

Yours perhaps too candidly,

G. Bernard Shaw

'A letter to John Barrymore' by George Bernard Shaw (Ladies Home Journal, XLIII, Febrary 1926). Reprinted in *Shaw on Theatre*, ed. by E. J. West (Hill and Wang Dramabooks)

Suggestions for Further Reading

There is, of course, far more criticism about *Hamlet* than about any other play; and Waldock's book (above), as well as offering its own comments on the play, is perhaps the most convenient guide through some of the earlier critics. The list that follows must perforce be an even more arbitrary selection than is the case with the other plays.

H. GRANVILLE-BARKER: *Prefaces to Shakespeare III.*

T. S. ELIOT: *'Hamlet'* (in *The Sacred Wood*: reprinted in *Selected Essays*). Suggests that the play is not really an artistic success, because 'Hamlet (the man) is dominated by an emotion which is inexpressible, because it is in *excess* of the facts as they appear'. To clarify this point, Eliot introduces his now famous notion of the 'objective correlative'.

WILLIAM EMPSON: *'Hamlet* when New' (*Sewanee Review*, Winter and Spring, 1953). 'The real "Hamlet problem", it seems clear, is a problem about his first audiences.' Empson, however, uses a historical approach to draw far more imaginative and daring conclusions about the Revenge Play than literary historians ever allow themselves.

H. D. F. KITTO: *Form and Meaning in Drama.* Contains a discussion of *Hamlet.*

G. WILSON KNIGHT: 'The Embassy of Death' (in *The Wheel of Fire*). Comes very close to suggesting that Hamlet is the villain, and so has often been dismissed as eccentric, even lunatic. Eccentric it is: but it may nonetheless be offering an insight into this eccentric play.

JULES LAFORGUE: *'Hamlet'* (in *Moralités légendaires*). Not concerned with the play; but a fascinating attempt to express, in terms of the sensibility of the late nineteenth century, the mood – or a version of the mood – of Shakespeare's prince.

HARRY LEVIN: *The Question of Hamlet.*

MAYNARD MACK: 'The World of *Hamlet*' (*Yale Review*, 1952; reprinted in *Shakespeare: Modern Essays in Criticism*, ed. by Leonard F. Dean; and in *Tragic Themes in Western Literature*, ed. by Cleanth Brooks).

SALVADOR DE MADARIAGA: *On Hamlet.*

GEORGE SANTAYANA: *'Hamlet'* (printed in *Life and Letters*, vol. I (1926), and reprinted in Santayana's *Obiter Scripta*). 'It is the tragedy of a soul buzzing in the glass prison of a world which it can neither escape nor understand, in which it flutters about without direction, without clear hope, and yet with many a keen pang, many a dire imaginary problem, and much exquisite music.'

E. M. W. TILLYARD: *Shakespeare's Problem Plays.*

J. DOVER WILSON: *What Happens in Hamlet.* Tries to re-emphasize those aspects of the play (e.g. the political element, the question of the ghost's true nature) which were clearer or more prominent to the original audience than they are to us.

OTHELLO

NINE

Iago

A. C. BRADLEY

... CERTAINLY he assigns motives enough; the difficulty is that he assigns so many. A man moved by simple passions due to simple causes does not stand fingering his feelings, industriously enumerating their sources, and groping about for new ones. But this is what Iago does. And this is not all. These motives appear and disappear in the most extraordinary manner. Resentment at Cassio's appointment is expressed in the first conversation with Roderigo, and from that moment is never once mentioned again in the whole play. Hatred of Othello is expressed in the first act alone. Desire to get Cassio's place scarcely appears after the first soliloquy, and when it is gratified Iago does not refer to it by a single word. The suspicion of Cassio's intrigue with Emilia emerges suddenly, as an after-thought, not in the first soliloquy but the second, and then disappears for ever. Iago's 'love' of Desdemona is alluded to in the second soliloquy; there is not the faintest trace of it in word or deed either before or after. The mention of jealousy of Othello is followed by declarations that Othello is infatuated about Desdemona and is of a constant nature, and during Othello's sufferings Iago never shows a sign of the idea that he is now paying his rival in his own coin. In the second soliloquy he declares that he quite believes Cassio to be in love with Desdemona: it is obvious that he believes no such thing, for he never alludes to the idea again, and within a few hours describes Cassio in soliloquy as an honest fool. This final reason for ill-will to Cassio never appears till the fifth act.

What is the meaning of all this? Unless Shakespeare was out of his mind, it must have a meaning. And certainly this meaning is not contained in any of the popular accounts of Iago.

Is it contained then in Coleridge's word 'motive-hunting'? Yes, 'motive-hunting' exactly answers to the impression that Iago's soliloquies produce. He is pondering his design, and unconsciously trying to justify it to himself. He speaks of one or two real feelings, such as resentment against Othello, and he mentions one or two real causes of these feelings. But these are not enough for him. Along with them, or alone, there come into his head, only to leave it again, ideas and suspicions, the creations of his own baseness or uneasiness, some old, some new, caressed for a moment to feed his purpose and give it a reasonable look, but never really believed in, and never the main forces which are determining his action. In fact, I would venture to describe Iago in these soliloquies as a man setting out on a project which strongly attracts his desire, but at the same time conscious of a resistance to the desire, and unconsciously trying to argue the resistance away by assigning reasons for the project. He is the counterpart of Hamlet, who tried to find reasons for his delay in pursuing a design which excites his aversion. And most of Iago's reasons for actions are no more the real ones than Hamlet's reasons for delay were the real ones. Each is moved by forces which he does not understand; and it is probably no accident that these two studies of states psychologically so similar were produced at about the same period.

What then were the real moving forces of Iago's action? . . . To find these, let us return to our half-completed analysis of the character. Let us remember especially the keen sense of superiority, the contempt of others, the sensitiveness to everything which wounds these feelings, the spite against goodness in men as a thing not only stupid but, both in its nature and by its success, contrary to Iago's nature and irritating to his pride. Let us remember in addition the annoyance of having always to play a part, the consciousness of exceptional but unused ingenuity and address, the enjoyment of action, and the absence of fear. And let us ask what would be the greatest pleasure of such a man, and what the situation which might tempt him to abandon his habitual prudence and pursue this pleasure. Hazlitt and Mr Swinburne do not put this question, but the answer I proceed to give to it is in principle theirs.

The most delightful thing to such a man would be something that gave an extreme satisfaction to his sense of power and superiority; and if it involved, secondly, the triumphant exertion of his abilities, and, thirdly, the excitement of danger, his delight would be consummated. And the moment most dangerous to such a man would be one when his sense of superiority had met with an affront, so that its habitual craving was reinforced by resentment, while at the same time he saw an opportunity of satisfying it by subjecting to his will the very persons who had affronted it. Now, this is the temptation that comes to Iago. Othello's eminence, Othello's goodness, and his own dependence on Othello, must have been a perpetual annoyance to him. At *any* time he would have enjoyed befooling and tormenting Othello. Under ordinary circumstances he was restrained, chiefly by self-interest, in some slight degree perhaps by the faintest pulsations of conscience or humanity. But disappointment at the loss of the lieutenancy supplied the touch of lively resentment that was required to overcome these obstacles; and the prospect of satisfying the sense of power by mastering Othello through an intricate and hazardous intrigue now became irresistible. Iago did not clearly understand what was moving his desire; though he tried to give himself reasons for his action, even those that had some reality made but a small part of the motive force; one may almost say they were no more than the turning of the handle which admits the driving power into the machine. Only once does he appear to see something of the truth. It is when he uses the phrase 'to *plume up my will* in double knavery'.

To 'plume up the will', to heighten the sense of power or superiority – this seems to be the unconscious motive of many acts of cruelty which evidently do not spring chiefly from ill-will, and which therefore puzzle and sometimes horrify us most. It is often this that makes a man bully the wife or children of whom he is fond. The boy who torments another boy, as we say, 'for no reason', or who without any hatred for frogs tortures a frog, is pleased with his victim's pain, not from any disinterested love of evil or pleasure in pain, but mainly because this pain is the unmistakable proof of his own power over his victim. So it is with Iago. His thwarted sense of superiority wants satisfaction. What fuller satisfaction could it find than the consciousness that he is the master of the General who has undervalued him and of the rival who has been preferred to him; that these worthy people, who are so successful and popular and stupid, are mere puppets in his hands, but living puppets, who at the motion of his finger must contort themselves in agony while all the time they believe that he is their one true friend and comforter? It must have been an ecstasy of bliss to him. And this, granted a most abnormal deadness of human feeling, is, however horrible, perfectly intelligible. There is no mystery in the psychology of Iago; the mystery lies in a further question, which the drama has not to answer, the question why such a being should exist.

Iago's longing to satisfy the sense of power is, I think, the strongest of the forces that drive him on. But there are two others to be noticed. One is the pleasure in an action very difficult and perilous and, therefore, intensely exciting. This action sets all his powers on the strain. He feels the delight of one who executes successfully a feat thoroughly congenial to his special aptitude, and only just within his compass; and, as he is fearless by nature, the fact that a single slip will cost him his life only increases his pleasure. His exhilaration breaks out in the ghastly words with which he greets the sunrise after the night of the drunken tumult which has led to Cassio's disgrace: 'By the mass, 'tis morning. Pleasure and action make the hours seem short.' Here, however, the joy in exciting action is quickened by other feelings. It appears more simply elsewhere in such a way as to suggest that nothing but such actions gave him happiness, and that his happiness was greater if the action was destructive as well as exciting. We find it, for instance, in his gleeful cry to Roderigo, who proposes to shout to Brabantio in order to wake him and tell him of his daughter's flight:

> Do, with like timorous accent and dire yell
> As when, by night and negligence, the fire
> Is spied in populous cities.   I. I. 76

All through that scene; again, in the scene where Cassio is attacked and Roderigo murdered; everywhere where Iago is in physical action, we catch this sound of almost feverish enjoyment. His blood, usually so cold and slow, is racing through his veins.

But Iago, finally, is not simply a man of action; he is an artist. His action is a plot, the intricate plot of a drama, and in the conception and execution of it he experiences the tension and the joy of artistic creation. 'He is,' says Hazlitt, 'an amateur of tragedy in real life; and, instead of employing his invention on imaginary characters or long-forgotten incidents, he takes the bolder and more dangerous course of getting up his plot at home, casts the principal parts among his nearest friends and connexions, and rehearses it in downright earnest, with steady nerves and unabated resolution.' Mr Swinburne lays even greater stress on this aspect of Iago's character, and even declares that 'the very subtlest and strongest component of his complex nature' is 'the instinct of what Mr Carlyle would call an inarticulate poet'. And those to whom this idea is unfamiliar, and who may suspect it at first sight of being fanciful, will find, if they examine the play in the light of Mr Swinburne's exposition, that it rests on a true and deep perception, will stand scrutiny, and might easily be illustrated. They may observe, to take only one point, the curious analogy between the early stages of dramatic composition and those soliloquies in which Iago broods over his plot, drawing at first only an outline, puzzled how to fix more than the main idea, and gradually seeing it develop and clarify as he works upon it or lets it work. Here at any rate Shakespeare put a good deal of himself into Iago. But the tragedian in real life was not the equal of the tragic poet. His psychology, as we shall see, was at fault, at a critical point, as Shakespeare's never was. And so his catastrophe came out wrong, and his piece was ruined.

Such, then, seem to be the chief ingredients of the force which, liberated by his resentment at Cassio's promotion, drives Iago from inactivity into action, and sustains him through it. And, to pass to a new point, this force completely possesses him; it is his fate. It is like the passion with which a tragic hero wholly identifies himself, and which bears him on to his doom. It is true that, once embarked on this course, Iago *could* not turn back, even if this passion did abate; and it is also true that he is compelled, by his success in convincing Othello, to advance to conclusions of which at the outset he did not dream. He is thus caught in his own web, and could not liberate himself if he would. But, in fact, he never shows a trace of wishing to do so, not a trace of hesitation, of looking back, or of fear, any more than of remorse; there is no ebb in the tide. As the crisis approaches there passes through his mind a fleeting doubt whether the deaths of Cassio and Roderigo are indispensable; but that uncertainty, which does not concern the main issue, is dismissed, and he goes forward with undiminished zest. Not even in his sleep – as in Richard's before his final battle – does any rebellion of outraged conscience or pity, or any foreboding of despair, force itself into clear consciousness. His fate – which is himself – has completely mastered him: so that, in the later scenes, where the improbability of the entire success of a design built on so many different falsehoods forces itself on the reader, Iago appears for moments not as a consummate schemer, but as a man absolutely infatuated and delivered over to certain destruction.

from Lecture VI of *Shakespearean Tragedy*, 1904

TEN

The Hero and the Devil

MAUD BODKIN

IN this essay we shall consider the image of man, or the hero, as
expressing the sense of self in relation to forces that appear under
the names of God, or Fate, and of the Devil.

It will be convenient first to follow up the reference already
made, when considering *Faust*, to a mode of representing a factor
of human experience by a figure man-like yet not concretely human
– the Devil in the form of a man. I shall attempt some study of the
tragedy of *Othello*, in order to examine the figure of Iago in relation to Othello, and to compare it with Mephistopheles in relation
to Faust.

I would ask the reader to recall his experience of the play of
Othello, focusing it at the moment, in Act II, of the meeting of
Othello and Desdemona, in the presence of Iago. This appears to
me one of those moments where the poet's choice of words and
shaping of the action leads us to look back and forward, concentrating in its timeless significance the procession of the play's
temporal unfolding. Each of the chief figures at this moment
appears charged with full symbolic value for feeling. The character
of the situation – the fury of the storm braved, Othello's military
task accomplished by the elements' aid – prepares for that idealization of the hero and his bride communicated through the words of
Cassio:

> Tempests themselves, high seas, and howling winds,
> The gutter'd rocks and congregated sands,
> Traitors ensteep'd to enclog the guiltless keel,
> As having sense of beauty, to omit
> Their mortal natures, letting go safely by
> The divine Desdemona. . . .
> . . . Great Jove, Othello guard,
> And swell his sail with thine own powerful breath,
> That he may bless this bay with his tall ship,

Make love's quick pants in Desdemona's arms,
Give renew'd fire to our extincted spirits,
[And bring all Cyprus comfort!]   II. I. 68

The words of Othello greeting Desdemona communicate the
experience of that high rapture which in a tragic world brings fear.
We feel a poise of the spirit like that of the sun at its zenith, or of
the wheel of fate, before the downward plunge. Consider these
words in their place:

OTHELLO: O my fair warrior!
DESDEMONA: My dear Othello!
OTHELLO: It gives me wonder great as my content
          To see you here before me. O my soul's joy!
          If after every tempest come such calms,
          May the winds blow till they have waken'd death,
          And let the labouring bark climb hills of seas
          Olympus-high, and duck again as low
          As hell's from heaven. If it were now to die,
          'Twere now to be most happy; for I fear
          My soul hath her content so absolute
          That not another comfort like to this
          Succeeds in unknown fate.   II. I. 179

The name Othello gives his lady, 'my fair warrior', recalls the
events that have led up to this meeting. It reminds us of Othello's
story of his wooing – how, moved by his life's tale of warlike
adventure,

    She swore, in faith, 'twas strange, 'twas passing strange;
    'Twas pitiful, 'twas wondrous pitiful.
    She wish'd she had not heard it; yet she wish'd
    That heaven had made her such a man . . .
    She lov'd me for the dangers I had pass'd
    And I lov'd her that she did pity them.   I. 3. 160

And of Desdemona's confession:

    That I did love the Moor to live with him,
    My downright violence, and storm of fortunes,
    May trumpet to the world. My heart's subdu'd:
    Even to the very quality of my lord:
    I saw Othello's visage in his mind;

And to his honors and his valiant parts
Did I my soul and fortunes consecrate.
So that, dear lords, if I be left behind,
A moth of peace, and he go to the war,
The rites for which I love him are bereft me.   I. 3. 248

Desdemona – the 'maiden never bold; Of spirit so still and quiet that her motion Blushed at herself' – has found, we divine, in Othello the warrior hidden in the depth of her woman's heart. She lives in him as 'essential man in all his prowess and protective strength', while he finds in her 'essential woman', and lives in her adoring trust and love as in the secret place his own later words describe:

where I have garner'd up my heart,
Where either I must live or bear no life,
The fountain from the which my current runs,
Or else dries up . . .   IV. 2. 58

In the light that these passages throw upon the relation of the lovers, their high moment appears as, in a manner, a fulfilment of fantasy – the almost inevitable, archetypal fantasy of man and woman in their turning to one another – and this sense of it contributes to the presage of disaster. We may recall Shakespeare's rendering in his sonnets of the tragic aspect that belongs to love in its very nature. 'Love's not Time's fool,' he cries, but to prove that Love is not so, against 'reckoning Time, whose million'd accidents Creep in twixt vows', is a desperate venture of faith and will.

To the menace immanent in the form of the ecstatic moment substantial shape is given in the figure of Iago. Already in earlier scenes Iago has become known to us, his hatred of Othello, his pose of the honest clear-sighted friend. Here, as the lovers embrace, the harsh impact of his threatening aside gains intensity from the shadowing fear that lies in excess of happiness:

O, you are well tun'd now!
But I'll set down the pegs that make this music,
As honest as I am.   II. I. 198

In his essay entitled 'The Othello music', Wilson Knight has

enriched our apprehension of the metaphor in these words of Iago
by relating it to his view of the main contrast within the play and
of the manner in which it is presented. He gives detailed illustration
of the way in which Shakespeare has utilized the resources of style
in speech to convey the relation between the different worlds, or
forces, which the characters represent. The unrealistic beauty of
Othello's speech, when he is master of himself, suggests the romantic world of varied colour, form, and sound, to which Othello
belongs:

> The spirit-stirring drum, th' ear-piercing fife,
> The royal banner, and all quality,
> Pride, pomp, and circumstance of glorious war!   III. 3. 356

'Othello's speech reflects not a soldier's language, but the quality of
soldiership in all his glamour of romantic adventure.' Othello is a
symbol of faith in human values of love and war, romantically conceived. Desdemona, as she appears in relation to Othello, is not so
much individual woman as the Divinity of love. Iago is cynicism
incarnate. He stands for a 'devil-world', unlimited, formless,
negative. He is the spirit of denial of all romantic values. His
hatred of Othello is something intrinsic to his nature, needing no
external motive. Othello's world of colour, shape, and music is
undermined by him, poisoned, disintegrated. We are made to
feel the disintegration through the direct impact of speech, as
Othello's verbal music is transformed by the working of Iago's
'poison' into incoherence – something chaotic, absurd, hideous:

> – pish! noses, ears, and lips. Is't possible? Confess!
> Handkerchief! O devil!   IV. 1. 41

Only at the end we feel the partial, hard-won self-maintenance of
the world of romantic values in Othello's recovery of his speech-
music; as when he gives expression to that longing – recurrent in
the Shakespearian tragic hero – for the survival of his memory and
his true story among men:

> Speak of me as I am. Nothing extenuate,
> Nor set down aught in malice. Then must you speak
> Of one that loved not wisely but too well;
> Of one not easily jealous, but, being wrought,

Perplexed in the extreme; of one whose hand,
Like the base Indian, threw a pearl away
Richer than all his tribe; . . .

v. 2. 349

Upon this characterization of the different worlds or forces that contend within the play, I wish to base a further psychological consideration of the figure of Iago in relation to Othello. Wilson Knight has noted that while Othello and Desdemona have symbolic significance, they are also 'warmly human, concrete'. Iago, on the other hand, is mysterious, inhuman, 'a kind of Mephistopheles'. Iago illustrates, we may say, that different plane of representation noted in relation to Greek and medieval art; and we may raise the question how far it is possible to identify Iago as a projected image of forces present in Othello, in some such fashion as Apatê of the vase-painting represents the blindness of ambition in the Persian king.

We may note first that even when a critic sets out, as A. C. Bradley does, to study Iago's character as if he were an actual living man, what seems to emerge most clearly is the dominance of the man by a certain force, or spirit. We can feel, says Bradley, the part of himself that Shakespeare put into Iago – the artist's delight in the development of a plot, a design, which, as it works itself out, masters and possesses him. In regard to this plot it concerns us, as psychological critics, to note that it is built not merely, as Bradley remarks, on falsehood, but also on partial truths of human nature that the romantic vision ignores. It is such a truth that a woman, 'a super-subtle Venetian', suddenly wedding one in whom she sees the image of her ideal warrior, is liable to experience moments of revulsion from the strange passionate creature she as yet knows so little, movements of nature toward those more nearly akin to her in 'years, manners and beauties'. There is an element of apt truth in Iago's thought that a woman's love may be won, but not held, by 'bragging and telling her fantastical lies'. There is terrible truth in the reflection that if a man is wedded to his fantasy of woman as the steadfast hiding-place of his heart, the fountain whence his current flows, so that he grows frantic and blind with passion at the thought of the actual woman he has married as a creature of natural varying impulse – then he lies at the mercy of life's chances, and of his own secret fears and suspicions.

What is the meaning of that reiteration by Othello of his trust in Iago's honesty? Before Iago has fashioned accident into a trap for Othello, and woven a web of falsehood to ensnare him, at his very first insinuations, Othello shows signs of terror. He fears the monster 'too hideous to be shown' that he discerns lurking in Iago's thought. He begins to harp upon his honesty:

> ... for I know thou art full of love and honesty
> And weigh'st thy words before thou giv'st them breath,
> Therefore these stops of thine fright me the more;   III. 3. 122

As soon as Iago has left him:

> Why did I marry? This honest creature doubtless
> Sees and knows more much more, than he unfolds.
>
> III. 3. 246

And again:

> This fellow's of exceeding honesty,
> And knows all qualities, with a learned spirit,
> Of human dealing . . .   III. 3. 262

The whole of this dialogue between Othello and Iago, at the very beginning of Iago's plot, shows the uncanny insight of genius, illustrating in anticipation the discoveries of science. Our halting psychological theory has begun to describe for us the manner in which those aspects of social experience that a man's thought ignores leave their secret impress on his mind; how from this impress spring feelings and impulses that work their way toward consciousness, and if refused entrance there project themselves into the words, looks, and gestures of those around, arming these with a terrible power against the willed personality and its ideals. Iago seems to Othello so honest, so wise beyond himself in human dealings, possessed of a terrible power of seeing and speaking truth, because into what he speaks are projected the half truths that Othello's romantic vision ignored, but of which his mind held secret knowledge.

If we attempt to define the devil in psychological terms, regarding him as an archetype, a persistent or recurrent mode of apprehension, we may say that the devil is our tendency to represent in personal form the forces within and without us that threaten our supreme values. When Othello finds those values, of confident love, of honour, and pride in soldiership, that made up his purposeful life, falling into ruin, his sense of the devil in all around him becomes acute. Desdemona has become 'a fair devil'; he feels 'a young and sweating devil' in her hand. The cry 'O devil' breaks out among his incoherent words of raving. When Iago's falsehoods are disclosed, and Othello at last, too late, wrenches himself free from the spell of Iago's power over him, his sense of the devil incarnate in Iago's shape before him becomes overwhelming. If those who tell of the devil have failed to describe Iago, they have lied:

> I look down towards his feet – but that's a fable.
> If that thou be'st a devil, I cannot kill thee.

V. 2. 288

We also, watching or reading the play, experience the archetype. Intellectually aware, as we reflect, of natural forces, within a man himself as well as in society around, that betray or shatter his ideals, we yet feel these forces aptly symbolized for the imagination by such a figure as Iago – a being through personal yet hardly human, concentrated wholly on the hunting to destruction of its destined prey, the proud figure of the hero.

from Archetypal Patterns in Poetry,
1934: Part V, Chapter I

ELEVEN

Honest in Othello

WILLIAM EMPSON

This extract is taken from a long, famous, and difficult book on the borderland between literary criticism and linguistic theory; and it may be helpful to the reader to be told something of Mr Empson's approach to a Shakespeare play. His discussion of *Othello* concentrates on the contrast between Iago and Othello, and his view of the play is compatible with that of Maud Bodkin, perhaps even indebted to it: what distinguishes the Empsonian method, however, is his insistence that the best way to contrast the two characters is not to speak about 'character' at all, but to concentrate on the interplay of meaning within some (in this case only one) of the key words of the play. Hence the title of the book, *The Structure of Complex Words*.

A complex word, to Empson, is one which the common reader would tend to think of as a very ordinary word: it is a word whose meaning includes important areas of our beliefs and values. 'A word may become a sort of solid entity, able to direct opinion, thought of as like a person; also it is often said (whether this is the same idea or not) that a word can become a "compacted doctrine", or even that all words are compacted doctrines inherently.' The words Empson mainly discusses are *fool, dog, honest,* and *sense.* Interesting uses of these words, he believes, assert unexplained relations between two or more of their many meanings; and these relations he represents by means of equations. Empson does not deny that such uses affect our emotions, often very powerfully; but he does not find it useful to talk about the emotional part of a word's meaning. The best way to describe this emotional impact is to examine the equations between the various senses of the word.

The key word of *Othello* is 'honest '. Though the essay on the play is self-contained, it follows two chapters analysing the meanings of this word; and if you find it valuable, it is well worth while turning these up.

This extract includes most of the first .section of the essay, in which Empson states his own theory; and all the analyses of particular uses of 'honest'. The later sections compare this theory with those of other critics, and I have included part of the discussion of Bradley: it seems to me one of those rare occasions where criticism of criticism really throws important light on the original work. Perhaps I should add that the selection from Bradley, included above, contains most of the ideas that Empson discusses, though it was not chosen for that reason. Bradley is at his very best (though not his most typical) on Iago.

*

THE fifty-two uses of *honest* and *honesty* in Othello are a very queer business; there is no other play in which Shakespeare worries a word like that. *King Lear* uses *fool* nearly as often but does not treat it as a puzzle, only as a source of profound metaphors. In *Othello* divergent uses of the key word are found for all the main characters; even the attenuated clown plays on it; the unchaste Bianca, for instance, snatches a moment to claim that she is more honest than Emilia the thief of the handkerchief; and with all the variety of use the ironies on the word mount up steadily to the end. Such is the general power of the writing that this is not obtrusive, but if all but the phrases involving *honest* were in the style of Ibsen the effect would be a symbolical charade. Everybody calls Iago honest once or twice, but with Othello it becomes an obsession; at the crucial moment just before Emilia exposes Iago he keeps howling the word out. The general effect has been fully recognized by critics, but it looks as if there is something to be found about the word itself.

What Shakespeare hated in the word, I believe, was a peculiar use, at once hearty and individualist, which was then common among raffish low people but did not become upper-class till the Restoration; here as in Iago's heroic couplets the play has a curious effect of prophecy. But to put it like this is no doubt to over-simplify; the Restoration use, easy to feel though hard to define, seems really different from its earlier parallels, and in any case does not apply well to Iago. . . . The word was in the middle of a rather complicated process of change, and what emerged from it was a sort of jovial cult of independence. At some stage of the development (whether by the date of *Othello* or not) the word came to have in it a covert assertion that the man who accepts the natural desires, who does not live by principle, will be fit for such warm uses of *honest* as imply 'generous' and 'faithful to friends', and to believe this to disbelieve the Fall of Man. Thus the word, apart from being complicated, also came to raise large issues, and it is not I think a wild fancy to suppose that Shakespeare could feel the way it was going. . . .

Most people would agree with what Bradley, for example, implied, that the way everybody calls Iago honest amounts to a criticism of the word itself; that is, Shakespeare means 'a bluff forthright manner, and amusing talk, which get a man called honest, may go with extreme dishonesty'. Or indeed that this is treated as normal, and the satire is on our nature not on language. But they would probably maintain that Iago is not honest and does not think himself so, and only calls himself so as a lie or an irony. It seems to me, if you leave the matter there, that there is much to be said for what the despised Rymer decided, when the implications of the hearty use of *honest* had become simpler and more clear-cut. He said that the play is ridiculous, because that sort of villain (silly-clever, full of secret schemes, miscalculating about people) does not get mistaken for that sort of honest man. This if true is of course a plain fault, whatever you think about 'character-analysis'. It is no use taking short cuts in these things, and I should fancy that what Rymer said had a large truth when he said it, and also that Iago was a plausible enough figure in his own time. The only main road into this baffling subject is to find how the characters actually use the term and thereby think about themselves.

I must not gloss over the fact that Iago once uses the word to say that he proposes to tell Othello lies:

> The Moor is of a free and open nature
> That thinks men honest that but seem to be so; . . . I. 3. 393

This is at the end of the first act. And indeed, the first use of the word in the play seems also to mean that Iago does not think himself honest. . . .

Both Iago and Othello oppose honesty to mere truth-telling:

OTHELLO:	I know, Iago,	
	Thy honesty and love doth mince this matter,	
	Making it light to Cassio . . .	II. 3. 237
IAGO:	It were not for your quiet nor your good,	
	Nor for my manhood, honesty, or wisdom,	
	To let you know my thoughts.	III. 3. 156

No doubt the noun tends to be more old-fashioned than the adjective, but anyway the old 'honourable' sense is as broad and vague as the new slang one; it was easy enough to be puzzled by the word. Iago means partly 'faithful to friends', which would go with the Restoration use, but partly I think 'chaste', the version normally used of women; what he has to say is improper. Certainly one cannot simply treat his version of *honest* as the Restoration one – indeed, the part of the snarling critic involves a rather puritanical view, at any rate towards other people. It is the two notions of being ready to blow the gaff on other people and frank to yourself about your own desires that seem to me crucial about Iago; they grow on their own, independently of the hearty feeling that would normally humanize them; though he can be a good companion as well.

One need not look for a clear sense when he toys with the word about Cassio; the question is how it came to be so mystifying. But I think a queer kind of honesty is maintained in Iago through all the puzzles he contrives; his emotions are always expressed directly, and it is only because they are clearly genuine ('These stops of thine', Othello tells him, 'are close dilations, working from the heart') that he can mislead Othello as to their cause.

OTHELLO: Is he not honest? (*Faithful, etc.*)

IAGO: Honest, my lord? (*Not stealing, etc. Shocked.*)

OTHELLO: Honest. Ay, honest. ('*Why repeat? The word is clear enough.*')

IAGO: My lord, for aught I know ... ('*In some sense.*')

IAGO: For Michael Cassio,
I dare be sworn I think that he is honest.

OTHELLO: I think so too.

IAGO: Men should be what they seem;
Or those that be not, would they might seem none!

OTHELLO: Certain, men should be what they seem.

IAGO: Why then, I think Cassio's an honest man.   III. 3. 104

Othello has just said that Cassio 'went between them very oft', so Iago now learns that Cassio lied to him in front of Brabantio's house when he pretended to know nothing about the marriage.

Iago feels he has been snubbed,* as too coarse to be trusted in such a matter, and he takes immediate advantage of his discomposure. The point of his riddles is to get 'not hypocritical' – 'frank about his own nature' accepted as the relevant sense; Iago will readily call him honest on that basis, and Othello cannot be reassured. 'Chaste' (the sense normally used of women) Cassio is not, but he is 'not a hypocrite' about Bianca. Iago indeed, despises him for letting her make a fool of him in public; for that and for other reasons (Cassio is young and without experience) Iago can put a contemptuous tone into the word; the feeling is genuine, but not the sense it may imply. This gives room for a hint that Cassio has been 'frank' to Iago in private about more things than may honestly be told. I fancy too, that the idea of 'not being men' gives an extra twist. Iago does not think Cassio manly nor that it is specially manly to be chaste; this allows him to agree that Cassio may be honest in the female sense about Desdemona and still keep a tone which seems to deny it – if he is, after so much encouragement, he must be 'effeminate' (there is a strong idea of 'manly' in *honest*, and an irony on that gives its opposite). Anyway, Iago can hide what reservations he makes but show that he makes reservations; this suggests an embarrassed defence – 'Taking a broad view, with the world as it is, and Cassio my friend, I can decently call him honest.' This forces to me the Restoration idea – 'an honest dog of a fellow, straightforward about women', and completes the suspicion. It is a bad piece of writing unless you are keyed up for the shifts of the word.

The play with the feminine version is doubtful here, but he certainly does it the other way round about Desdemona, where it had more point; in the best case it is for his own amusement when alone.

> And what's he, then, that says I play the villain?
> When this advice is free I give and honest,

* Cassio does not call Iago *honest* till he can use the word warmly (II. 3. 108); till then he calls him good Iago (II. 1. 97; II. 3. 34) – apparently a less obtrusive form of the same trick of patronage. Possibly as they have been rivals for his present job he feels it more civil to keep his distance. However the social contempt which he holds in check is hinted jovially to Desdemona (II. 1. 165) and comes out plainly when he is drunk; Iago returns the 'good' to him and is firmly snubbed for it as not a man of quality (II. 3. 108).

> Probal to thinking, and indeed the course
> To win the Moor again? For 'tis most easy
> Th' inclining Desdemona to subdue
> In any honest suit; she's fram'd as fruitful
> As the free elements.   II. 3. 325

Easy, inclining, fruitful, free all push the word the same way, from 'chaste' to 'flat, frank, and natural'; all turn the ironical admission of her virtue into a positive insult against her. The delight in juggling with the word here is close to the Machiavellian interest in plots for their own sake, which Iago could not resist and allowed to destroy him. But a good deal of the 'motive-hunting' of the soliloquies must, I think, be seen as part of Iago's 'honesty'; he is quite open to his own motives or preferences and interested to find out what they are.

The clear cases where Iago thinks himself honest are at a good distance from the Restoration use; they bring him into line with the series of sharp unromantic critics like Jacques and Hamlet:

> For I am nothing if not critical   II. 1. 119

he tells Desdemona to amuse her; his faults, he tells Othello, are due to an excess of this truthful virtue –

> ... I confess it is my nature's plague
> To spy into abuses, and oft my jealousy
> Shapes faults that are not.   III. 3. 150

There seems no doubt that he believes this and thinks it creditable, whatever policy made him say it here; indeed we know it is true from the soliloquies. Now this kind of man is really very unlike the Restoration 'honest fellow', and for myself I find it hard to combine them in one feeling about the word. But in a great deal of Iago's talk to Roderigo – 'drown thyself! drown cats and blind puppies ... why, thou silly gentleman, I will never love thee after' – he is a wise uncle, obviously honest in the cheerful sense, and for some time this is our main impression of him.* It is still strong during the business of making Cassio drunk; there is no reason why he should praise the English for their powers of drinking except to make sure that the groundlings are still on his side.

* It is a very bold and strange irony to make Othello repeat the phrase 'love thee after' just before he kills Desdemona.

Perhaps the main connexion between the two sorts of honest men is not being indulgent towards romantic love:

OTHELLO: I cannot speak enough of this content;
It stops me here; it is too much of joy.
And this, and this, the greatest discords be
That e'er our hearts shall make! [*Kissing her.*]

IAGO: O, you are well tun'd now!
But I'll set down the pegs that make this music,
As honest as I am.   II. I. 194

The grammar may read 'because I am so honest' as well as 'though I am so honest' and the irony may deny any resultant sense. He is ironical about the suggestions in the patronizing use, which he thinks are applied to him – 'low-class, and stupid, but good-natured'. But he feels himself really 'honest' as the kind of man who can see through nonsense; Othello's affair is a passing lust which has become a nuisance, and Iago can get it out of the way.

It may well be objected that this is far too mild a picture of Iago's plot, and indeed he himself is clearly impressed by its wickedness; at the end of the first act he calls it a 'monstrous birth' and invokes Hell to assist it. But after this handsome theatrical effect the second act begins placidly, in a long scene which includes the 'As honest as I am' passage, and at the end of this scene we find that Iago still imagines he will only

Make the Moor thank me, love me, and reward me
For making him egregiously an ass   II. I. 302

– to be sure, the next lines say he will practise on Othello 'even to madness', but even this can be fitted into the picture of the clown who makes 'fools' of other people; it certainly does not envisage the holocaust of the end of the play. Thinking in terms of character, it is clear that Iago has not yet decided how far he will go.

The suggestion of 'stupid' in a patronizing use of *honest* (still clear in 'honest Thompson, my gardener', a Victorian if not a present-day use) brings it near to *fool*; there is a chance for these two rich words to overlap. There is an aspect of Iago in which he is the Restoration 'honest fellow', who is good company because he blows the gaff; but much the clearest example of it is in the beginning of the second act, when he is making sport for his betters.

While Desdemona is waiting for Othello's ship, which may have
been lost in the tempest, he puts on an elaborate piece of clowning
to distract her; and she takes his real opinion of love and women
for a piece of hearty and good-natured fun. Iago's kind of honesty,
he feels, is not valued as it should be; there is much in Iago of the
Clown in Revolt, and the inevitable clown is almost washed out in
this play to give him a free field. It is not, I think, dangerously far-
fetched to take almost all Shakespeare's uses of *fool* as metaphors
from the clown, whose symbolism certainly rode his imagination
and was explained to the audience in most of his early plays. Now
Iago's defence when Othello at last turns on him, among the rich
ironies of its claim to honesty, brings in both *Fool* and the Vice
used in *Hamlet* as an old name for the clown.

IAGO: O wretched fool,
That lov'st to make thine honesty, a vice!*
O monstrous world! Take note, take note, O World,
To be direct and honest is not safe.
I thank you for this profit; and from hence
I'll love no friend, sith love breeds such offence.
OTHELLO: Nay, stay. Thou shouldst be honest.
IAGO: I should be wise; for honesty's a fool
And loses that it works for.
OTHELLO: By the world,
I think my wife be honest, and think she is not.   III. 3. 379

What comes out here is Iago's unwillingness to be the fool he
thinks he is taken for; but it is dramatic irony as well, and that
comes back to his notion of *honest*; he is fooled by the way his
plans run away with him; he fails in knowledge of others and perhaps even of his own desires.

Othello swears *by the world* because what Iago has said about
being honest in the world, suggesting what worldly people think, is
what has made him doubtful; yet the senses of *honest* are quite
different – chastity and truth-telling. Desdemona is called a super-
subtle Venetian, and he may suspect she would agree with what
Iago treats as worldly wisdom; whereas it was her simplicity that
made her helpless; though again, the fatal step was her lie about the
handkerchief. *Lov'st* in the second line (Folios) seems to be better

* And make thyself a motley to the view. Sonnet 110.

than *liv'st* (Quarto), as making the frightened Iago bring in his main claim at once; the comma after *honesty* perhaps makes the sense 'loves with the effect of making' rather than 'delights in making'; in any case *love* appears a few lines down. *Breeds* could suggest sexual love, as if Iago's contempt for that has spread to his notions of friendship; Othello's marriage is what has spoilt their relations (Cassio 'came a-wooing with' Othello, as a social figure, and then got the lieutenantship). In the same way Othello's two uses of *honest* here jump from 'loving towards friends, which breeds honour' to (of women) 'chaste'. It is important I think that the feminine sense, which a later time felt to be quite distinct, is so deeply confused here with the other ones.

It is not safe to be *direct* either way, to be honest in Othello's sense or Iago's. The sanctimonious metaphor *profit* might carry satire from Iago on Puritans or show Iago to be like them. Iago is still telling a good deal of truth; the reasons he gives have always made him despise those who are faithful to their masters, if not to their friends. It is not clear that he would think himself a bad friend to his real friends. He believes there is a gaff to blow about the ideal love affair, though his evidence has had to be forced. Of course he is using *honest* less in his own way than to impose on Othello, yet there is a real element of self-pity in his complaint. It is no whitewashing of Iago – you may hate him the more for it – but he feels he is now in danger because he has gone the 'direct' way to work, exposed false pretensions, and tried to be 'frank' to himself about the whole situation. I do not think this is an oversubtle treatment of his words; behind his fear he is gloating over his cleverness, and seems to delight in the audience provided by the stage.

In the nightmare scene where Othello clings to the word to justify himself he comes near accepting Iago's use of it.

EMILIA: My husband?
OTHELLO: Ay, 'twas he that told me first.
           An honest man he is, and hates the slime
           That sticks on filthy deeds. . . .
EMILIA: My husband say that she was false?
OTHELLO: He, woman.
           I say thy husband. Dost understand the word?
           My friend, thy husband; honest, honest Iago.   v. 2. 149

From the sound of the last line it seems as bitter and concentrated as the previous question; to the audience it is. Yet Othello means no irony against Iago, and it is hard to invent a reason for his repetition of *honest*. He may feel it painful that the coarse Iago, not Desdemona or Cassio, should be the only honest creature, or Iago's honest may suggest the truth he told; or indeed you may call it a trick on the audience, to wind up the irony to its highest before Iago is exposed. Yet Iago would agree that one reason why he was honest was that he hated the slime. The same slime would be produced, by Desdemona as well as by Othello one would hope, if the act of love were of the most rigidly faithful character; the disgust in the metaphor is disgust at all sexuality. Iago playing 'honest' as prude is the rat who stands up for the ideal; as soon as Othello agrees he is finely cheated; Iago is left with his pleasures and Othello's happiness is destroyed. Iago has always despised his pleasures, always treated sex without fuss, like the lavatory; it is by this that he manages to combine the 'honest dog' tone with honesty as Puritanism. The twist of the irony here is that Othello now feels humbled before such clarity. It is a purity he has failed to attain, and he accepts it as a form of honour. The hearty use and the horror of it are united in this appalling line.

Soon after there is a final use of *fool*, by Emilia, which sums up the clown aspect of Iago, but I ought to recognize that it may refer to Othello as well:

EMILIA:	He begged of me to steal't.
IAGO:	Villainous whore!
EMILIA:	She give it Cassio? No, alas, I found it,
	And I did give't my husband.
IAGO:	Filth, thou liest!
EMILIA:	By heaven, I do not, I do not, gentlemen.
	O murd'rous coxcomb! what should such a fool
	Do with so good a wife?

[*Iago stabs Emilia and escapes*]   V. 2. 232

On the face of it she praises herself to rebut his insults, which are given because she is not a 'good wife' in the sense of loyal to his interests. But her previous speech takes for granted that 'she' means Desdemona, and we go straight on to Emilia's death-scene, which is entirely selfless and praises Desdemona only. I think she is meant to turn and upbraid Othello, so that she praises Desdemona in this sentence: it would be a convenience in acting, as it explains why she does not notice Iago's sword. *Coxcomb* in any case insists on the full meaning of 'fool', which would make a startling insult for Othello; the idea becomes not that he was stupid to be deceived (a reasonable complaint) but that he was vain of his clownish authority, that is, self-important about his position as a husband and his suspicions, murderous merely because he wanted to show what he could do, like a child. She is the mouthpiece of all the feelings in us which are simply angry with Othello, but this judgement of him is not meant to keep its prominence for long. Indeed as her death-scene goes on the interpretation which the producer should reject is I think meant to come back into our minds; the real murderous coxcomb, the clown who did kill merely out of vanity, was Iago. The cynic had always hated to be treated as a harmless joker, and what finally roused him into stabbing her was perhaps that he thought she had called him a clown. The Lion and the Fox are thus united in the word, but, as so many things happen in the play, by a misunderstanding. It is perhaps an unnecessarily elaborate interpretation (the reference to Iago is much the more important one) but I think it is needed for our feelings about Emilia that she should not deliberately give herself the praise which we none the less come to feel she deserves. . . .

It struck me on reading this over that it is not likely to convince a supporter of Bradley, since it bows to the master as if taking his results for granted and then appears to include him among the nineteenth-century critics who are denounced; also, what is more important, it does not answer the central question that Bradley put – 'Why does Iago plot at all?' I shall try now to summarize Bradley's position and explain the points at which I disagree from it.

We are shown, says Bradley, that Iago is clear-sighted, and he appears to have been prudent till the play begins; he must have realized that his plot was extremely dangerous to himself (in the event it was fatal); and yet we feel that he is not actuated by any passion of hatred or ambition – in fact, so far as he pretends that he is, he seems to be wondering what his motives for action can be, almost as Hamlet (in the immediately previous play by Shakespeare) wonders what his motives can be for inaction.* Some recent critics have objected to this sort of analysis, but I think it is clearly wrong to talk as if coherence of character is not needed in poetic drama, only coherence of metaphor and so on. The fair point to make against Bradley's approach (as is now generally agreed) is that the character of Iago must have been intended to seem coherent to the first-night audience; therefore the solution cannot be reached by learned deductions from hints in the text about his previous biography, for instance; if the character is puzzling nowadays, the answer must be a matter of recalling the assumptions of the audience and the way the character was put across. Of course it is also possible that Shakespeare was cheating, and that the audience would not care as long as they got their melodrama. Indeed there are lines in Iago's soliloquies which seem to be using the older convention, by which the villain merely announced his villainy in terms such as the good people would have used about him. But I should maintain that the character was an eminently interesting one to the first-night audience (they did not take the villain for granted) and that even the crudities could be absorbed into a realistic view of him. Such at any rate is the question at issue.

Bradley's answer is in brief that Iago is tempted by vanity and love of plotting. Iago says he likes 'to plume up his will in double knavery', to heighten his sense of power by plots, and Bradley rightly points out that this reassurance to the sense of power is a common reason for apparently meaningless petty cruelties. Iago particularly wants to do it at this time, because he has been slighted by Cassio's appointment and is in irritating difficulties with Roderigo, so that 'his thwarted sense of superiority demands satisfaction'. But he knows at the back of his mind that his plot is dangerous to the point of folly, and that is why he keeps inventing excuses for himself. Bradley opposes what seems to have been a common Victorian view that Iago had 'a general disinterested love of evil', and says that if he had a 'motiveless malignity' (Coleridge) it was only in the more narrow but more psychologically plausible way that Bradley has defined.

* One might indeed claim that Iago is a satire on the holy thought of Polonius – 'To thine own self be true . . . thou canst not then be false to any man.'

All this I think is true, and satisfies the condition about the first-night audience. . . .

Iago's opinions, so far as he has got them clear, are shared by many people around him, and he boasts about them freely. To be sure, he could not afford to do this if they were not very confused, but even the confusion is shared by his neighbours. When Iago expounds his egotism to Roderigo, in the first scene of the play, he is not so much admitting a weak criminal to his secrets as making his usual claim to Sturdy Independence in a rather coarser form. He is not subservient to the interests of the men in power who employ him, he says; he can stand up for himself, as they do. No doubt an Elizabethan employer, no less than Professor Bradley, would think this a shocking sentiment; but it does not involve Pure Egotism, and I do not even see that it involves Machiavelli. It has the air of a spontaneous line of sentiment among the lower classes, whereas Machiavelli was interested in the deceptions necessary for a ruler. Certainly it does not imply that the Independent man will betray his friends (as apart from his employer), because if it did he would not boast about it to them. This of course is the answer to the critics who have said that Roderigo could not have gone on handing all his money to a self-confessed knave. And, in the same way, when it turns out that Iago does mean to betray Roderigo, he has only to tell the audience that this fool is not one of his real friends; indeed he goes on to claim that it would be *wrong* to treat him as one. I do not mean to deny there is a paradox about the whole cult of the Independent Man (it is somehow felt that his selfishness makes him more valuable as a friend); but the paradox was already floating in the minds of the audience. No doubt Shakespeare thought that the conception was a false one, and gave a resounding demonstration of it, but one need not suppose that he did this by inventing a unique psychology for Iago, or even by making Iago unusually conscious of the problem at issue. . . .

It is clear I think that all the elements of the character are represented in the range of meanings of 'honest', and (what is more important) that the confusion of moral theory in the audience, which would make them begin by approving of Iago (though perhaps only in the mixed form of the 'ironical cheer') was symbolized or echoed in a high degree by the confusion of the word. When opinion had become more settled or conventionalized, and the word had itself followed this movement by becoming simpler, there were of course two grounds for finding a puzzle in the character; but, of the two, I should say that failure to appreciate the complexity of the word was the more important ground, because after all the complexity of moral judgement had not become so difficult – what people had lost was the verbal pointer directing them to it. I think indeed that the Victorians were not ready enough to approve the good qualities of being 'ready to blow the gaff' and 'frank to yourself about your own desires'; and it is not likely that any analysis of one word would have altered their opinions. And I must admit (as a final effort to get the verbalist approach into its right proportion) that my opinions about the play date from seeing an actual performance of it, with a particularly good Iago, and that I did not at the time think about the word 'honest' at all. The verbal analysis came when I looked at the text to see what support it gave to these impressions. But I do not feel this to be any reason for doubting that the puns on 'honest' really do support them.

from 'Honest in *Othello*' in *The Structure of Complex Words,*
1951

TWELVE

Modes of Irony in Othello

R. B. HEILMAN

WITHOUT ignoring irony as a characteristic value of a mature literary work – the maintenance of disparate perspectives – I wish to regard it here as also a mode of inter-connexion, as illuminating discrepancy. Awareness of discrepancy means awareness of at least the two elements required to create a discrepancy; in a non-ironic work such nexus would be lacking, and the texture would be correspondingly thinner. The ironic connexion may be between elements close or distant; it may be completed in actional or verbal terms; and it may have different temporal aspects. It may complete itself in the 'present' in which it comes into view, either as a contradiction of terms within that situation or as an overturn of a universal expectancy. Or it may bind past and present, or present and future, by a reversal of 'ordinary probability' or of specific expectancies created by the terms of the plot.

The standard dramatic irony is that of a character's taking an action which does not lead where he expects it to; e.g. Othello, trying to punish an apparent wrong, commits a real wrong, much greater than the supposed one, and leaves himself infinitely worse off than if he had foregone the punitive satisfaction. A lesser irony, though it may be valuable connectively, is that of circumstance, in which the human will operates minimally or not at all: Cassio is the first person whose death is formally plotted, but he is the principal survivor. As he says to his nocturnal assailant, Roderigo, 'That thrust had been mine enemy indeed But that my coat is better than thou know'st' (v. i. 24–5). Thus he is able to succeed the very commander who fired him.

There are a number of ironic relations in which the future reverses the certainty, promise, oath, or hope expressed in the present. Othello is sure that his love of Desdemona will not interfere with his execution of duties at the front: if it happens, he says, 'That my disports corrupt and taint my business, Let huswives make a skillet of my helm' (I. 3. 272). It is just this domestication of the warrior that takes place: Othello is overcome by the 'family problem' and formally gives up the career of war. Desdemona assures Cassio that she 'will have my lord and you again As friendly as you were' (III. 3. 6–7). This comes true but not in the intended sense: they are re-united only after her death and for a short time before Othello's. When Othello wagers, 'My life upon her faith!' (I. 3. 295), both terms ironically come true: she is faithful, and he pays with his life. Or a literal statement may be countered by facts not known or foreseen: when Desdemona fears that Othello may 'shake me off To beggarly divorcement' (IV. 2. 157–8), he has already resolved on steps that would make divorce seem like a friendly act.

Again, there are relations of irony in which a character 'speaks better than he knows', expressing truths which would not be expected of him, or making statements that are true in a way he does not intend or is not conscious of. When Desdemona asserts her faithfulness as Cassio's attorney, she uses a metaphor of fidelity which is literally prophetic: 'For thy solicitor shall rather die Than give thy cause away.' (III. 3. 27–8.) Characters stumble into words which would be guides to right understanding or action if the speakers were not in some way inhibited from seizing upon the validity of their perceptions, as when Brabantio says to Iago and Roderigo, 'Upon malicious bravery dost thou come To start my quiet' (I. 1. 100–1). When Othello repeats Iago's 'lie on her', he annotates, 'We say lie on her when they belie her' (IV. 1. 35–6), i.e. 'tell a lie on her'. Half-mad as he is, he is toying, like a virtuoso in language, with the ambiguity of meaning in the phrase: the very verbal play leads him to the doorstep of truth. What is more, Iago's own provocative embellishment of his lie – 'lie with her, lie on her' – has led his victim to the point from which he might see truth.

The villain, who is by definition outside the community of tragic awareness, defines the tragic hero. Iago's phrase, 'loving his own pride and purposes' (I. 1. 12), though it refers only to Othello's appointment of a lieutenant, actually describes Othello's tragic role generally. Derogatory statements, indeed, are often vibrant with strange accuracies that the reader perceives, indeed cannot help perceiving, if he is aware of the interplay of contexts. Iago's account of Othello's style, 'bombast circumstance. Horribly stuffed with epithets of war' (I. I. 13–14), is partly justified by Othello's addiction to rhetorical bravura. In a simpler kind of play, the villain would merely speak unjustly. When Brabantio calls Iago 'profane wretch' (I. I. 115) and Desdemona playfully calls him 'a most profane and liberal counsellor' (II. I. 162), we are aware, in each case, of the unfelt truth, and, additionally, of the kind of verbal echo frequently woven into the fabric of the play. When Othello says sneeringly of Desdemona, 'And she's obedient; as you say, obedient, Very obedient' (IV. I. 248–9), i.e. obedient to any man that asks, the word that he uses sarcastically is true literally, in the sense in which he thinks it is not. Or a character may ignorantly speak an untruth and then compound the irony by the inadvertent use of specifically corrective terms, as when Othello, having described the living Desdemona's hand as 'Hot, hot, and moist' (III. 4. 39), uses these words of Desdemona dead: 'Cold, cold, my girl? Even like thy chastity' (V. 2. 276–7). Note his repetition of the antonyms.

Irony as a linking agent appears also in the variations of dynamic ideas held by different characters – for instance, the idea that one injury justifies another. But here I aim not at inconclusiveness, nor am I ready to approach the larger structural design, just as in describing certain ironic modes I am intent not upon their significance for tone and theme, nor yet upon an exhaustive catalogue and a refined analytical differentiation of them. The sampling and the rough classifications, in this section and the notes, should be enough to suggest the pervasiveness and multifariousness of irony as one source of the rich interwovenness of the dramatic web.

from *Magic in the Web: Action and Language in Othello*, 1956: Ch. I sec. 2

Suggestions for Further Reading

H. GRANVILLE-BARKER: *Prefaces to Shakespeare IV*.

HELEN GARDNER: *The Noble Moor* (British Academy Shakespeare Lecture for 1955).

LEO KIRSCHBAUM: 'The Modern Othello' (*English Literary History II*, 1944; reprinted in Leonard F. Dean's *Casebook on Othello*, which is a very useful collection).

G. WILSON KNIGHT: 'The *Othello* Music' (in *The Wheel of Fire*).

LAURENCE LERNER: 'The Machiavel and the Moor' (in *Essays in Criticism*, October 1959).

F. R. LEAVIS: 'Diabolic Intellect and the Noble Hero' (in *The Common Pursuit*). Attacks Bradley's conception of Othello as completely noble and blameless. Leavis places the responsibility for the murder within Othello, and claims that the importance of Iago has been overrated.

KING LEAR

THIRTEEN

On Sitting Down to Read King Lear Once Again

JOHN KEATS

O GOLDEN-TONGUED Romance with serene lute!
    Fair plumed Syren! Queen of far away!
    Leave melodizing on this wintry day,
Shut up thine olden pages, and be mute.
Adieu! for once again the fierce dispute,
    Betwixt damnation and impassion'd clay
    Must I burn through; once more humbly assay
The bitter-sweet of this Shakespearian fruit.
Chief Poet! and ye clouds of Albion,
    Begetters of our deep eternal theme,
When through the old oak forest I am gone,
    Let me not wander in a barren dream,
But when I am consumed in the fire
Give me new Phoenix wings to fly at my desire.

(1818)

FOURTEEN

The Moral of King Lear

GEORGE ORWELL

THE subject of *Lear* is renunciation, and it is only by being wilfully blind that one can fail to understand what Shakespeare is saying.

Lear renounces his throne but expects everyone to continue treating him as a king. He does not see that if he surrenders power, other people will take advantage of his weakness: also that those who flatter him the most grossly, i.e. Regan and Goneril, are exactly the ones who will turn against him. The moment he finds that he can no longer make people obey him as he did before, he falls into a rage which Tolstoy describes as 'strange and unnatural', but which in fact is perfectly in character. In his madness and despair, he passes through two moods which again are natural enough in his circumstances, though in one of them it is probable that he is being used partly as a mouthpiece for Shakespeare's own opinions. One is the mood of disgust in which Lear repents, as it were, for having been a king, and grasps for the first time the rottenness of formal justice and vulgar morality. The other is a mood of impotent fury in which he wreaks imaginary revenges upon those who have wronged him. 'To have a thousand with red burning spits come hissing in upon 'em!', and:

> It were a delicate stratagem to shoe
> A troop of horse with felt; I'll put't in proof;
> And when I have stol'n upon these son-in-laws,
> Then kill, kill, kill, kill, kill, kill! IV. 6. 185

Only at the end does he realize, as a sane man, that power, revenge, and victory are not worth while:

> No, no, no, no! Come, let's away to prison . . .
> and we'll wear out,
> In a wall'd prison, packs and sects of great ones
> That ebb and flow by th' moon. V. 3. 8

But by the time he makes this discovery it is too late, for his death and Cordelia's are already decided on. That is the story, and, allowing for some clumsiness in the telling, it is a very good story. . . .

What exactly *is* the moral of *Lear*? Evidently there are two morals, one explicit, the other implied in the story.

Shakespeare starts by assuming that to make yourself powerless is to invite an attack. This does not mean that *everyone* will turn against you (Kent and the Fool stand by Lear from first to last), but in all probability *someone* will. If you throw away your weapons, some less scrupulous person will pick them up. If you turn the other cheek, you will get a harder blow on it than you got on the first one. This does not always happen, but it is to be expected, and you ought not to complain if it does happen. The second blow is, so to speak, part of the act of turning the other cheek. First of all, therefore, there is the vulgar, common-sense moral drawn by the Fool: 'Don't relinquish power, don't give away your lands.' But there is also another moral. Shakespeare never utters it in so many words, and it does not very much matter whether he was fully aware of it. It is contained in the story, which, after all, he made up, or altered to suit his purposes. It is: 'Give away your lands if you want to, but don't expect to gain happiness by doing so. Probably you won't gain happiness. If you live for others, you must live *for others*, and not as a roundabout way of getting an advantage for yourself.'

from 'Lear, Tolstoy, and the Fool', 1947
(available in Orwell's *Selected Essays*, Penguin)

FIFTEEN

King Lear *and the Comedy of the Grotesque*

G. WILSON KNIGHT

IT may appear strange to search for any sort of comedy as a primary theme in a play whose abiding gloom is so heavy, whose reading of human destiny and human actions so starkly tragic. Yet it is an error of aesthetic judgement to regard humour as essentially trivial. Though its impact usually appears vastly different from that of tragedy, yet there is a humour that treads the brink of tears, and tragedy which needs but an infinitesimal shift of perspective to disclose the varied riches of comedy. Humour is an evanescent thing, even more difficult of analysis and intellectual location than tragedy. To the coarse mind lacking sympathy an incident may seem comic which to the richer understanding is pitiful and tragic. So, too, one series of facts can be treated by the artist as either comic or tragic, lending itself equivalently to both. Sometimes a great artist may achieve significant effects by a criss-cross of tears and laughter. Chekhov does this, especially in his plays. A shifting flash of comedy across the pain of the purely tragic both increases the tension and suggests, vaguely, a resolution and a purification. The comic and the tragic rest both on the idea of incompatibilities, and are also, themselves, mutually exclusive: therefore to mingle them is to add to the meaning of each; for the result is then but a new sublime incongruity.

King Lear is roughly analogous to Chekhov where *Macbeth* is analogous to Dostoevsky. The wonder of Shakespearian tragedy is ever a mystery – a vague, yet powerful, tangible, presence; an interlocking of the mind with a profound meaning, a disclosure to the inward eye of vistas undreamed, and but fitfully understood. *King Lear* is great in the abundance and richness of human delineation, in the level focus of creation that builds a massive oneness, in fact, a universe, of single quality from a multiplicity of differentiated units; and in a positive and purposeful working out of a purgatorial philosophy. But it is still greater in the perfect fusion of psychological realism with the daring flights of a fantastic imagination. The heart of a Shakespearian tragedy is centred in the imaginative, in the unknown; and in *King Lear*, where we touch the unknown, we touch the fantastic. The peculiar dualism at the root of this play which wrenches and splits the mind by a sight of incongruities displays in turn realities absurd, hideous, pitiful. This incongruity is Lear's madness: it is also the demonic laughter that echoes in the *Lear* universe. In pure tragedy the dualism of experience is continually being dissolved in the masterful beauty of passion, merged in the sunset of emotion. But in comedy it is not so softly resolved – incompatibilities stand out till the sudden relief of laughter or its equivalent of humour: therefore incongruity is the especial mark of comedy. Now in *King Lear* there is a dualism continually crying in vain to be resolved either by tragedy or comedy. Thence arises its peculiar tension of pain: and the course of the action often comes as near to the resolution of comedy as to that of tragedy. So I shall notice here the imaginative core of the play, and, excluding much of the logic of the plot from immediate attention, analyse the fantastic comedy of *King Lear*.

From the start, the situation has a comic aspect. It has been observed that Lear has, so to speak, staged an interlude, with himself as chief actor, in which he grasps expressions of love to his heart, and resigns his sceptre to a chorus of acclamations. It is childish, foolish – but very human. So, too, is the result. Sincerity forbids play-acting, and Cordelia cannot subdue her instinct to any judgement advising tact rather than truth. The incident is profoundly comic and profoundly pathetic. It is, indeed, curious that so storm-furious a play as *King Lear* should have so trivial a domestic basis: it is the first of our many incongruities to be noticed. The absurdity of the old King's anger is clearly indicated by Kent:

> Kill thy physician, and the fee bestow
> Upon the foul disease.   I. I. 163

The result is absurd. Lear's loving daughter Cordelia is struck from his heart's register, and he is shortly, old and grey-haired and a king, cutting a cruelly ridiculous figure before the cold sanity of his unloving elder daughters. Lear is selfish, self-centred. The

images he creates of his three daughters' love are quite false, sentimentalized: he understands the nature of none of his children, and
demanding an unreal and impossible love from all three, is disillu-
sioned by each in turn. But, though sentimental, this love is not
weak. It is powerful and firm-planted in his mind as a mountain
rock embedded in earth. The tearing out of it is hideous, cata-
clysmic. A tremendous soul is, as it were, incongruously geared to
a puerile intellect. Lear's senses prove his idealized love-figments
false, his intellect snaps, and, as the loosened drive flings limp, the
disconnected engine of madness spins free, and the ungeared revo-
lutions of it are terrible, fantastic. This, then, is the basis of the
play: greatness linked to puerility. Lear's instincts are themselves
grand, heroic – noble even. His judgement is nothing. He understands neither himself nor his daughters:

REGAN: 'Tis the infirmity of his age; yet he hath ever but slenderly
known himself.
GONERIL: The best and soundest of his time hath been but rash ...
I. I. 292

Lear starts his own tragedy by foolish misjudgement. Lear's fault
is a fault of the mind, a mind unwarrantably, because selfishly,
foolish. And he knows it:

O Lear, Lear, Lear!
Beat at this gate that let thy folly in,
And thy dear judgment out.   I. 4. 270

His purgatory is to be a purgatory of the mind, of madness. Lear
has trained himself to think he cannot be wrong: he finds he is
wrong. He has fed his heart on sentimental knowledge of his
children's love: he finds their love is not sentimental. There is
now a gaping dualism in his mind, thus drawn asunder by incongruities, and he endures madness. Thus the theme of the play is
bodied continually into a fantastic incongruity, which is implicit
in the beginning – in the very act of Lear's renunciation, retaining
the 'title and addition' of King, yet giving over a king's authority
to his children. As he becomes torturingly aware of the truth,
incongruity masters his mind, and fantastic madness ensues; and
this peculiar fact of the Lear-theme is reflected in the *Lear*-universe:

GLOUCESTER: These late eclipses in the sun and moon portend no
good to us. Though the wisdom of nature can reason it thus and
thus, yet nature finds itself scourg'd by the sequent effects. Love
cools, friendship falls off, brothers divide; in cities, mutinies; in
countries, discord; in palaces, treason; and the bond crack'd 'twixt
son and father. This villain of mine comes under the prediction,
there's son against father. The King falls from bias of nature, there's
father against child. We have seen the best of our time. Machinations,
hollowness, treachery, and all ruinous disorders follow us disquietly
to our graves.   I. 2. 100

Gloucester's words hint a universal incongruity here: the fantastic
incongruity of parent and child opposed. And it will be most helpful later to notice the Gloucester-theme in relation to that of Lear.

From the first signs of Goneril's cruelty, the Fool is used as a
chorus, pointing us to the absurdity of the situation. He is truly
an admirable chorus, increasing our pain by his emphasis on a
humour which yet will not serve to merge the incompatible in a
unity of laughter. He is not all wrong when he treats the situation
as matter for a joke. Much here that is always regarded as essentially
pathetic is not far from comedy. For instance, consider Lear's
words:

> I will have such revenges on you both
> That all the world shall – I will do such things –
> What they are yet I know not; but they shall be
> The terrors of the earth.   II. 4. 278

What could be more painfully incongruous, spoken, as it is, by an
old man, a king, to his daughter? It is not far from the ridiculous.
The very thought seems a sacrilegious cruelty, I know: but ridicule
is generally cruel. The speeches of Lear often come near comedy.
Again, notice the abrupt contrast in his words:

> But yet thou art my flesh, my blood, my daughter;
> Or rather a disease that's in my flesh,
> Which I must needs call mine. Thou art a boil,
> A plague-sore, or embossed carbuncle
> In my corrupted blood. But I'll not chide thee ...   II. 4. 219

This is not comedy, nor humour. But it is exactly the stuff of which
humour is made. Lear is mentally a child; in passion a titan. The

absurdity of his every act at the beginning of his tragedy is contrasted wth the dynamic fury which intermittently bursts out, flickers – then flames and finally gives us those grand apostrophes lifted from man's stage of earth to heaven's rain and fire and thunder:

> Blow, winds, and crack your cheeks; rage, blow.
> You cataracts and hurricanoes, spout
> Till you have drench'd our steeples, drown'd the cocks.
>
> III. 2. I

Two speeches of this passionate and unrestrained volume of Promethean curses are followed by:

> No, I will be the pattern of all patience;
> I will say nothing.
>
> III. 2. 37

Again we are in touch with potential comedy: a slight shift of perspective, and the incident is rich with humour. A sense of self-directed humour would clearly have saved Lear. It is a quality he absolutely lacks.

Herein lies the profound insight of the Fool: he sees the potentialities of comedy in Lear's behaviour. This old man, recently a king, and, if his speeches are fair samples, more than a little of a tyrant, now goes from daughter to daughter, furious because Goneril dares criticize his pet knights, kneeling down before Regan, performing, as she says, 'unsightly tricks' (II. 4. 155) – the situation is excruciatingly painful, and its painfulness is exactly of that quality which embarrasses in some forms of comedy. In the theatre, one is terrified lest some one laugh: yet, if Lear could laugh – if the Lears of the world could laugh at themselves – there would be no such tragedy. In the early scenes old age and dignity suffer, and seem to deserve, the punishments of childhood:

> Now, by my life,
> Old fools are babes again, and must be us'd
> With checks as flatteries . . .
>
> I. 3. 19

The situation is summed up by the Fool:

LEAR: When were you wont to be so full of songs, sirrah?
FOOL: I have us'd it, nuncle, e'er since thou mad'st thy daughters

thy mothers; for when thou gav'st them the rod, and put'st down
thine own breeches . . .   I. 4. 169

The height of indecency in suggestion, the height of incongruity.
Lear is spiritually put to the ludicrous shame endured bodily by
Kent in the stocks: and the absurd rant of Kent, and the unreasonable childish temper of Lear, both merit in some measure what they
receive. Painful as it may sound, that is, provisionally, a truth
we should realize. The Fool realizes it. He is, too, necessary. Here,
where the plot turns on the diverging tugs of two assurances in the
mind, it is natural that the action be accompanied by some symbol
of humour, that mode which is built of unresolved incompatibilities. Lear's torment is a torment of this dualistic kind, since he
scarcely believes his senses when his daughters resist him. He
repeats the history of Troilus, who cannot understand the faith-
lessness of Cressid. In *Othello* and *Timon of Athens* the transition
is swift from extreme love to revenge or hate. The movement of
Lear's mind is less direct: like Troilus, he is suspended between
two separate assurances. Therefore Pandarus, in the latter acts
of *Troilus and Cressida*, plays a part similar to the Fool in *King
Lear*: both attempt to heal the gaping wound of the mind's incongruous knowledge by the unifying, healing release of laughter.
They make no attempt to divert, but rather to direct the hero's
mind to the present incongruity. The Fool sees, or tries to
see, the humorous potentialities in the most heart-wrenching of
incidents:

LEAR: O me, my heart, my rising heart! But down!
FOOL: Cry to it, nuncle, as the cockney did to the eels when she put
    'em i' th' paste alive. She knapp'd 'em o' th' coxcombs with a stick,
    and cried, 'Down, wantons, down!' 'Twas her brother that, in pure
    kindness to his horse, buttered his hay.   II. 4. 119

Except for the last delightful touch – the antithesis of the other –
that is a cruel, ugly sense of humour. It is the sinister humour at the
heart of this play: we are continually aware of the humour of
cruelty and the cruelty of humour. But the Fool's use of it is not
aimless. If Lear could laugh he might yet save his reason.

But there is no relief. Outside, in the wild country, the storm
grows more terrible:

KENT: ... Since I was man,
Such sheets of fire, such bursts of horrid thunder,
Such groans of roaring wind and rain, I never
Remember to have heard. ...   III. 2. 45

Lear's mind keeps returning to the unreality, the impossibility of what has happened:

Your old kind father, whose frank heart gave all!
O, that way madness lies; let me shun that;
No more of that.   III. 4. 20

He is still self-centred; cannot understand that he has been anything but a perfect father; cannot understand his daughters' behaviour. It is

as this mouth should tear this hand
For lifting food to't? ...   III. 4. 15

It is incongruous, impossible. There is no longer any 'rule in unity itself'. Just as Lear's mind begins to fail, the Fool finds Edgar disguised as 'poor Tom'. Edgar now succeeds the Fool as the counterpart to the breaking sanity of Lear; and where the humour of the Fool made no contact with Lear's mind, the fantastic appearance and incoherent words of Edgar are immediately assimilated, as glasses correctly focused to the sight of oncoming madness. Edgar turns the balance of Lear's wavering mentality. His fantastic appearance and lunatic irrelevancies, with the storm outside, and the Fool still for occasional chorus, create a scene of wraithlike unreason, a vision of a world gone mad:

... Bless thy five wits! Tom's acold. O, do, de, do, de, do, de. Bless thee from whirlwinds, star-blasting, and taking! Do poor Tom some charity, whom the foul fiend vexes. There could I have him now – and there – and there again, and there –   III. 4. 56

To Lear his words are easily explained. His daughters 'have brought him to this pass'. He cries:

LEAR: Is it the fashion that discarded fathers
Should have thus little mercy on their flesh?
Judicious punishment! 'twas this flesh begot
Those pelican daughters.

EDGAR: Pillicock sat on Pillicock Hill.
   Alow, alow, loo, loo!
FOOL: This cold night will turn us all to fools and madmen.

III. 4. 71

What shall we say of this exquisite movement? Is it comedy? Lear's profound unreason is capped by the blatant irrelevance of Edgar's couplet suggested by the word 'pelican'; then the two are swiftly all but unified, for us if not for Lear, in the healing balm of the Fool's conclusion. It is the process of humour, where two incompatibles are resolved in laughter. The Fool does this again. Lear speaks a profound truth as the wild night and Edgar's fantastic impersonation grip his mind and dethrone his conventional sanity:

LEAR: Is man no more than this? Consider him well. Thou ow'st the worm no silk, the beast no hide, the sheep no wool, the cat no perfume. Ha! Here's three on 's are sophisticated! Thou art the thing itself: unaccommodated man is no more but such a poor, bare, forked animal as thou art. Off, off, you lendings! Come unbutton here. [*Tearing off his clothes.*]
FOOL: Prithee, nuncle, be contented; 'tis a naughty night to swim in.

III. 4. 101

This is the furthest flight, not of tragedy, but of philosophic comedy. The autocratic and fiery-fierce old king, symbol of dignity, is confronted with the meanest of men: a naked lunatic beggar. In a flash of vision he attempts to become his opposite, to be naked, 'unsophisticated'. And then the opposing forces which struck the lightning-flash of vision tail off, resolved into a perfect unity by the Fool's laughter, reverberating, trickling, potent to heal in sanity the hideous unreason of this tempest-shaken night: ''tis a naughty night to swim in.' Again this is the process of humour: its flash of vision first bridges the positive and negative poles of the mind, unifying them, and then expresses itself in laughter.

This scene grows still more grotesque, fantastical, sinister. Gloucester enters, his torch flickering in the beating wind:

FOOL: ... Look, here comes a walking fire.
    [*Enter* Gloucester, *with a torch.*]
EDGAR: This is the foul Flibbertigibbet; he begins a curfew, and walks till the first cock. . . .

III. 4. 112

Lear welcomes Edgar as his 'philosopher', since he embodies that philosophy of incongruity and the fantastically-absurd which is Lear's vision in madness. 'Noble philosopher', he says (III. 4. 167), and 'I will keep still with my philosopher' (III. 4. 172). The unresolved dualism that tormented Troilus and was given metaphysical expression by him (*Troilus and Cressida*, V. 2. 134–57) is here more perfectly bodied into the poetic symbol of poor Tom: and since Lear cannot hear the resolving laugh of foolery, his mind is focused only to the 'philosopher' mumbling of the foul fiend. Edgar thus serves to lure Lear on: we forget that he is dissimulating. Lear is the centre of our attention, and as the world shakes with tempest and unreason, we endure something of the shaking and the tempest of his mind. The absurd and fantastic reign supreme. Lear does not compass for more than a few speeches the 'noble anger' (II. 4. 275) for which he prayed, the anger of Timon. From the start we wavered between affection and disillusionment, love and hate. The heavens in truth 'fool' (II. 4. 295) him. He is the 'natural fool of fortune' (IV. 6. 192). Now his anger begins to be a lunatic thing, and when it rises to any sort of magnificent fury or power it is toppled over by the ridiculous capping of Edgar's irrelevancies:

LEAR: To have a thousand with red burning spits
         Come hissing in upon 'em –
EDGAR: The foul fiend bites my back.   III, 6, 15

The mock trial is instituted. Lear's curses were for a short space terrible, majestic, less controlled and purposeful than Timon's but passionate and grand in their tempestuous fury. Now, in madness, he flashes on us the ridiculous basis of his tragedy in words which emphasize the indignity and incongruity of it, and make his madness something nearer the ridiculous than the terrible, something which moves our pity, but does not strike awe:

> Arraign her first. 'Tis Goneril. I here take my oath before this honourable assembly she kick'd the poor King her father.
>
> III. 6. 46

This stroke of the absurd – so vastly different from the awe we experience in face of Timon's hate – is yet fundamental here. The core of the play is an absurdity, an indignity, an incongruity.

In no tragedy of Shakespeare does incident and dialogue so recklessly and miraculously walk the tight-rope of our pity over the depths of bathos and absurdity.

This particular region of the terrible bordering on the fantastic and absurd is exactly the playground of madness. Thus the setting of Lear's madness includes a sub-plot where these same elements are presented with stark nakedness, and no veiling subtleties. The Gloucester-theme is a certain indication of our vision and helps us to understand, and feel, the enduring agony of Lear. As usual, the first scene of this play strikes the dominant note. Gloucester jests at the bastardy of his son Edmund, remarking that, though he is ashamed to acknowledge him, 'there was good sport at his making' (I. I. 23). That is, we start with humour in bad taste. The whole tragedy witnesses a sense of humour in 'the gods' which is in similar bad taste. Now all the Lear effects are exaggerated in the Gloucester theme. Edmund's plot is a more Iago-like, devilish, intentional thing than Goneril's and Regan's icy callousness. Edgar's supposed letter is crude and absurd:

... I begin to find an idle and fond bondage in the oppression of aged tyranny ...   I. 2. 47

But then Edmund, wittiest and most attractive of villains, composed it. One can almost picture his grin as he penned those lines, commending them mentally to the limited intellect of his father. Yes – the Gloucester theme has a beginning even more fantastic than that of Lear's tragedy. And not only are the Lear effects here exaggerated in the directions of villainy and humour: they are even more clearly exaggerated in that of horror. The gouging out of Gloucester's eyes is a thing unnecessary, crude, disgusting: it is meant to be. It helps to provide an accompanying exaggeration of one element – that of cruelty – in the horror that makes Lear's madness. And not only horror: there is even again something satanically comic bedded deep in it. The sight of physical torment, to the uneducated, brings laughter. Shakespeare's England delighted in watching both physical torment and the comic ravings of actual lunacy. The dance of madmen in Webster's *Duchess of Malfi* is of the same ghoulish humour as Regan's plucking Gloucester by the beard: the groundlings will laugh at both. Moreover,

139

the sacrilege of the human body in torture must be, to a human mind, incongruous, absurd. This hideous mockery is consummated in Regan's final witticism after Gloucester's eyes are out:

> Go thrust him out at gates, and let him smell
> His way to Dover.   III. 7. 92

The macabre humoresque of this is nauseating: but it is there, and integral to the play. These ghoulish horrors, so popular in Elizabethan drama, and the very stuff of the *Lear* of Shakespeare's youth, *Titus Andronicus*, find an exquisitely appropriate place in the tragedy of Shakespeare's maturity which takes as its especial province this territory of the grotesque and the fantastic which is Lear's madness. We are pointed to this grim fun, this hideous sense of humour, at the back of tragedy:

> As flies to wanton boys are we to th' gods –
> They kill us for their sport.   IV. I. 37

This illustrates the exact quality I wish to emphasize: the humour a boy – even a kind boy – may see in the wriggles of an impaled insect. So, too, Gloucester is bound, and tortured, physically; and so the mind of Lear is impaled, crucified on the cross-beams of love and disillusion.

There follows the grim pilgrimage of Edgar and Gloucester towards Dover Cliff: an incident typical enough of *King Lear* –

> 'Tis the time's plague when madmen lead the blind. IV. I. 47

They stumble on, madman and blind man, Edgar mumbling:

> ... Five fiends have been in poor Tom at once; of lust, as Obidicut; Hobbididance, prince of dumbness; Mahu, of stealing; Modo of murder; Flibbertigibbet, of mopping and mowing, who since possesses chambermaids and waiting-women ...   IV. I. 59

They are near Dover. Edgar persuades his father that they are climbing steep ground, though they are on a level field, that the sea can be heard beneath:

GLOUCESTER: Methinks the ground is even.
EDGAR: Horrible steep.
                    Hark, do you hear the sea?
GLOUCESTER: No, truly.
EDGAR: Why, then, your other senses grow imperfect
                    By your eyes' anguish.   IV. 6. 3

Gloucester notices the changed sanity of Edgar's speech, and remarks thereon. Edgar hurries his father to the supposed brink, and vividly describes the dizzy precipice over which Gloucester thinks they stand:

> How fearful
> And dizzy 'tis to cast one's eyes so low!
> The crows and choughs that wing the midway air
> Show scarce so gross as beetles. Half-way down
> Hangs one that gathers sampire – dreadful trade. . . . . IV. 6. II

Gloucester thanks him, and rewards him; bids him move off; then kneels, and speaks a prayer of noble resignation – breathing that stoicism which permeates the suffering philosophy of this play:

> O you mighty gods!
> This world I do renounce, and in your sights
> Shake patiently my great affliction off.
> If I could bear it longer and not fall
> To quarrel with your great opposeless wills,
> My snuff and loathed part of nature should
> Burn itself out.   IV. 6. 34

Gloucester has planned a spectacular end for himself. We are given these noble descriptive and philosophical speeches to tune our minds to a noble, tragic sacrifice. And what happens? The old man falls from his kneeling posture a few inches, flat, face foremost. Instead of the dizzy circling to crash and spill his life on the rocks below – just this. The grotesque merged into the ridiculous reaches a consummation in this bathos of tragedy: it is the furthest, most exaggerated, reach of the poet's towering fantastically. We have a sublimely daring stroke of technique, unjustifiable, like Edgar's emphasized and vigorous madness throughout, on the plane of plot-logic, and even to a superficial view somewhat out of place imaginatively in so dire and stark a limning of human destiny as is *King Lear*; yet this scene is in reality a consummate stroke of art. The Gloucester-theme throughout reflects and emphasizes and exaggerates all the percurrent qualities of the Lear-theme. Here the incongruous and fantastic element of the Lear-theme is boldly reflected into the tragically-absurd. The stroke is audacious, unashamed, and magical of effect. Edgar keeps up the deceit;

persuades his father that he has really fallen; points to the empty sky, as to a cliff:

> ... the shrill-gorg'd lark so far
> Cannot be seen or heard. ...   IV. 6. 58

and finally paints a fantastic picture of a ridiculously grotesque devil that stood with Gloucester on the edge:

> As I stood here below, methought his eyes
> Were two full moons; he had a thousand noses,
> Horns whelk'd and waved like the enridged sea.
> It was some fiend ...   IV. 6. 69

Some fiend, indeed.

There is masterful artistry in all this. The Gloucester-theme has throughout run separate from that of Lear, yet parallel, and continually giving us direct villainy where the other shows cold callousness; horrors of physical torment where the other has a subtle mental torment; culminating in this towering stroke of the grotesque and absurd to balance the fantastic incidents and speeches that immediately follow. At this point we suddenly have our first sight of Lear in the full ecstasy of his later madness. Now, when our imaginations are most powerfully quickened to the grotesque and incongruous, the whole surge of the Gloucester-theme, which has just reached its climax, floods as a tributary the main stream of our sympathy with Lear. Our vision has thus been uniquely focused to understand that vision of the grotesque, the incongruous, the fantastically-horrible, which is the agony of Lear's mind:

> Enter Lear, *fantastically dressed with wild flowers*
>   IV. 6. 79

So runs Capell's direction. Lear, late 'every inch a king', the supreme pathetic figure of literature, now utters the wild and whirling language of furthest madness. Sometimes his words hold profound meaning. Often they are tuned to the orthodox Shakespearian hate and loathing, especially sex-loathing, of the hate-theme. Or again, they are purely ludicrous, or would be, were it not a Lear who speaks them:

> ... Look, look, a mouse! Peace, peace; this piece of toasted cheese
> will do't ...   IV. 6. 89

It is, indeed, well that we are, as it were, prepared by now for the grotesque. Laughter is forbidden us. Consummate art has so forged plot and incident that we may watch with tears rather than laughter the cruelly comic actions of Lear:

LEAR: I will die bravely,
             Like a smug bridegroom. What, I will be jovial!
             Come, come, I am a king; masters, know you that?
GENTLEMAN: You are a royal one, and we obey you.
LEAR: Then there's life in't. Come, an you get it, you shall get
             it by running. Sa, sa, sa, sa!   IV. 6. 200

Lear is a child again in his madness. We are in touch with the exquisitely pathetic, safeguarded only by Shakespeare's masterful technique from the bathos of comedy.

This recurring and vivid stress on the incongruous and the fantastic is not a subsidiary element in *King Lear*: it is the very heart of the play. We watch humanity grotesquely tormented, cruelly and with mockery impaled: nearly all the persons suffer some form of crude indignity in the course of the play. I have noticed the major themes of Lear and Gloucester: there are others. Kent is banished, undergoes the disguise of a servant, is put to shame in the stocks; Cornwall is killed by his own servant resisting the dastardly mutilation of Gloucester; Oswald, the prim courtier, is done to death by Edgar in the role of an illiterate country yokel –

   . . . Keep out, che vore ye, or Ise try whether your costard or my ballow be the harder. . . .   IV. 6. 241

Edgar himself endures the utmost degradation of his disguise as 'poor Tom', begrimed and naked, and condemned to speak nothing but idiocy. Edmund alone steers something of an unswerving tragic course, brought to a fitting, deserved, but spectacular end, slain by his wronged brother, nobly repentant at the last:

EDMUND: What you have charged me with, that have I done,
          And more, much more. The time will bring it out.
          'Tis past, and so am I. But what art thou
          That hast this fortune on me? If thou'rt noble,
          I do forgive thee.

143

EDGAR: Let's exchange charity.
I am no less in blood than thou art, Edmund;
If more, the more th' hast wronged me.
My name is Edgar . . .   v. 3. 163

The note of forgiving chivalry reminds us of the deaths of Hamlet
and Laertes. Edmund's fate is nobly tragic: 'The wheel has come
full circle; I am here' (v. 3. 175). And Edmund is the most
villainous of all. Again, we have incongruity; and again, the
Gloucester-theme reflects the Lear-theme. Edmund is given a
noble, an essentially tragic, end, and Goneril and Regan, too, meet
their ends with something of tragic fineness in pursuit of their evil
desires. Regan dies by her sister's poison; Goneril with a knife.
They die, at least, in the cause of love – love of Edmund. Compared
with these deaths, the end of Cordelia is horrible, cruel, unnecessarily cruel – the final grotesque horror in the play. Her villainous
sisters are already dead. Edmund is nearly dead, repentant. It is a
matter of seconds – and rescue comes too late. She is hanged by a
common soldier. The death which Dostoevsky's Stavrogin singled
out as of all the least heroic and picturesque, or rather, shall we say,
the most hideous and degrading: this is the fate that grips the
white innocence and resplendent love-strength of Cordelia. To
be hanged, after the death of her enemies, in the midst of friends.
It is the last hideous joke of destiny: this – and the fact that Lear is
still alive, has recovered his sanity for this. The death of Cordelia is
the last and most horrible of all the horrible incongruities I have
noticed:

Why should a dog, a horse, a rat, have life,
And thou no breath at all?   v. 3. 306

We remember: 'Upon such sacrifices, my Cordelia, the gods themselves throw incense' (v. 3. 20). Or do they laugh, and is the _Lear_
universe one ghastly piece of fun?

We do not feel that. The tragedy is most poignant in that it is
purposeless, unreasonable. It is the most fearless artistic facing of
the ultimate cruelty of things in our literature. That cruelty would
be less were there not this element of comedy which I have emphasized, the insistent incongruities, which create and accompany the
madness of Lear, which leap to vivid shape in the mockery of

Gloucester's suicide, which are intrinsic in the texture of the whole play. Mankind is, as it were, deliberately and comically tormented by 'the gods'. He is not even allowed to die tragically. Lear is 'bound upon a wheel of fire' and only death will end the victim's agony:

> Vex not his ghost. O, let him pass! He hates him
> That would upon the rack of this tough world
> Stretch him out longer.
>
> v. 3. 313

King Lear is supreme in that, in this main theme, it faces the very absence of tragic purpose: wherein it is profoundly different from *Timon of Athens*. Yet, as we close the sheets of this play, there is no horror, nor resentment. The tragic purification of the essentially untragic is yet complete.

Now in this essay it will, perhaps, appear that I have unduly emphasized one single element of the play, magnifying it, and leaving the whole distorted. It has been my purpose to emphasize. I have not exaggerated. The pathos has not been minimized: it is redoubled. Nor does the use of the words 'comic' and 'humour' here imply disrespect to the poet's purpose: rather I have used these words, crudely no doubt, to cut out for analysis the very heart of the play – the thing that man dares scarcely face: the demonic grin of the incongruous and absurd in the most pitiful of human struggles with an iron fate. It is this that wrenches, splits, gashes the mind till it utters the whirling vapourings of lunacy. And, though love and music – twin sisters of salvation – temporarily may heal the racked consciousness of Lear, yet, so deeply planted in the facts of our life is this unknowing ridicule of destiny, that the uttermost tragedy of the incongruous ensues, and there is no hope save in the broken heart and limp body of death. This is the most agonizing of all tragedies to endure: and if we are to feel more than a fraction of this agony, we must have sense of this quality of grimmest humour. We must beware of sentimentalizing the cosmic mockery of the play.

And is there, perhaps, even a deeper and less heart-searing, significance in its humour? Smiles and tears are most curiously interwoven here. Gloucester was saved from his violent and tragic suicide that he might recover his wronged son's love, and that his heart might

> 'Twixt two extremes of passion, joy and grief,
> Burst smilingly.   v. 3. 198

Lear dies with the words

> Do you see this? Look on her! Look, her lips,
> Look there, look there . . .   v. 3. 370

What smiling destiny is this he sees at the last instant of racked mortality? Why have we that strangely beautiful account of Cordelia's first hearing of her father's pain:

> . . . Patience and sorrow strove
> Who should express her goodliest. You have seen
> Sunshine and rain at once – her smiles and tears
> Were like a better way: those happy smilets,
> That played on her ripe lip seemed not to know
> What guests were in her eyes, which parted thence
> As pearls from diamonds dropped. In brief,
> Sorrow would be a rarity most beloved,
> If all could so become it.   iv. 3. 16

What do we touch in these passages? Sometimes we know that all human pain holds beauty, that no tear falls but it dews some flower we cannot see. Perhaps humour, too, is inwoven in the universal pain, and the enigmatic silence holds not only an unutterable sympathy, but also the ripples of an impossible laughter whose flight is not for the wing of human understanding; and perhaps it is this that casts its darting shadow of the grotesque across the furrowed pages of King Lear.

'King Lear and the Comedy of the Grotesque',
from The Wheel of Fire, 1930

SIXTEEN

The Catharsis of King Lear

J. STAMPFER

THE overriding critical problem in *King Lear* is that of its ending. The deaths of Lear and Cordelia confront us like a raw, fresh wound where our every instinct calls for healing and reconciliation. This problem, moreover, is as much one of philosophic order as of dramatic effect. In what sort of universe, we ask ourselves, can wasteful death follow suffering and torture? Nor is this concern an extrapolation from our own culture. It is, rather, implicit in Lear's own image, when he calls for tongues and eyes to howl 'That heaven's vault should crack' (v. 3. 259), and in his despairing question:

> Why should a dog, a horse, a rat, have life,
> And thou no breath at all? v. 3. 306

The problem becomes more overwhelming when we consider that, unlike the problems Shakespeare may have inherited with the plot of *Hamlet*, this tragic ending was imposed by Shakespeare on a story which, in its source, allowed Cordelia's forces to win the war. Moreover, the massive intrusion into *King Lear* of Christian elements of providence, depravity, and spiritual regeneration make it impossible to shunt aside the ending as a coincidence of its pre-Christian setting. The antiquity of setting may have had the irrelevant effect of releasing certain inhibitions in the playwright's mind; but the playgoers in Shakespeare's audience did not put on pagan minds to see the play. Rather, the constant references to retributive justice, perhaps greater here than in any other of Shakespeare's tragedies, make it an issue in a way that it is not in such 'pagan' plays as *Timon of Athens*, *Antony and Cleopatra*, and *Coriolanus*. Indeed, part of the poignance of *King Lear* lies in the fact that its issues, and the varieties of evil that it faces, are so central to Christianity, while it is denied any of the mitigation offered by a well-defined heaven and hell, and a formal doctrine of supernatural salvation.

The impression of unreconciled savagery and violence in the ending has been mitigated, in our generation, by a critical reading that would interpret Lear's last emotion as one of joy, even ecstasy, rather than one of unbearable agony. Bradley advances this reading, though hedged with a considerable qualification, in the following passage:

And, finally, though he is killed by an agony of pain, the agony in which he actually dies is not one of pain but of ecstasy. Suddenly, with a cry represented in the oldest text by a four-times repeated 'O', he exclaims:

> Do you see this? Look on her! Look her lips,
> Look there, look there . . .   v. 3. 310

These are the last words of Lear. He is sure, at last, that she *lives*: and what had he said when he was still in doubt?

> She lives. If it be so,
> It is a chance which does redeem all sorrows
> That ever I have felt.   v. 3. 265

To us, perhaps, the knowledge that he is deceived may bring a culmination of pain: but, if it brings *only* that, I believe we are false to Shakespeare, and it seems almost beyond question that any actor is false to the text who does not attempt to express, in Lear's last accents and gestures and look, an unbearable *joy*.

Some recent critics have gone much further than Bradley in an attempt to build from Lear's momentary emotion at death a 'chance which doth redeem all sorrows', and make the play's ending a transfigured vision of attained salvation.

Before disputing the weight this penultimate moment in Lear's life can bear in counterbalancing all that precedes it, one must first consider whether the reading itself is defensible; for, in a sense, everything in the play hangs in the balance with Lear's death. If it is one of transfiguring joy, then one might, for all the enormous difficulties involved, affirm that a species of order is re-established. If not, however, then the impression is irresistible that in *King Lear* Shakespeare was confronting chaos itself, unmitigated, brutal, and utterly unresolved. The problems of justice and order, however interpreted, finally rest in the mystery of Lear's last moment, and not in the ambiguity of whether Edgar will or will not take over, by default, the throne of England. Like the news of Edmund's death, the problem of the succession is 'but a trifle' (v. 3. 296) alongside the supreme issue of whether any 'comfort' was applied by Shakespeare to the 'great decay' of Lear, as was evidently applied by him to the deaths of Hamlet and to a lesser extent Othello.

Bradley and those who follow him in this matter rest their case on the observation that Lear died persuaded that Cordelia still lived. He leaves unremarked, however, the fact that this illusion is not a new and sudden turn, but recurs three or four times in the last scene. It is, indeed, the main concern of Lear's first three speeches on re-entering the stage, before he goes temporarily out of his mind:

> She's gone for ever.
> I know when one is dead, and when one lives.
> She's dead as earth. Lend me a looking glass.
> If that her breath will mist or stain the stone,
> Why then she lives.   v. 3. 260

The tension here, and it is the underlying tension in Lear until his death, lies between an absolute knowledge that Cordelia is dead, and an absolute inability to accept it. Lear 'knows when one is dead, and when one lives'. His very faculties of reason and know-ledge would be in question if he could not distinguish life from death. 'She's gone for ever . . . She's dead as earth,' he repeats over and over. If he is to grasp reality in the face of madness, it is the reality of Cordelia's death that he must grasp. But this is the one reality that sears him whenever he attempts to grasp it, and so he tries, by the test of the looking glass, to prove that she lives, despite his emphatically underlined knowledge to the contrary.

Three brief speeches by Kent, Edgar, and Albany intervene between this and Lear's next speech. One would guess that Lear is very active on stage at this point, possibly getting a looking glass, holding it up to Cordelia's lips, registering either momentary hope or immediate despair, then, when his test fails, snatching a feather and trying a second test. He would seem to be oblivious to all reality but Cordelia's body and his attempts to prove that she is alive. His second speech shows what is at stake in the effort:

> This feather stirs; she lives! If it be so,
> It is a chance which does redeem all sorrows
> That ever I have felt.   v. 3. 265

This effort, too, fails, and Kent's painful attempt, on his knees, to wrest Lear's attention away from Cordelia only makes Lear momentarily turn on his companions with the savage outcry of 'murderers' and 'traitors' before trying again to prove her alive, this time by putting his ear to her lips in the thought that she might be speaking:

> A plague upon you murderers, traitors all!
> I might have sav'd her; now she's gone for ever.
> Cordelia, Cordelia, stay a little. Ha,
> What is't thou say'st? Her voice was ever soft,
> Gentle, and low – an excellent thing in woman.
> I kill'd the slave that was a-hanging thee.   v. 3. 269

His outcry, 'Ha!' like his cry 'This feather stirs', registers an illusion that Cordelia has spoken to him. This is a wilder self-deception than the thought that she has breathed, and remains with him beyond the end of the speech. His 'I killed the slave' is said almost lovingly and protectively to Cordelia's body, as if she heard him. Thus he struggles simultaneously for sanity and for the belief that Cordelia lives. Under the strain of these two irreconcilable psychic needs, his mind simply slips and relaxes into temporary madness:

> He knows not what he says; and vain is it
> That we present us to him.   v. 3. 293

But agonized sanity breaks through Lear's madness once more, as the words of Kent, Albany, and Edgar could not. Albany sees it rising, ominously convulsing Lear's features, and exclaims, 'O, see, see!' (l. 305) as Lear cries out:

> And my poor fool is hanged: no, no, no life?
> Why should a dog, a horse, a rat, have life,
> And thou no breath at all? Thou'lt come no more,
> Never, never, never, never, never.   v. 3. 305

The repeated cries of 'Never!' are the steady hammering of truth on a mind unable to endure it. Lear's life-blood rushes to his head. He chokes, and asks someone to undo the button of his collar

(l. 309). Then, against the unendurable pressure of reality, the counterbalancing illusion that Cordelia lives rushes forth once more. Once again, it is at her lips, breathing or speaking, that he seeks life and dies:

> Do you see this? Look on her! Look her lips,
> Look there, look there   (*dies*)   l. 310

Who is to say, given this cycle of despair, insanity, and the illusion of hope, if it really matters at what point of the cycle Lear expires, or even if his last words establish it decisively? On the contrary, on purely aesthetic grounds, we have an indication from another point in Act v that all of Lear's emotions have been gathering to an unendurable head at the moment of death. Gloucester, the counterpart to Lear in the subplot, was, like him, driven out by his false offspring, tormented in the storm, and finally preserved by a faithful, though rejected child. And Gloucester's death, which is described in considerable detail by Edgar, contains just such a welter of conflicting feelings as does Lear's. and might well be the model for understanding Lear's death:

> Never – O fault! – reveal'd myself unto him
> Until some half-hour past, when I was arm'd,
> Not sure, though hoping of this good success,
> I ask'd his blessing, and from first to last
> Told him my pilgrimage. But his flaw'd heart –
> Alack, too weak the conflict to support –
> 'Twixt two extremes of passion, joy and grief,
> Burst smilingly.   v. 3. 192

Gloucester's heart burst from its inability to contain two conflicting emotions, his psyche torn apart by a thunderclap of simultaneous joy and grief. And such, by aesthetic parallel, we may presume was the death of Lear, whose 'flawed heart', too, as is evident throughout the last scene, was

> Alack, too weak the conflict to support

But the similarity only serves to accentuate the basic difference between the two deaths. Gloucester died between extremes of joy and grief, at the knowledge that his·son was miraculously preserved, Lear between extremes of illusion and truth, ecstasy and the blackest despair, at the knowledge that his daughter was needlessly butchered. Gloucester's heart 'burst smilingly' at his reunion with Edgar; Lear's, we are driven to conclude, burst in the purest agony at his eternal separation from Cordelia.

There is, then, no mitigation in Lear's death, hence no mitigation in the ending of the play. On the contrary, either the play has no aesthetic unity, or everything in it, including Lear's spiritual regeneration, is instrumental to the explosive poignance of Lear's death. Nor can there be any blenching from the implications of Lear's last sane question:

> Why should a dog, a horse, a rat, have life,
> And thou no breath at all? Thou'lt come no more,
> Never, never, never, never, never.   v. 3. 306

It is only by giving Lear's death a fleeting, ecstatic joy that Bradley can read some sort of reconciliation into the ending, some renewed synthesis of cosmic goodness to follow an antithesis of pure evil. Without it, this is simply, as Lear recognized, a universe where dogs, horses, and rats live, and Cordelias are butchered. There may be mitigations in man himself, but none in the world which surrounds him. Indeed, unless Lear's death is a thoroughly anomalous postscript to his pilgrimage of life, the most organic view of the plot would make almost a test case of Lear, depicting, through his life and death, a universe in which even those who have fully repented, done penance, and risen to the tender regard of sainthood can be hunted down, driven insane, and killed by the most agonizing extremes of passion.

The plot of *King Lear* is generally not read in this fashion. On the contrary, its *dénouement* is generally interpreted as another 'turn of the screw', an added, and unnecessary, twist of horror to round out a play already sated with horrors. If it is defended, it is generally on grounds like those of Lamb, who contended that it was 'fair dismissal' from life after all Lear had suffered, or those of Bradley, that Lear's death is a transfiguration of joy to counterbalance all that has preceded it. Neither reading is satisfactory, Lamb's because it makes the ending, at best, an epilogue rather than a *dénouement* to the main body of the action, Bradley's because the textual evidence points to the opposite interpretation of Lear's death. If Lear's spiritual regeneration, however, with the fearful penance he endures, is taken as the play's 'middle', and his death, despite that regeneration, as its *dénouement*, then the catharsis of *King Lear*, Shakespeare's profoundest tragedy, has as yet escaped definition. This catharsis, grounded in the most universal elements of the human condition, can be formulated only when one has drawn together some of the relevant philosophical issues of the play.

Thus, the ending is decisive in resolving the plethora of attitudes presented in the play concerning the relationship between God and man. Set side by side, out of context, and unrelated to the *dénouement*, these attitudes, and their religious frames of reference, can be made to appear an absolute chaos. Certainly almost every possible point of view on the gods and cosmic justice is expressed, from a malevolent, wanton polytheism (IV. 1. 36–7) to an astrological determinism (IV. 3. 32–3), from an amoral, personified Nature-goddess (I. 2. 1) to 'high-judging Jove' (II. 4. 223). But the very multitude, concern, and contradictory character of these references do not cancel each other out, but rather show how precarious is the concept of cosmic justice. Surely if the play's ending is an ending, and cosmic justice has hung in the balance with such matters as Goneril's cruelty (IV. 2. 40–44), Gloucester's blinding (III. 7. 83–4), and Edmund's death (V. 3. 151), it collapses with Lear's ultimate question: 'Why should a dog, a horse, a rat, have life, And thou no breath at all?' Despite the pagan setting, the problem of theodicy, the justification of God's way with man, is invoked by so many characters, and with such concern, that it emerges as a key issue in the play. As such, either the *dénouement* vindicates it, or its integrity is universally destroyed. In point of fact, this is implied in the deaths of Lear and Cordelia.

The force of evil, perhaps the most dynamic element in the Christian tragedies, is extended to wide dimensions in *King Lear*, where two distinct modes of evil emerge, evil as animalism, in Goneril and Regan, and evil as doctrinaire atheism, in Edmund. These modes are not to be confused. Goneril, in particular, is, from the point of view of conscience, an animal or beast of prey. She and Regan never discuss doctrine, as does Edmund, or offer motives, as does Iago. Their actions have the immediacy of animals, to whom consideration never interposes between appetite and deed. It is in this spirit that Lear compares Goneril, in a single scene (I. 4), to a sea-monster, a detested kite, a serpent and a wolf, and Albany, in another (IV. 2), to a tiger, a bear, a monster of the deep, and a fiend, as though, through them, animalism were bursting through civil society.

Edmund, on the other hand, is a doctrinaire atheist with regard not only to God, but also to the traditional, organic universe, a heterodoxy equally horrifying to the Elizabethans. This doctrinaire atheism involves an issue as basic in *King Lear* as that of a retributive justice, and that is the bond between man, society, and nature. Here, there is no plethora of attitudes, but two positions, essentially, that of Cordelia, and that of Edmund. Cordelia's position is perhaps best expressed by Albany, after he learns of Goneril's treatment of Lear:

> That nature which contemns its origin
> Cannot be border'd certain in itself;
> She that herself will sliver and disbranch
> From her material sap, perforce must wither
> And come to deadly use.   IV. 2. 32

According to Albany, an invisible bond of sympathy binds human beings like twigs to the branches of a tree. This bond is no vague universal principle, but closely rooted in one's immediate family and society. This is natural law in its most elemental possible sense, not a moral code, but almost a biochemical reaction. Hierarchical propriety is a necessity for life, like sunlight and water, its violation an act of suicide or perversion. It is Cordelia, in response to this law, who says firmly, 'I love your Majesty According to my bond, no more or less' (I. I. 91–2). This bond, the central concept of the play, is the bond of nature, made up at once of propriety and charity.

In contrast to this concept of Nature is Edmund's soliloquy affirming his doctrinaire atheism (I. 2. 1–15), where natural law is summed up in two phrases, 'the plague of custom', and 'the curiosity of nations'. The bond of human relations, as understood by Cordelia and Albany, is a tissue of extraneous, artificial constraints. Edmund recognizes a hierarchy, but rather than growing out of society, this hierarchy goes wholly against its grain. This is the hierarchy of animal vitality, by which 'the lusty stealth of nature', even in the act of adultery, creates a more worthy issue than the 'dull, stale, tired bed' of marriage. And in response to Gloucester's superstitious references to the larger concept of the organic universe, Edmund repudiates any relationship between the 'orbs from whom we do exist' and his own destiny (I. 2. 121–7).

Strangely enough, however, while the *dénouement* seems to destroy any basis for providential justice, it would seem to vindicate Cordelia with regard to the bond of human nature. Thus, the deaths of Cornwall, Goneril, and Regan are, as Albany prophesied, the swift and monstrous preying of humanity upon itself. Cornwall is killed by his own servant; Regan is poisoned by her sister; and Goneril finally commits suicide. Even more is Cordelia vindicated in Edmund, who is mortally wounded by his brother, and then goes through a complete, and, to this reader, sincere repentance before his death. Critics have expressed bewilderment at Edmund's delay in attempting to save Lear and Cordelia. They do not, however, remark the significance of the point at which Edmund acts. For it is not until Goneril confesses the poisoning of Regan and commits suicide, thus persuading Edmund that he was loved, that he bestirs himself to save Lear and Cordelia if it is not too late. Intellectual assent is not sufficient. Only to those wholly caught up in the bond of love is charity possible:

EDMUND: Yet Edmund was beloved.
    The one the other poison'd for my sake,
    And after slew herself.
ALBANY: Even so. Cover their faces.
EDMUND: I pant for life. Some good I mean to do,
    Despite of mine own nature.   V. 3. 240

Herein, however, lies a sardonic paradox; for Edmund deceived himself. He was the object of lust, but was not encompassed by love. Goneril slew Regan for his sake, but it was out of lust and ambition; she was incapable of that love which brings to self-transcendence, such as Cordelia's love of Lear, or his own act of 'good', in spite of his 'own nature'. And far from killing herself for Edmund's sake, she committed suicide, utterly alone, at the implicit threat of arrest for treason. Edmund, ever the doctrinaire logician, took false evidence of the bond of love at face value, and died as isolated as he lived. The two forms of evil in *King Lear* were ultimately opaque to one another.

But an even more sardonic paradox is implicit in Edmund's death. For Edmund, by abandoning his atheistic faith and acknowledging the power of love, accepts Cordelia's instinctual affirmation of natural law. But the *dénouement* itself, with the gratuitous, harrowing deaths of Cordelia and Lear, controverts any justice in the universe. Chance kills, in despite of the maidenly stars. It would seem, then, by the *dénouement*, that the universe belongs to Edmund, but mankind belongs to Cordelia. In a palsied cosmos, orphan man must either live by the moral law, which is the bond of love, or swiftly destroy himself. To this paradox, too, Shakespeare offers no mitigation in *King Lear*. The human condition is as inescapable as it is unendurable.

To so paradoxical an ending, what catharsis is possible? This question can be answered only by re-examining the structure of the plot. There can be observed, in *Hamlet*, a radical break from the mode of redemption in such earlier plays as *Romeo and Juliet*. In *Romeo and Juliet*, redemption comes when the tragic hero affirms the traditional frame of values of society, love, an appropriate marriage, peace, and the like, though society has, in practice, ceased to follow them. The result is to enhance the *sancta* of society by the sacrifice of life itself. In *Hamlet*, redemption only comes, finally, when the tragic hero spurns and transcends the *sancta* of society, and appeals to a religious mysticism into which human wisdom can have no entry, and in which, at most, 'the readiness is all'. The final result, however, is none the less the redemption of society and the reconciliation of the tragic hero to it; for Hamlet's last act is to cast a decisive vote for the next king of Denmark. Even *Othello*, domestic tragedy though it is, ends with the reconciliation of the tragic hero and society; and Othello's last act is an affirmation of loyalty to Venice and the execution of judgement upon himself. *King Lear* is Shakespeare's first tragedy in which the tragic hero dies unreconciled and indifferent to society.

The opening movement of *King Lear* is, then, not merely a physical exile from, but an abandonment of the formal *sancta* and institutions of society, which is pictured as even more bankrupt than in *Hamlet*. In *Hamlet*, only one man's deliberate crime corrupts the Danish state, 'mining all within'; in *King Lear*, animalism, atheism, brutal ambition, superstition, self-indulgence, and lethargy all contribute to society's decay. In this opening movement of abandonment, Lear is stripped of all that majesty and reverence clothing him in the opening scene, of kingdom, family, retainers, shelter, and finally reason and clothing themselves, until he comes, at the nadir of his fortunes, to 'the king itself . . . a poor, bare, forked animal' (III. 4. 106). Romeo found his touchstone of truth against the rich texture of the Capulet feast, Lear in an abandoned and naked madman. Romeo and Juliet formed, from the first, an inviolate circle of innocence that was the fulfilment of their previous lives; Lear found no innocence until all his previous life had been stripped away from him.

In contrast to this movement of abandonment, and the basis of the second, counter-movement, stands not, as in *Hamlet*, religious mysticism, but an elemental bond that we can, in this play, indifferently call charity or natural law, one that binds man to man, child to parent, husband to wife, and servant to master almost by a biological impulsion. From first to last, charity is discovered, not as the crown of power and earthly blessings, but in their despite. This theme is enunciated by France in taking Cordelia for his wife:

> Fairest Cordelia, that art most rich being poor;
> Most choice forsaken and most lov'd despised!
> Thee and thy virtues here I seize upon.
> Be it lawful to take up what's cast away.
> Gods, gods! 'Tis strange that from their cold'st neglect
> My love should kindle to inflam'd respect.   I. I. 250

The same affirmation is made by Kent, in entering the impoverished Lear's service:

LEAR: If thou be'st as poor for a subject as he's for a king, thou art poor enough. What wouldst thou?

KENT: Service.

LEAR: Who wouldst thou serve?

KENT: You.

LEAR: Dost thou know me, fellow?

KENT: No, sir; but you have that in your countenance which I would fain call master.

LEAR: What's that?
KENT: Authority.   I. 4. 20

Indeed, organized society dulls people to an awareness of charity,
so that it is only in Lear's abandonment that he becomes bound to
all men:

> Poor naked wretches, wheresoe'er you are,
> That bide the pelting of this pitiless storm,
> How shall your houseless heads and unfed sides,
> Your loop'd and widow'd raggedness, defend you
> From seasons such as these? O, I have ta'en
> Too little care of this! Take physic, pomp;
> Expose thyself to what these wretches feel,
> That thou mayst shake the superflux to them
> And show the heavens more just.   III. 4. 28

Shakespeare could, of course, have used this more elemental level of
charity or natural law as he used the force of love in *Romeo and
Juliet*, to redeem and renew society. Had he chosen to do so, it
would have become politically effective in Cordelia's invading
army, overwhelmed the corrupt elements then in power, and
restored the throne to Lear, as is suggested in Shakespeare's con-
ventionally pious source. But society, in Shakespeare, is now no
longer capable of self-renewal. And so the counter-movement of
the play, the reclothing of Lear, by charity and natural law, with
majesty, sanity, family, and shelter, after the most terrible of
penances, does not close the play. At its close, the completion only
of its dramatic 'middle', Lear is utterly purged of soul, while the
hierarchy of society is reduced, as at the end of *Hamlet*, to an
equation of 'court news' with 'gilded butterflies' (v. 3. 13–14).
At this point, if the universe of the play contained a transcendent
providence, it should act as in the closing movement of *Hamlet*,
mysteriously to redeem a society unable to redeem itself.

Shakespeare's pessimism, however, has deepened since *Hamlet*,
and the deaths to no purpose of Lear and Cordelia controvert any
providential redemption in the play's decisive, closing movement,
so that another resolution entirely is called for. Narrowing our
problem somewhat, the catharsis of any play lies in the relationship
of the *dénouement* to the expectations set up in the play's 'middle'.
In *King Lear*, this middle movement has to do primarily with

Lear's spiritual regeneration after his 'stripping' in the opening movement of the play. These two movements can be subsumed in a single great cycle, from hauteur and spiritual blindness through purgative suffering to humility and spiritual vision, a cycle that reaches its culmination in Lear's address of consolation to Cordelia before they are taken off to prison (v. 3. 8–17). The catharsis of *King Lear* would seem to lie, then, in the challenge of Lear's subsequent death to the penance and spiritual transcendence that culminates the play's second movement. This challenge can be described as follows:

All men, in all societies, make, as it were, a covenant with society in their earliest infancy. By this covenant, the dawning human consciousness accepts society's deepest ordinances, beliefs, and moral standards in exchange for a promise of whatever rewards and blessings society offers. The notion of intelligible reward and punishment, whether formulated as a theological doctrine and called retributive justice or as a psychological doctrine and called the reality principle, is as basic to human nature as the passions themselves. But given the contingency of human life, that covenant is constantly broken by corruption within and without. A man's life and that of his family are at all times hostages of his limited wisdom, his tainted morality, the waywardness of chance, and the decay of institutions. Indeed, social ritual, whether religious in character, like confession or periodic fasting, or secular, like the ceremonial convening of a legislature, is an attempt to strengthen the bond of a covenant inevitably weakened by the attrition of evil and the brute passage of time. These are all, in a sense, acts of penance, that is, acts whose deepest intent is to purge us of guilt and the fear of being abandoned, to refresh our bond with one another and with our private and collective destiny.

Lear, at the beginning of the play, embodies all that man looks forward to in a world in which, ultimately, nothing is secure. He has vocation, age, wealth, monarchy, family, personal followers, and long experience. Like Oedipus and Othello, he would have seemed to have attained, before the play begins, what men strive for with indifferent success all their lives. In this sense, Lear engages our sympathies as an archetype of mankind. And just as Othello discovers areas of experience which he never cultivated and which destroy him, Lear discovers that even in those areas he most cultivated he has nothing. Thus, like Oedipus and more than Othello, Lear activates the latent anxiety at the core of the human condition, the fear not only of unexpected catastrophe but that even what seems like success may be a delusion, masking corruption, crime, and almost consummated failure.

This opening movement, however, leads not to dissolution, exposure, and self-recognition, as in *Oedipus* and *Othello*, but to purgation. And Lear's purgation, by the end of the play's middle movement, like his gifts and his vulnerability at its start, is so complete as to be archetypal. By the time he enters prison, he has paid every price and been stripped of everything a man can lose, even his sanity, in payment for folly and pride. He stands beyond the veil of fire, momentarily serene and alive. As such he activates an even profounder fear than the fear of failure, and that is the fear that whatever penance a man may pay may not be enough once the machinery of destruction has been let loose, because the partner of his covenant may be neither grace nor the balance of law, but malignity, intransigence, or chaos.

The final, penultimate tragedy of Lear, then, is not the tragedy of *hubris*, but the tragedy of penance. When Lear, the archetype not of a proud, but of a penitential man, brutally dies, then the uttermost that can happen to man has happened. One can rationalize a passing pedestrian struck down by a random automobile; there is no blenching from this death. Each audience harbours this anxiety in moments of guilt and in acts of penance. And with Lear's death, each audience, by the ritual of the drama, shares and releases the most private and constricting fear to which mankind is subject, the fear that penance is impossible, that the covenant, once broken, can never be re-established, because its partner has no charity, resilience, or harmony – the fear, in other words, that we inhabit an imbecile universe. It is by this vision of reality that Lear lays down his life for his folly. Within its bounds lies the catharsis of Shakespeare's profoundest tragedy.

'The Catharsis of *King Lear*',
Shakespeare Survey, Vol. 13, 1960

SEVENTEEN

Shakespeare's Rituals and the Opening Scene of King Lear

WILLIAM FROST

RITUAL is probably connected with the nature of dramatic art at its very core, if the theories of anthropologists and classical scholars be correct. And like disguise again, ritual can operate to free both actor and playwright from the demands of strict verisimilitude, for the participants in a rite are assumed *a priori* to act parts and to speak language not simply their own or natural to them as individuals, but traditional or appropriate in some way to a publicly acknowledged occasion. I should like to extend the term 'ritual' here to include any speech or situation which will be felt by participants or spectators to be predictable in important respects. . . .

Ritual has these characteristics, at least: it is ordinarily public, it is deliberate, and it is presumed to be predictable, in outline if not in detail. When Richard is sent for it is known that he will give up the crown; when Claudius assembles his court he has already decided what action to take against Fortinbras. Such a scene as the opening of *I Henry IV* has some of the elements of a state-of-the-union message, and some of those of a presidential press conference. Like such throne-room scenes, trial scenes are normally intensely public; and while their outcome – as in *Measure for Measure* – may actually astonish participants and spectators alike the fact that there will be an outcome, and of a certain kind, is well understood in advance. Since ritual is frequently felt to express simple appropriateness to an occasion at least as much as practical purposive utility, the sort of language used in it can be heightened in various ways without appearing needlessly artificial; this fact no doubt partly accounts for its frequent appearance in verse-drama especially, whether of the seventeenth or the twentieth century.

The various advantages of ritual to drama, however, probably do not need stressing at the moment. Any one who has seen a good performance of the conjuring scene in *Doctor Faustus* or of the conclusion of the first act of *Heartbreak House* will be aware of its theatrical effectiveness. Furthermore, western theatre has been for so long predominantly naturalistic and antiritualistic, and life today is so intent on discarding whatever vestigial rituals may still be about (we don't have speeches from the throne, we have fireside chats), that criticism is perhaps occasionally in danger of becoming hypnotized by idealized visions of a more largely ceremonial stagecraft. One particularly ritual-happy critic, for example, has observed of *Hamlet* that 'on stage, the music and the drums and the marching of royal and military pageantry are directly absorbing, and they assure us that something of great and general significance is going on'. If they only could, how easy to write a tragedy! Or how little eccentric would have appeared the man in the Broadway farce who *liked* to attend commencements! Against the strong intoxication of boom-boom, tramp-tramp dramaturgy perhaps it is time to make the point that, like patriotism, ritual is not enough. In this essay I should like to comment on some of its drawbacks, and to conclude with an example of Shakespeare's power to transcend them.

'The trick of that voice I do well remember,' says the blinded Gloucester on being addressed as Goneril-with-a-white-beard; 'Is't not the King?' 'The trick of that voice' – for all the patterns of imagery, the ironic paradoxes, and the strong concatenated plots, it is still by the tricks of their voices that we remember the Shakespearean tribe: by Falstaff's 'They hate us youth' or Regan's 'What need one?' But a primary effect of much ritual is to damp down the oscillations of personality, subduing them to the exigencies of what is ceremonial, appropriate, and expected. For me the basic objection to Gertrude's obituary on Ophelia ('There is a willow grows aslant a brook That shows his hoar leaves in the grassy stream') is not the standard naturalistic one that Gertrude, if she saw all this, should have jumped in and stopped it; but rather that the all-too-appropriate pastoral-cum-phallic imagery in her oration has an inevitably depersonalizing effect on Gertrude herself. . . .

Besides its possible blotting-out effects on individuality of character, ritual also involves the danger of mechanizing action, of replacing possible real significance with an illusion of built-in significance. The very guarantee-in-advance of drama carried by a marriage or a trial may be disastrous; having one's initials engraved on an electric toaster does not essentially 'personalize' the operations of the gadget. The more obviously ingenious the contrivance, the greater the danger of its developing into a marionette dance:

> – Good shepherd, tell this youth what 'tis to love.
> – It is to be made all of sighs and tears,
> – And so am I for Phebe.
> – And I for Ganymede.
> – And I for Rosalind.
> – And I for no woman.

What might have been an emotion becomes in effect a conundrum.

There is also the temptation for the dramatist to extract an added *frisson* from ritual by interrupting it, as when the King throws down his gage in *Richard II*, the bridegroom answers 'No!' in *Much Ado About Nothing*, or an unexpected guest appears for dinner in *Macbeth*. . . .

Probably no scene in any of Shakespeare's mature tragedies is more overtly ritualistic in construction and in language than the holding of court that opens *King Lear*; all the force of Dryden's comment on rhyme in drama – that it will sound as though the speakers in a dialogue had got together and composed it in advance – would seem to apply to this gathering. First Lear speaks, announcing fully and formally what is about to happen; then come the questioning of the daughters in order of age; the breakdown of the four-part liturgy (challenge, response, comment, award) on its third performance; the ceremonial quarrel with Cordelia, followed by formal disinheritance; the ceremonial quarrel with Kent, followed by formal banishment; Kent's elaborate farewells; the public rejection of Cordelia by Burgundy; her ritual wooing by France; and a cluster of antiphonal farewells as the court breaks up. Except for Cordelia's sudden 'Nothing' – a violent momentary break in the proceedings – the scene, even at its most passionate moments, is conducted in blank verse of a Byzantine stateliness, if not, indeed, in rhyme:

> Thy dow'rless daughter, King, thrown to my chance,
> Is queen of us, of ours, and our fair France.
> Not all the dukes of wat'rish Burgundy
> Can buy this unprized precious maid of me.   I. I. 256

It used to be fashionable to call couplets not unlike those of France – at least when produced a century or so later by Pope or Dryden – frigid and lifeless; and indeed as recently as 1927 Professor Allardyce Nicoll has written that 'One could have wished it were possible to prove that these lines were not by Shakespeare or that they were remnants of an earlier *Lear* of his callow youth, but we may accept them I think, as his own, manifesting in their stiffness and mental rigidity the dramatist's recognition of his own failure to make this scene live and his obvious desire to push on to more congenial subject-matter.' For Nicoll, as a matter of fact, the whole first scene of *Lear* is 'a failure' and 'easily the most uninteresting long scene of the drama'. Here, surely, by contrast to the point of view of some more recent critics, we find modern uneasiness with ritual, and opposition to it, stated in the most uncompromising terms.

What can be said in defence of the scene?

In the first place, if it must be viewed as allegory, then as allegory, at least, it holds together extremely well. Its basic constituents are simply two contests of affection, the first among Goneril, Regan, and Cordelia, the second between France and Burgundy. That the second is a neat and ironic commentary on the first comes out in France's courteous lines to the reluctant Burgundy –

> My Lord of Burgundy,
> What say you to the lady? Love's not love
> When it is mingled with regards that stand
> Aloof from th' entire point. Will you have her?
> She is herself a dowry.   I. I. 237

The aphorism about the nature of love, though not so intended by France, who was absent from the earlier contest, sums up the moral issue involved in that contest, and prepares for the appropriately religious formality of France's ensuing proposal:

> Fairest Cordelia, that art most rich, being poor;
> Most choice forsaken and most lov'd despised, . . .
>
>   I. I. 250

To the level of the preceding action no other style of declaration could possibly be adequate. It is no wonder that Granville-Barker finds 'an actor of authority and distinction' requisite for this briefest, but not least important, of roles in the scene.

In the second place, the balanced ceremony of the scene accords well with the mythic, the folk tale nature of the story as it came down from the old chronicles to Shakespeare: the story of an ancient king of Britain who had three daughters, of whom two were evil, and one was good. Such fairy-tale materials, of course, underlie more than one of Shakespeare's plots, and he has various ways of handling them; here, his method is the simplest and boldest possible; all questions of motivation are bypassed at the outset, and we start with the naked myth. For given such a myth, to raise the question of motive would be to undermine dramatic effect in advance. As the earlier play *King Lear* surely demonstrates sufficiently, any conceivable rationalization is bound to be weak and inadequate.

In the third place, the machine-like quality of ritual, produces, in the first part of the scene, precisely the effect of nightmarish inevitability most useful, I think, for certain sorts of tragedy. The driver is fully and terrifyingly in control of the car; every piston functions smoothly; and the road ends in a precipice just around the next corner. Any suggestion of deliberation, hesitation, or wavering between alternatives would but confuse and perplex the appalling spectacle.

I have so far mentioned only elements *within* the scene. There is also the question of its relation to the play as a whole, a relation mainly one of several sorts of contrast. In the first place there is the contrast, well commented on by S. L. Bethell among other critics, between the rituals and their framework, those brief prose interchanges between Kent and Gloucester before the ceremonies start and between Goneril and Regan after they conclude. The prose dialogues are casual, colloquial, and the reverse of mythic in atmosphere. Because they allude to the motivation of the central figure in the rites, without really attempting to explain it, they give the effect of going backstage and hearing the actors comment on the play. By this means the gap between ritual and more naturalistic drama is bridged, at the same time that ritual itself is thrown into high relief.

Second, there is the contrast between Lear's courtroom and

Goneril's household, where we get our second look at the King. In the household, action and imagery alike are trivial, domestic, and haphazard; again the effect is of going backstage, where fancy dress is partly thrown off, make-up smudged, and wigs awry. This effect is only temporary, however; for tension rises throughout the scene till at its close, in curses and quarrel, Lear is evidently remounting an imaginary throne – how pathetically and ironically imaginary Goneril's reassurances of Albany remind us. The Lear who had disinherited Cordelia and banished Kent retains a power of banishment, but only over himself.

The third contrast is with the storm-and-madness scenes at the centre of the play. In these Lear, now unable to distinguish imaginary thrones from real ones, pardons Gloucester for adultery and pronounces a death sentence on Kent for treason:

KENT [*speaking of Edgar*]: He hath no daughters, sir.
LEAR: Death, traitor; nothing could have subdued nature
      To such a lowness but his unkind daughters.   III. 4. 68

In these scenes are embodied one enormous parody after another of the ritualistic opening of the play. Of the trial scene in the farmhouse Granville-Barker remarks: 'Where Lear, such a short while since, sat in his majesty, there sit the Fool and the outcast, with Kent whom he banished beside them; and he, witless, musters his failing strength to beg justice upon a joint stool. Was better justice done, the picture ironically asks, when he presided in majesty and sanity and power?' The trial scene in the farmhouse, moreover, is followed immediately by a yet more monstrous parody, the justice done on Gloucester by Regan and Cornwall.

Disorder of various sorts is basic to these central scenes. It is no longer as though we had passed backstage to observe the actors in their dressing-gowns, but as though the theatre itself had suddenly been shaken by an earthquake, and the actors were improvising amid falling masonry. They seem continually to grasp for some shred of ceremony as the boards tremble beneath them and the footlights flicker uncertainly. 'Come, sit thou here, most learned justicer,' Lear beseeches the blanketed Edgar in the farmhouse. 'Though well we may not pass upon his life Without the form of justice,' begins Cornwall at the trial of Gloucester, towards the end of which two stagehands, panic-stricken, suddenly refuse to co-operate longer and one of them hastily murders the chief actor. On the cliffs of Dover, even scenery has to be openly improvised out of nothing.

The final contrast is between the opening and the conclusion of the play. At this conclusion, both in the reunion with Cordelia and in the final spectacle, ritual has lost all relevance to the King. His 'I am a very foolish fond old man, Fourscore and upward' is like Cleopatra's 'No more but e'en a woman, and commanded By such poor passion as the maid that milks And does the meanest chares'; but it is more final than Cleopatra's self-regarding momentary dethronement. We are now in the presence, not of the ceremonies by which human beings encompass their condition, the *rites de passage* of the anthropologists; but of the barest facts of that condition itself. King and daughter, no longer figures in myth or allegory, come before us fragile, irreplaceable, and particular, a pair of jailbirds and losers.

Meanwhile, however, the earthquake is subsiding, and the stage getting swept up so that orderly drama can go forward. Act v is emphatically not without ritual, the chief rite being, of course, the trial by combat which restores Edgar to status and inheritance, eliminates Edmund, and leaves the political field clear for Albany at last. Many commentators have analysed the double plot structure of *King Lear*, mostly in regard to its universalizing effect on the conflict of the generations; another important result of the subplot is that it keeps everybody so busy, especially at the end of the play. Wars have to be fought, traitors unmasked, and a final contest of affection adjudicated between Regan and Goneril, whose love-rivalry for Edmund ironically parallels that of France and Burgundy for Cordelia earlier, just as Edgar's restoration restores some semblance of order to the judicial processes of primitive Britain. So much has been happening, in fact, that Kent creates a sensation by appearing on the stage and asking for his master. 'Great thing of us forgot!' cries Albany, stupefied; 'Speak, Edmund, where's the King? and where's Cordelia?'

This moment in the play, which some have criticized as fortuitous, melodramatic, and contrived, needs to be regarded in the light of the ritual which started the whole chain of events in motion. In that opening scene, everything depended on Lear and Cordelia; around the conflict of their wills the fates of nations, literally, revolved. Now, they are of no importance; no role is left to them; what happens to them scarcely matters; it is as though they had been dropped from the play. Contrast the death of Hamlet, in the instant of Claudius's exposure; or the death of Cleopatra, foiling the purposes of Caesar. Left without function in the mechanism of society, Lear will not be, like Hamlet, carried to a stage and exhibited to the tune of a military dead march. He will not be given a few last words, like Othello, about the service he has done the state. Nor can Cordelia be arrayed like Cleopatra in the robes and crown of a princess and made to embrace her death as a bride embraces a bridegroom. So 'formal and megalithic' at the beginning, these two personages have passed beyond ritual altogether at the close. They cannot be expressed or comprehended by any of its forms – this fact is their greatness and their tragedy.

from 'Shakespeare's Rituals and the Opening Scene of *King Lear*', *The Hudson Review*, vol. x, No. 4, 1957–8

KING LEAR

Suggestions for Further Reading

H. GRANVILLE-BARKER: *Prefaces to Shakespeare I.*

EDMUND BLUNDEN: 'Shakespeare's Significances' (Shakespeare Association Lecture 1929); reprinted both in Blunden's *The Mind's Eye,* and in Bradby's *Shakespeare Criticism, 1919–1935* (World's Classics).

A. C. BRADLEY: *Shakespearean Tragedy.* Bradley suggests the play might be called 'The Redemption of King Lear'.

JOHN F. DANBY: *Shakespeare's Doctrine of Nature: A Study of King Lear.*

WILLIAM EMPSON: 'Fool in *Lear*' (in *The Structure of Complex Words*). Examines the play through the uses made of the metaphor of the Fool. 'Nature is the most prominent of the many clowns in view ... Divine goodness and gentleness in Lear has been learned through madness: not merely through suffering, but through having been a clown. ... Where there does seem room for a religious view is through a memory of the Erasmus fool, that is, by being such a complete fool Lear may become in some mystical way superlatively wise and holy.'

BARBARA EVERETT: 'The New King Lear' (*Critical Quarterly,* Winter 1960). This article sparked off a long controversy about the play, to which many of the leading English Shakespearians contributed; this can be found in the two subsequent issues of the *Critical Quarterly,* Spring and Summer, 1961.

L. C. KNIGHTS: '*King Lear*' (in *Some Shakespearean Themes*; a shorter but quite coherent and self-contained version of this article appeared in Vol. 11 of *The Pelican Guide to English Literature*).

WINIFRED NOWOTTNY: 'Some Aspects of the Style of *King Lear*' (in *Shakespeare Survey 13*).

WILLIAM ROSEN: '*King Lear*' (in *Shakespeare and the Craft of Tragedy*). 'Lear ... loses himself to find himself part of all humanity. ... Nevertheless, his insight into truth and happiness is not negotiable in this tough world.'

ENID WELSFORD: *The Fool.* This historical survey makes interesting background reading to Empson's approach, and also contains a chapter on the play.

MACBETH

EIGHTEEN

The Atmosphere of Macbeth

A. C. BRADLEY

A SHAKESPEARIAN tragedy, as a rule, has a special tone or atmosphere of its own, quite perceptible, however difficult to describe. The effect of this atmosphere is marked with unusual strength in *Macbeth*. . . .

Darkness, we may even say blackness, broods over this tragedy. It is remarkable that almost all the scenes which at once recur to memory take place either at night or in some dark spot. The vision of the dagger, the murder of Duncan, the murder of Banquo, the sleep-walking of Lady Macbeth, all come in night-scenes. The Witches dance in the thick air of a storm, or, 'black and midnight hags', receive Macbeth in a cavern. The blackness of night is to the hero a thing of fear, even of horror; and that which he feels becomes the spirit of the play. The faint glimmerings of the western sky at twilight are here menacing: it is the hour when the traveller hastens to reach safety in his inn and when Banquo rides homeward to meet his assassins; the hour when 'light thickens', when 'night's black agents to their prey do rouse', when the wolf begins to howl, and the owl to scream, and withered murder steals forth to his work. Macbeth bids the stars hide their fires that his 'black' desires may be concealed; Lady Macbeth calls on thick night to come, palled in the dunnest smoke of hell. The moon is down and no stars shine when Banquo, dreading the dreams of the coming night, goes unwillingly to bed, and leaves Macbeth to wait for the summons of the little bell. When the next day should dawn, its light is 'strangled', and 'darkness does the face of earth entomb'.

from Lecture IX, *Shakespearean Tragedy*, 1904

NINETEEN

The Capital Difficulty of Macbeth

SIR ARTHUR QUILLER-COUCH

LET us exclude the supernatural for a moment. Having excluded it, we shall straightway perceive that the story of the *Chronicle* has one fatal defect as a theme of tragedy. For tragedy demands some sympathy with the fortunes of its hero: but where is there room for sympathy in the futures of a disloyal, self-seeking murderer?

Just there lay Shakespeare's capital difficulty. . . .

Aristotle says this concerning the hero, or protagonist, of tragic drama, and Shakespeare's practice at every point supports him:

(1) A tragedy must not be the spectacle of a perfectly good man brought from prosperity to adversity. For this merely shocks us.

(2) Nor, of course, must it be that of a bad man passing from adversity to prosperity: for that is not tragedy at all, but the perversion of tragedy, and revolts the moral sense.

(3) Nor, again, should it exhibit the downfall of an utter villain: since pity is aroused by undeserved misfortunes, terror by misfortunes befalling a man like ourselves.

(4) There remains, then, as the only proper subject for tragedy, the spectacle of a man not absolutely or eminently good or wise, who is brought to disaster not by sheer depravity but by some error or frailty.

(5) Lastly, this man must be highly renowned and prosperous – an Oedipus, a Thyestes, or some other illustrious person.

Before dealing with the others, let us get this last rule out of the way; for, to begin with, it presents no difficulty in *Macbeth*, since in the original – in Holinshed's *Chronicles* – Macbeth is an illustrious warrior who makes himself a king; and moreover the rule is patently a secondary one, of artistic expediency rather than of artistic right or wrong. . . .

But, touching the other and more essential rules laid down by Aristotle, let me – very fearfully, knowing how temerarious it is,

how imprudent to offer to condense so great and close a thinker –
suggest that, after all, they work down into one: that a hero of
tragic drama must, whatever else he miss, engage our sympathy;
that, however gross his error or grievous his frailty, it must not
exclude our feeling that he is a man like ourselves; that, sitting in
the audience, we must know in our hearts that what is befalling
him might conceivably in the circumstances have befallen us, and
say in our hearts, 'There, but for the grace of God, go I'.

I think, anticipating a little, I can drive this point home by a
single illustration. When the ghost of Banquo seats itself at that
dreadful supper, who sees it? Not the company. Not even Lady
Macbeth. Whom does it accuse? Not the company, and, again, not
even Lady Macbeth. Those who see it are Macbeth and you and I.
Those into whom it strikes terror are Macbeth and you and I.
Those whom it accuses are Macbeth and you and I. And what it
accuses is what, of Macbeth, you and I are hiding in our own
breasts.

So, if this be granted, I come back upon the capital difficulty that
faced Shakespeare as an artist.

(1) It was not to make Macbeth a grandiose or a conspicuous
figure. He was already that in the *Chronicle*.

(2) It was not to clothe him in something to illude us with the
appearance of real greatness. Shakespeare, with his command of
majestic poetical speech, had that in his work-bag surely enough,
and knew it. When a writer can make an imaginary person talk
like this:

> She should have died hereafter.
> There would have been a time for such a word –
> Tomorrow, and tomorrow, and tomorrow,
> Creeps in this petty pace from day to day
> To the last syllable of recorded time;
> And all our yesterdays have lighted fools
> The way to dusty death.   v. 5. 17

I say, when a man knows he can make his Macbeth talk like that, he
needs not distrust his power to drape his Macbeth in an illusion of
greatness. Moreover, Shakespeare – artist that he was – had other
tricks up his sleeve to convince us of Macbeth's greatness. One of
these I hope to discuss in a subsequent chapter.

But (here lies the crux) how could he make us sympathize with him – make us, sitting or standing in the Globe Theatre some time (say) in the year 1610, feel that Macbeth was even such a man as you or I? He was a murderer, and a murderer for his private profit – a combination which does not appeal to most of us, to unlock the flood-gates of sympathy or (I hope) as striking home upon any private and pardonable frailty. The *Chronicle* does, indeed, allow just one loop-hole for pardon. It hints that Duncan, nominating his boy to succeed him, thereby cut off Macbeth from a reasonable hope of the crown, which he thereupon (and not until then) by process of murder usurped, 'having,' says Holinshed, 'a juste quarrell so to do (as he took the mater).'

Did Shakespeare use that one hint, enlarge that loophole? He did not.

The more we study Shakespeare as an artist, the more we must worship the splendid audacity of what he did, just here, in this play of *Macbeth*.

Instead of using a paltry chance to condone Macbeth's guilt, he seized on it and plunged it threefold deeper, so that it might verily

the multitudinous seas incarnadine.

Think of it:

He made this man, a sworn soldier, murder Duncan, his liege-lord.

He made this man, a host, murder Duncan, a guest within his gates.

He made this man, strong and hale, murder Duncan, old, weak, asleep and defenceless.

He made this man commit murder for nothing but his own advancement.

He made this man murder Duncan, who had steadily advanced him hitherto, who had never been aught but trustful, and who (that no detail of reproach might be wanting) had that very night, as he retired, sent, in most kindly thought, the gift of a diamond to his hostess.

To sum up: instead of extenuating Macbeth's criminality, Shakespeare doubles and redoubles it. Deliberately this magnificent artist locks every door on condonation, plunges the guilt deep as hell, and then – tucks up his sleeves . . .

How could it lie within the compass even of Shakespeare, master-workman though he was and lord of all noble persuasive language, to make a tragic hero of this Macbeth – traitor to his king, murderer of his sleeping guest, breaker of most sacred trust, ingrate, self-seeker, false kinsman, perjured soldier? Why, it is sin of this quality that in *Hamlet*, for example, outlaws the guilty wretch beyond range of pardon – our pardon, if not God's.

> Upon my secure hour thy uncle stole . . .   I. 5. 61

Why, so did Macbeth upon Duncan's. Hear the wretch himself on his knees:

> Forgive me my foul murder?
> That cannot be; since I am still possess'd
> Of those effects for which I did the murder . . .   III. 3. 52

Why, so was Macbeth again.

> O bosom black as death!
> O limèd soul, that, struggling to be free,
> Art more engag'd!   III. 3. 67

How could Shakespeare make his audience feel pity or terror for such a man? Not for the deed, not for Duncan; but for Macbeth, doer of the deed; how make them sympathize, saying inwardly, 'There, but for the grace of God, might you go, or I'?

He could, by majesty of diction, make them feel that Macbeth was somehow a great man: and this he did. He could conciliate their sympathy at the start by presenting Macbeth as a brave and victorious soldier: and this he did. He could show him drawn to the deed, against will and conscience, by persuasion of another, a woman: and this – though it is extremely dangerous, since all submission of will forfeits something of manliness, lying apparently on the side of cowardice, and ever so little of cowardice forfeits sympathy – this, too, Shakespeare did. He could trace the desperate act to ambition, 'last infirmity of noble minds': and this again he did. All these artifices, and more, Shakespeare used. But yet are they artifices and little more. They do not begin – they do not

pretend – to surmount the main difficulty which I have indicated,
How of such a criminal to make a hero?

Shakespeare did it: *solutum est agendo*. How?

There is (I suppose) only one possible way. It is to make our
hero – supposed great, supposed brave, supposed of certain win-
ning natural gifts – proceed to his crime *under some fatal hallucination* . . .

Now let us return to Holinshed. The *Chronicle* relates that Macbeth and Banquo 'went sporting by the way together without
other companie save only themselves, passing the woodes and
fieldes, when sodenly, in the middes of a launde there met them 3
women in strange and ferly apparell, resembling creatures of an
elder worlde': and it adds that by common opinion these women
'were eyther the weird sisters, that is (as ye would say) ye God-
desses of destinee, or else some Nimphes or Faieries'. I have
already announced my readiness to make affidavit that Shakespeare's mind, as he read, seized on this passage at once. Following
this up, I will suggest (as a diversion from my main argument) a
process – rough indeed, yet practical – by which a dramatist's
mind would operate.

He would say to himself, 'I have to treat of a murder; which is,
of its nature, a deed of darkness. Here to my hand is a passage
which, whether I can find or not in it the motive of my plot, already
drapes it in the supernatural, and so in mystery, which is next door
to darkness.' . . .

Let us pause here, on the brink of the deed, and summarize:

(1) Shakespeare, as artificer of this play, meant the Witches, with
their suggestions, to be of capital importance.

(2) Shakespeare, as a workman, purposely left vague the extent
of their influence; purposely left vague the proportions of their
influence and Macbeth's own guilty promptings, his own acceptance of the hallucination, contribute to persuade him; vague as the
penumbra about him in which – for he is a man of imagination –
he sees that visionary dagger. For (let us remember) it is not on
Macbeth alone that this horrible dubiety has to be produced; but
on us also, seated in the audience. We see what he does not see,
and yearn to warn him; but we also see what he sees – the dagger,
Banquo's ghost – and understand why he doubts.

THE CAPITAL DIFFICULTY OF 'MACBETH'

(3) As witchcraft implies a direct reversal of the moral order, so the sight and remembrance of the witches, with the strange fulfilment of the Second Witch's prophecy, constantly impose the hallucination upon him – 'Fair is foul, and foul is fair.' 'Evil, be thou my good.'

from *Shakespeare's Workmanship*, 1918, Chapters I and II

TWENTY

Shakespeare's Tragic Villain

WAYNE BOOTH

CONSIDERED even in its simplest terms, the problem Shakespeare gave himself in *Macbeth* was immense: take a 'noble' man, full of 'conscience' and 'the milk of human kindness', and make of him a 'dead butcher', yet maintain him as a tragic hero with full stature commanding our sympathy to the end. To portray a credible path of moral degeneration is difficult enough in itself; to do so in a form requiring undiminished pity is next to impossible. The attempt would be brash even in fiction, or epic, with all of their additional resources for portraying subtle changes and for building sympathy. But to attempt a moral transformation of such scope in a short play, without muddling the audience's responses, is to court disaster.

One need only consider how rarely authors have achieved tragedy with their sympathetic villains to realize the difficulties involved. In place of the tragic experience offered by *Macbeth*, one usually finds one or another of the following transformations: (1) The protagonist is never really made very wicked, after all: he only *seems* wicked by conventional, unsound standards and is really a highly admirable reform-candidate. (2) The abhorrence for the protagonist becomes so strong that all sympathy is lost, and the work becomes 'punitive', as in *Richard III*. (3) The protagonist reforms in the end, before ever really doing anything very bad (innumerable motion pictures and tragi-comedies). (4) The wickedness is mitigated by comedy, so that the serious conflict between sympathy and moral judgement is diminished (*Lolita, The Ginger Man*). (5) The book or play itself becomes a 'wicked' work; that is, either deliberately or unconsciously the artist makes us take the side of his degenerated hero against morality (The Marquis de Sade). (6) The spectacle of decay is no longer exploited, as in *Macbeth*, for its greatest human effects, but these are subordinated to other, 'purer' ends, as Flaubert, in *Madame Bovary*, often deliberately undercuts the pathos of Emma's gradual corruption in order, as he puts it, 'to make the reader dream' rather than weep.

There is no real reason why fine works cannot be written using any of these transformations, but it is hard to find many works of any kind that make the fact of moral decline credible by providing sufficient motivation; too often the degeneration remains finally unconvincing, because the forces employed to destroy the man are not strong enough to destroy anyone. In the last few decades, in fact, authors have tended to write as if the course of degeneration were so natural that it needed no explanation: if all men are corrupt, then corruption is inherently sympathetic.

Even in works which more closely resemble the attempt in *Macbeth*, there is almost always some shrinking from a fully responsible engagement with the inherent difficulties. In *Tender is the Night*, for example, Fitzgerald mitigates the effect in several ways. Dick Diver's natural nobility is destroyed, but he moves only to helplessness – to unpopularity and drunkenness and poverty. There are no grotesque acts of cruelty of the kind committed by Macbeth. Rather, Dick speaks more sharply to people than he used to; he is no longer charming. This is indeed pitiful enough, but it is easy enough, too, especially since Fitzgerald chooses to report the final demoralization only vaguely and from a great distance: one never *sees* the hero's final awful moments as one sees Macbeth's. So that, at the end of his downward path, Diver has been more sinned against than sinning, and we have no obstacles to our pity. On the other hand, since the fall has not been nearly so great, our pity is attenuated. Other attenuations follow. If the fall is not very great, the forces needed to produce it need not be great – though one could argue that even in *Tender is the Night* they should have been greater. Nicole and a general atmosphere of gloom and decay are made to do a job which in *Macbeth* require some of the richest degenerative forces ever employed.

I

The first requirement, if we are to believe that Macbeth's fall is a genuinely tragic event, is to convince us that he is an admirable man, a man who matters. One way would be to show him, as Fitzgerald shows Dick Diver, in admirable action. But such a leisurely representation is not possible when great moral distance must be travelled quickly by the protagonist, and Shakespeare quite rightly begins with the first temptation to the fall, using testimony of the liveliest possible kind to establish Macbeth's prior goodness. From the beginning, we are given sign after sign that his greatest nobility was reached at a point just before the play opens. But he has already coveted the crown, as is shown by his extreme response to the witches' prophecy. It is indeed likely that he has already thought of murder. In spite of this, we have ample reason to think Macbeth worthy of our admiration. He is 'brave' and 'valiant', a 'worthy gentleman'; Duncan calls him 'noble Macbeth'. These epithets seem ironic only in retrospect; when they are first applied, one has no reason to doubt them. Indeed, they are accurate, or they would have been accurate if applied, say, a few days or months earlier.

This testimony to his prior virtue would carry little force, however, if it were not supported in several other forms. We have the word of Lady Macbeth (the unimpeachable testimony of a wicked character deploring goodness):

> Yet do I fear thy nature:
> It is too full o' the milk of human kindness
> To catch the nearest way. Thou wouldst be great,
> Art not without ambition, but without
> The illness should attend it. What thou wouldst highly,
> That wouldst thou holily, wouldst not play false,
> And yet wouldst wrongly win.   I. 5. 14

No testimony would be enough, however, if we did not see specific signs of its validity, since we already know of his temptations. Thus the best evidence of his essential goodness is his vacillation before the murder. Just as Raskolnikov is tormented and just as we ourselves – virtuous theatre viewers – would be tormented, so Macbeth is tormented before the prospect of his own crime. Much as he wants the kingship, he decides in Scene 3 against the murder:

> If chance will have me King, why chance may crown me
> Without my stir. . . .

And when he first meets Lady Macbeth he is resolved to resist temptation. Powerful as her rhetoric is, it is barely sufficient to pull him back on the course of murder.

More important is the ensuing soliloquy, since stage conventions give absolute authority to any character's secret thoughts. It shows him weighing not only the bad political consequences of his act but also the moral values involved:

> He's here in double trust:
> First, as I am his kinsman and his subject,
> Strong both against the deed; then, as his host,
> Who should against his murderer shut the door,
> Not bear the knife myself.   1. 7. 12

We see here again Shakespeare's economy: the very speech which shows just how bad the contemplated act is builds sympathy for the planner.

Macbeth announces once again that he will not go on ('We will proceed no further in this business'), but again Lady Macbeth's eloquence is too much for him. Under her jibes at his 'unmanliness' he progresses from a kind of petulant, but still honourable, boasting ('I dare do all that may become a man; Who dares do more is none'), through a state of amoral consideration of mere expediency ('If we should fail?'), to complete resolution, but still with a full understanding of the wickedness of his act (' ... this terrible feat'). There is never any doubt, first, that he is bludgeoned into the deed by Lady Macbeth and by the pressure of unfamiliar circumstances and, second, that even in his final decision he is tormented by a guilty conscience ('False face must hide what the false heart doth know'). In the dagger soliloquy he is clearly suffering from the horror of the 'bloody business' ahead. He sees fully and painfully the wickedness of the course he has chosen, but not until after the deed, when the knocking has commenced, do we realize how terrifyingly alive his conscience is: 'To know my deed, 'twere best not know myself. Wake Duncan with thy knocking! I would thou couldst.' This is the wish of a 'good' man who, though he has become a 'bad' man, still thinks and feels as a good man would.

Finally, we have the testimony to Macbeth's character offered by Hecate:

And, which is worse, all you have done
Hath been but for a wayward son,
Spiteful and wrathful, who, as others do,
Loves for his own ends, not for you.   III. 5. 10

This reaffirmation that Macbeth is not a true son of evil comes, interestingly enough, immediately after the murder of Banquo, at a time when the audience needs a reminder that Macbeth is not fundamentally evil.

His crimes are thus built upon our knowledge that he is not a naturally evil man but a man who has every potentiality for goodness. Indeed, this potentiality and its destruction are the chief ingredients of the tragedy. Macbeth is a man whose progressive external misfortunes seem to produce, and at the same time seem to be produced by, the parallel progression from great goodness to great wickedness.

Our response to his destruction is compounded of three kinds of regret, only one of them known in pre-Shakespearian tragedy. We of course lament the fall of a great man from happiness to misery, as in classical tragedy. To this is added what to most modern spectators is much more poignant: the pity one feels in observing the *moral* decline of a great man who has once known goodness. Perhaps most influential in the later history of drama and fiction, there is the even greater poignancy of observing the destruction of a highly individualized person, a person one knows and cares for. Later writers have tended to rely more and more on the third of these and to play down the first two; one difference between Macbeth going to destruction and the fall of a typical modern hero (Willy Loman say, or Hemingway's Jake) is that in Macbeth there is some going.

2

But perhaps the most remarkable achievement is Shakespeare's choice of how to represent the moral decline. He has the task of trying to keep two contradictory streams moving simultaneously: the events showing Macbeth's growing wickedness and the tide of our mounting sympathy. In effect, each succeeding atrocity, marking another step towards depravity, must be so surrounded by contradictory circumstances or technical blandishments as to make us feel that, in spite of the evidence before our eyes, Macbeth is still somehow sympathetic.

Our first sure sign that Shakespeare's attention is on the need for such manipulation is his care in avoiding any representation of the murder of Duncan. It is, in fact, not even narrated. We hear only the details of how the guards reacted and how Macbeth reacted to their cries. We *see* nothing. There is nothing about the actual dagger strokes; there is no report of the dying cries of the good old king. We have only Macbeth's conscience-stricken lament. What would be an intolerable act if depicted with any vividness becomes relatively forgivable when seen only afterward in the light of Macbeth's remorse. This treatment may seem ordinary enough; it is always convenient to have murders take place offstage. But if one compares the handling of this scene with that of the blinding of Gloucester, where the perpetrators must be hated, one can see how important such a detail can be. The blinding of Gloucester is not so wicked an act, in itself, as Duncan's murder: imagine a properly motivated Goneril wringing her hands and crying, 'Methought I heard a voice cry, "Sleep no more." Goneril does put out the eyes of sleep . . . I am afraid to think what I have done', and on thus for nearly a full scene.

A second precaution is the highly general portrayal of Duncan before his murder. It is necessary only that he be known as a 'good king', the murder of whom will be a wicked act. He must be clearly the best type of benevolent monarch. But more particular characteristics are carefully kept from us. There is little for us to love or attach our imaginations to. We hear of his goodness; we never see it. We know almost no details about him, and we have little personal interest in him at the time of his death. All of the personal interest is reserved for Macbeth and Lady Macbeth. Thus again the wickedness is played up in the narration but played down in the representation. We must identify Macbeth with the murder of a blameless king, but only intellectually; emotionally we should be attending only to the effects on Macbeth. We know that he has done the deed, but we feel primarily his own suffering.

Banquo is considerably more individualized than Duncan. Not only is he a good man, but we have seen him in action as a good man, and we know a good deal about him. We saw his reaction to the witches, and we know that he has resisted temptations similar to those Macbeth is yielding to. We have heard him in soliloquy, that infallible guide to inner quality. He thus has our lively sympathy; his death is more nearly a personal loss than was Duncan's. Perhaps more important, his murder is shown on the stage. His dying words are spoken in our presence, and they are unselfishly directed to saving his son. We are led to the proper, though illogical, inference: it is more wicked to kill Banquo than to have killed Duncan.

But we must still not lose our sympathy for the criminal. It is helpful, of course, that Macbeth is acting on the basis of a real threat to himself. But the important thing is again the choice of what is represented. The murder is done by accomplices, so that Macbeth is never shown in any act of wicked violence. When we do see him, he is suffering the torments of the banquet scene. Our unconscious inference: the self-torture has already expiated his crime.

The same devices work in the murder of Lady Macduff and her children, the third and last atrocity explicitly shown in the play (the killing of young Seyward, being military, is hardly an atrocity in this sense). Lady Macduff is more vividly portrayed even than Banquo, although she appears on the stage for a much briefer time. Her complaints against the absence of her husband, her loving banter with her son, and her stand against the murderers make her as admirable as the little boy himself, who dies in defence of his father's name. The murder of women and children of such quality is wicked indeed, we feel, and when we move to England and see the effect of the atrocity on Macduff, our active pity for Macbeth's victims – as distinct from our abstract awareness that they are victimized – is at its highest point. For the first time, pity for Macbeth's victims really wars with pity for him, and our desire for his downfall threatens to turn the play into what some critics have claimed it to be: a punitive tragedy like *Richard III*.

Yet even here Macbeth is kept as little to blame as possible. He does not do the deed himself, and we can believe that he would have been unable to, if he had seen the victims as we have. (The Orson Welles movie version contained many grotesque errors of reading, but none worse than showing Macbeth actively engaged on the scene of the crime.) He is much further removed from them than from his other victims; as far as we know, he has never seen them. They are as remote and impersonal to him as they are immediate and personal to the audience, and while this impersonal brutality may make his crime worse in theory, our personal blame against him is attenuated. More important, immediately after Macduff's tears we shift to Lady Macbeth's scene, one effect of which is to 'prove' once again that the suffering of these criminals is worse than their crimes.

All three murders, then, are followed immediately by scenes of suffering and self-torture. It is almost as if Shakespeare were following a rule that Aristotle never dreamed of because none of the plays he knew presented this kind of problem: by your choice of what to represent from the materials provided in your story, insure that each step in your protagonist's degeneration will be counter-acted by mounting pity.

This technical brilliance would be useless, of course, if the hard facts of Macbeth's character did not offer grounds for sympathy. Perhaps the most important of these, except for the initial moral stature, is his poetic gift. In his maturer work Shakespeare does not bestow this gift indiscriminately. We naturally tend to feel with the character who speaks the best poetry of the play, no matter what his deeds (Iago would never be misplayed as protagonist if his poetry did not rival, and sometimes surpass, Othello's). When we add to this poetic gift an extremely rich and concrete set of charac-teristics, we have a man who is more likely to compel our sym-pathy than any character portrayed only in moral colours. Even the forces of virtue gathering about his castle to destroy him seem petty compared with his mammoth sensitivity, his rich despair. When he says:

> My way of life
> Is fallen into the sere, the yellow leaf;
> And that which should accompany old age,
> As honour, love, obedience, troops of friends,
> I must not look to have . . .   v. 3. 22

we respond more to Macbeth, the poet of his own condition, whose imagination can still grasp what it has lost, than to the circum-stances of his decline.

3

If Macbeth's initial nobility, the manner of representation of his crimes, and his rich poetic gift are all calculated to sustain our sympathy, the kind of mistake he makes in initiating his own destruction is equally well suited to heighten our willingness to forgive while deploring. It could be said that he errs simply in being over-ambitious and under-scrupulous. But this is only part of the truth. What allows him to sacrifice his moral beliefs to his ambition is a mistake of another kind – a kind which is, at least to modern spectators, more credible than any conventional tragic flaw or any traditional tragic error, such as mistaking the identity of a brother or not knowing that one's wife is one's mother. Macbeth knows what he is doing, yet he does not know. He knows the immorality of the act, but he has no conception of the effects of the act on himself or his surroundings. Accustomed to heroic killing, in battle, and having valorously 'carv'd out his passage' with 'bloody execution' many times previously, he misunderstands what will be the effect on his own character if he tries to carve out his passage in civil life. And of course he cannot foresee that success in the first murder will only lead to the speech 'to be thus is nothing; But to be safely thus', and to ever increasing degradation and suffering for himself and for those around him. Even though he has a kind of double premonition of the effects of the deed both on his own conscience and on Duncan's subjects ('If it were done when 'tis done, then 'twere well . . .'), he does not really understand. If he did understand, he could not, being who he is, do the deed.

This ignorance is made more convincing by being extended to a misunderstanding of the forces leading him to the murder. Macbeth does not really understand that he has two spurs, besides his own vaulting ambition, 'to prick the sides' of his intent. The first of these, the witches and their prophecy, might seem in no way to mitigate his responsibility, since he chooses wilfully to misinterpret what they say. But to reason in this way is again to overplay the role of logic in our dramatic experience. Surely the effect on the spectator is complex: while it is true that Macbeth ought to realize that if they are true oracles both parts of their prophecy must be fulfilled, it is also true that almost any man could be thrown off his moral balance by such supernatural confirmations. His misunderstanding is thus obvious and dramatically effective and at the same time quite forgivable.

The second force which Macbeth does not understand works less equivocally for our sympathy. While Lady Macbeth fills several functions in the play, beyond her great inherent interest as a character, her chief task, as the textbook commonplace has it, is to incite and confuse Macbeth – and thus ultimately to excuse him. Her rhetoric is brilliant whether we think of it as designed to sway Macbeth or as designed to convince the spectators that Macbeth is worth bothering about. She does not paint the pleasures of rewarded ambition; she does not allow him to think about the moral issues, as he would if he were left to himself. Rather she shifts the whole ground to questions of Macbeth's valour. She twits him for cowardice, plays upon the word 'man', and exaggerates her own courage. Macbeth's whole reputation seems at last to be at stake, and even questions of success and failure are made to hang on his courage: 'But screw your courage to the sticking place And we'll not fail.' So that the meaning of his past achievement seems to hang on the decision to murder Duncan.

His tragic error, then, is at least three-fold: he does not understand the two forces working upon him from outside; he does not understand the difference between 'bloody execution' in civilian life and in military life; and he does not understand his own character – he does not know what will be the effects of the act on his own future happiness. Only one of these – the misunderstanding of the weird sisters – can be considered similar to, say, Iphigenia's ignorance of her brother's identity. The hero here must be really aware, in advance, of the wickedness of his act. The more aware he can be – and still commit the act convincingly – the greater the regret felt by the spectator.

All of these points are illustrated powerfully in the contrast between the final words of Malcolm concerning Macbeth – 'This dead butcher and his fiend-like queen' – and the spectator's own feelings toward Macbeth at the same point. We judge Macbeth, as Shakespeare intends, not merely for his actions but in the light of the total impression of the play. Malcolm and Macduff do not know Macbeth and the forces that have worked on him; the spectator does know him and can feel great pity that a man with so much potentiality for greatness should have fallen so low and should be so thoroughly misjudged. The pity is that everything was not otherwise, when it so easily could have been otherwise. The conclusion brings a flood of relief that the awful blunder has played itself out, that Macbeth has at last been able to die, still valiant, and is forced no longer to go on enduring the knowledge of what he has become.

Originally published as 'Macbeth as Tragic Hero' in the *Journal of General Education VI*, October 1951, and revised for this anthology

TWENTY-ONE

Macbeth *as a Dramatic Poem*

L. C. KNIGHTS

'MACBETH' is a statement of evil. I use the word 'statement' (unsatisfactory as it is) in order to stress those qualities that are 'non-dramatic', if drama is defined according to the canons of William Archer or Dr Bradley. It also happens to be poetry, which means that the apprehension of the whole can be obtained from a lively attention to the parts, whether they have an immediate bearing on the main action or 'illustrate character', or not. Two main themes, which can only be separated for the purpose of analysis, are blended in the play – the themes of the reversal of values and of unnatural disorder. And closely related to each is a third theme, that of the deceitful appearance, and consequent doubt, uncertainty, and confusion. All this is obscured by false assumptions about the category 'drama'; *Macbeth* has greater affinity with *The Waste Land* than with *The Doll's House*.

Each theme is stated in the first act. The first scene, every word of which will bear the closest scrutiny, strikes one dominant chord:

> Fair is foul, and foul is fair.
> Hover through the fog and filthy air.   I. I. 9

It is worth remarking that 'hurley-burley' implies more than 'the tumult of sedition or insurrection'. Both it and 'When the battle's lost and won' suggest the kind of metaphysical pitch-and-toss that is about to be played with good and evil. At the same time we hear the undertone of uncertainty: the scene opens with a question, and the second line suggests a region where the elements are disintegrated as they never are in nature; thunder and lightning are disjoined, and offered as alternatives. We should notice also that the scene expresses the same movement as the play as a whole: the general crystallizes into the immediate particular ('Where the place?' – 'Upon the Heath.' – 'There to meet with Macbeth.') and then dissolves again into the general presentment of hideous gloom. All is done with the greatest speed, economy, and precision.

The second scene is full of images of confusion. It is a general principle in the work of Shakespeare and many of his contemporaries that when A is made to describe X, a minor character or event, the description is not merely immediately applicable to X, it helps to determine the way in which our whole response shall develop. This is rather crudely recognized when we say that certain lines 'create the atmosphere' of the play. Shakespeare's power is seen in the way in which details of this kind develop, check, or provide a commentary upon the main interests that he has aroused. In the present scene the description

> – Doubtful it stood,
> As two spent swimmers that do cling together
> And choke their art –   I. 2. 7

applies not only to the battle but to the ambiguity of Macbeth's future fortunes. The impression conveyed is not only one of violence but of unnatural violence ('to bathe in reeking wounds') and of a kind of nightmare gigantism –

> Where the Norweyan banners flout the sky
> And fan our people cold.   I. 2. 50

(These lines alone should be sufficient answer to those who doubt the authenticity of the scene.) When Duncan says, 'What he hath lost, noble Macbeth hath won', we hear the echo,

> So from the spring whence comfort seemed to come
> Discomfort swells.   I. 2. 27

– and this is not the only time the Captain's words can be applied in the course of the play. Nor is it fantastic to suppose that in the account of Macdonwald, Shakespeare consciously provided a parallel with the Macbeth of the later acts when 'The multiplying villainies of nature Do swarm upon him'. After all, everybody has noticed the later parallel between Macbeth and Cawdor ('He was a Gentleman, on whom I built An absolute trust').

A poem works by calling into play, directing, and integrating certain interests. If we really accept the suggestion, which then becomes revolutionary, that *Macbeth* is a poem, it is clear that the impulses aroused in Act I, Scenes 1 and 2, are part of the whole response, even if they are not all immediately relevant to the fortunes of the protagonist. If these scenes are 'the botching work of an interpolator', he botched to pretty good effect.

In Act I Scene 3, confusion is succeeded by uncertainty. The Witches

> look not like th' inhabitants o' th' earth,
> And yet are on't.

Banquo asks Macbeth,

> Why do you start and seem to fear
> Things that do sound so fair?

He addresses the witches,

> You should be women,
> And yet your beards forbid me to interpret
> That you are so . . .
> . . . . I' the name of truth
> Are ye fantastical, or that indeed
> Which outwardly, ye show?

When they vanish, 'what seemed corporal' melts 'As breath into the wind'. The whole force of the uncertainty of the scene is gathered into Macbeth's soliloquy,

> This supernatural soliciting
> Cannot be ill, cannot be good. . . .   I. 3. 129

which with its sickening see-saw rhythm completes the impression of 'a phantasma, or a hideous dream'. Macbeth's echoing of the witches' 'Fair is foul' has often been commented upon.

In contrast to the preceding scenes, Act I, Scene 4 suggests the natural order which is shortly to be violated. It stresses: natural relationships – 'children', 'servants', 'sons', and 'kinsmen'; honourable bonds and the political order – 'liege', 'thanes', 'service', 'duty', 'loyalty', 'throne', 'state', and 'honour'; and the human 'love' is linked to the natural order of organic growth by images of husbandry. Duncan says to Macbeth,

> I have begun to plant thee and will labour
> To make thee full of growing.   I. 4. 29

When he holds Banquo to his heart Banquo replies,

There if I grow,
The harvest is your own.   I. 4. 33

Duncan's last speech is worth particular notice,

                    ... in his commendations I am fed;
    It is a banquet to me.   I. 4. 56

At this point something should be said of what is meant by 'the
natural order'. In *Macbeth* this comprehends both 'wild nature' –
birds, beasts, and reptiles – and humankind since 'humane statute
purged the gentle weal'. The specifically human aspect is related to
the concept of propriety and degree –

                            communities,
    Degrees in schools, and brotherhoods in cities,
    Peaceful commerce from dividable shores,
    The primogenity, and due of birth,
    Prerogative of age, crowns, sceptres, laurels.
                            Troilus and Cressida I. 3. 103

In short, it represents society in harmony with nature, bound by
love and friendship, and ordered by law and duty. It is one of the
main axes of reference by which we take our emotional bearings in
the play.

In the light of this the scene of Duncan's entry into the castle
gains in significance. The critics have often remarked on the irony.
What is not so frequently observed is that the key words of the
scene are 'loved', 'wooingly', 'bed', 'procreant Cradle', 'breed,
and haunt', all images of love and procreation, supernaturally
sanctioned, for the associations of 'temple-haunting' colour the
whole of the speeches of Banquo and Duncan. We do violence to
the play when we ignore Shakespeare's insistence on what may be
called the 'holy supernatural' as opposed to the 'supernatural
soliciting' of the witches. I shall return to this point. Meanwhile it is
pertinent to remember that Duncan himself is 'The Lord's anointed
temple'.

The murder is explicitly presented as unnatural. After the greeting of Ross and Angus, Macbeth's heart knocks at his ribs 'against
the use of nature'. Lady Macbeth fears his 'human kindness'; she
wishes herself 'unsexed', that she may be troubled by 'no com-
punctious visitings of nature', and invokes the 'murd'ring min-

isters' who 'wait on nature's mischief'. The murder is committed when

> Nature seems dead, and wicked dre ms abuse
> The curtained sleep.   II. I. 50

and it is accompanied by portents 'unnatural, Even like the deed that's done'. The sun remains obscured, and Duncan's horses 'Turned wild in nature'. Besides these explicit references to the unnatural we notice the violence of the imagery –

> I have given suck, and know
> How tender 'tis to love the babe that milks me:
> I would, while it was smiling in my face,
> Have plucked my nipple from his boneless Gums
> And dashed the brains out, . . .   I. 7. 54

Not only are the feelings presented unnatural in this sense, they are also strange – peculiar compounds which cannot be classified by any of the usual labels: 'fear', 'disgust', etc. Macbeth's words towards the end of Act II, Scene I, serve to illustrate this:

> Thou sure and firm-set earth,
> Hear not my steps which way they walk, for fear
> Thy very stones prate of my whereabout
> And take the present horror from the time,
> Which now suits with it.   l. 56

The first three lines imply a recognition of the enormity of the crime; Macbeth asks that the earth ('sure and firm-set' contrasted with the disembodied 'Murder' which 'moves like a ghost') shall not hear his steps, for if it does so the very stones will speak and betray him – thereby breaking the silence and so lessening the horror. 'Take' combines two constructions. On the one hand, 'for fear' . . . they 'take the present horror from the time' expresses attraction, identification with the appropriate setting of his crime. But 'take' is also an imperative, expressing anguish and repulsion. 'Which now suits with it' implies an acceptance of the horror, willing or reluctant according to the two meanings of the previous line. The unusual sliding construction (unusual in ordinary verse, there are other examples in Shakespeare, and in Donne) expresses the unusual emotion which is only crudely analysed if we call it a mixture of repulsion and attraction fusing into 'horror'.

'Confusion now hath made his master-piece', and in the lull that
follows the discovery of the murder, Ross and an Old Man, as
chorus, echo the theme of unnatural disorder. The scene (and the
act) ends with a 'sentence' by the Old Man:

> God's benison go with you, and with those
> That would make good of bad, and friends of foes.   II. 4. 40

This, deliberately pronounced, has an odd ambiguous effect. The
immediate reference is to Ross, who intends to make the best of a
dubious business by accepting Macbeth as king. But Macduff also
is destined to 'make good of bad' by destroying the evil. And an
overtone of meaning takes our thoughts to Macbeth, whose
attempt to make good of bad by restoring the natural order is the
theme of the next movement; the tragedy lies in his inevitable
failure.

A key is found in Macbeth's words spoken to the men hired to
murder Banquo (III. 1. 91–100). When Dr Bradley is discussing
the possibility that *Macbeth* has been abridged he remarks ('very
aptly' according to the Arden editor), 'surely, anyone who wanted
to cut the play down would have operated, say, on Macbeth's talk
with Banquo's murderers, or on Act III, Scene 6, instead of reducing
the most exciting part of the drama'. By accepted canons it is an
irrelevance; actually it stands as a symbol of the order that Macbeth
wishes to restore. In the catalogue,

> Hounds, and greyhounds, mongrels, spaniels, curs,
> Shoughs, water-rugs, and demi-wolves   III. 1. 92

are merely 'dogs', but Macbeth names each one individually; and

> The valued file
> Distinguishes the swift, the slow, the subtle,
> The house-keeper, the hunter, every one
> According to the gift which bounteous nature
> Hath in him closed.

It is an image of order, each one in his degree. At the beginning of
the scene, we remember Macbeth had arranged 'a feast', 'a solemn
supper', at which 'society' should be 'welcome'. And when alone
he suggests the ancient harmonies by rejecting in idea the symbols
of their contraries – 'a fruitless crown', 'a barren sceptre', and an

'unlineal' succession. But this new 'health' is 'sickly' whilst Banquo lives, and can only be made 'perfect' by his death. In an attempt to re-create an order based on murder, disorder makes fresh inroads. This is made explicit in the next scene (III. 2). Here the snake, usually represented as the most venomous of creatures, stands for the natural order which Macbeth has 'scotched' but which will 'close, and be herself'.

At this point in the play there is a characteristic confusion. At the end of Act III, Scene 2, Macbeth says, 'Things bad begun make strong themselves by ill', that is, all that he can do is to ensure his physical security by a second crime, although earlier (III. 1. 106–7) he had aimed at complete 'health' by the death of Banquo and Fleance, and later he says that the murder of Fleance would have made him

> perfect;
> Whole as the marble, founded as the rock.

The truth is only gradually disentangled from this illusion.

The situation is magnificently presented in the banquet scene. Here speech, action, and symbolism combine. The stage direction '*Banquet prepared*' is the first pointer. In Shakespeare, as Mr Wilson Knight has remarked in an essay in *The Imperial Theme* to which I am much indebted, banquets are almost invariably symbols of rejoicing, friendship, and concord. Significantly, the nobles sit in due order.

MACBETH: You know your own degrees – sit down:
At first and last, the hearty welcome.
LORDS: Thanks to your Majesty.
MACBETH: Ourself will mingle with society,
And play the humble host.
Our hostess keeps her state; but in best time
We will require her welcome.
LADY MACBETH: Pronounce it for me, sir, to all our friends,
For my heart speaks they are welcome.
Enter first Murderer

There is no need for comment. In a sense the scene marks the climax of the play. One avenue has been explored; 'society', 'host', 'hostess', 'friends' and 'welcome' repeat a theme which henceforward is heard only faintly until it is taken up in the final orchestration, when it appears as 'honour, love, obedience, troops of friends'. With the disappearance of the ghost, Macbeth may be 'a man again', but he has, irretrievably,

> displaced the mirth, broke the good meeting
> With most admired disorder.   III. 4. 108

The end of the scene is in direct contrast to its beginning.

> Stand not upon the order of your going,
> But go at once.   III. 4. 118

echoes ironically, 'You know your own degrees – sit down'.

Before we attempt to disentangle the varied threads of the last Act, two more scenes call for particular comment. The first is the scene in Macduff's castle. Almost without exception the critics have stressed the pathos of young Macduff, his 'innocent prattle', his likeness to Arthur, and so on – reactions appropriate to the work of Sir James Barrie which obscure the complex dramatic function of the scene. In the first place, it echoes in different keys the theme of the false appearance, of doubt and confusion. At its opening we are perplexed with questions: – Is Macduff a traitor? If so, to whom, to Macbeth or to his wife? Was his flight due to wisdom or to fear? Ross says,

> But cruel are the times when we are traitors
> And do not know ourselves; when we hold rumour
> From what we fear, yet know not what we fear ...   IV. 2. 18

Lady Macduff says of her son,

> Fathered he is, and yet he's fatherless.   IV. 2. 27

She teases him with riddles, and he replies with questions.

Secondly, the scene shows the spreading evil. As Fletcher has pointed out, Macduff and his wife are 'representatives of the interests of loyalty and domestic affection'. There is much more in the death of young Macduff than 'pathos'; the violation of the natural order is completed by the murder. But there is even more than this. That the tide is about to turn against Macbeth is suggested both by the rhythm and imagery of Ross's speech:

> But cruel are the times, when we are traitors
> And do not know ourselves; when we hold rumour
> From what we fear, yet know not what we fear,

> But float upon a wild and violent sea
> Each way, and move –

The comma after 'way', the complete break after 'move', give the rhythm of a tide, pausing at the turn. And when Lady Macduff answers the Murderer's question, 'Where is your husband?'

> I hope in no place so unsanctified
> Where such as thou mayst find him   IV. 2. 80

we recall the associations set up in Act III, Scene 6, a scene of choric commentary upon Macduff's flight to England, to the 'Pious Edward', 'the Holy King'.

Although the play moves swiftly, it does not move with a simple directness. Its complex subtleties include cross-currents, the ebb and flow of opposed thoughts and emotions. The scene in Macduff's castle, made up of doubts, riddles, paradoxes, and uncertainties, ends with an affirmation, 'Thou liest, thou shag-eared villain'. But this is immediately followed, not by the downfall of Macbeth, but by a long scene which takes up once more the theme of mistrust, disorder, and evil.

The conversation between Macduff and Malcolm has never been adequately explained. We have already seen Dr Bradley's opinion of it. The Clarendon editors say, 'The poet no doubt felt this scene was needed to supplement the meagre parts assigned to Malcolm and Macduff.' If this were all, it might be omitted. Actually the Malcolm–Macduff dialogue has at least three functions. Obviously Macduff's audience with Malcolm and the final determination to invade Scotland help on the story, but this is of subordinate importance. It is clear also that Malcolm's suspicion and the long testing of Macduff emphasize the mistrust that has spread from the central evil of the play. But the main purpose of the scene is obscured unless we realize its function as choric commentary. In alternating speeches the evil that Macbeth has caused is explicitly stated, without extenuation. And it is stated impersonally.

> Each new morn
> New widows howl, new orphans cry, new sorrows
> Strike heaven on the face, that it resounds
> As if it felt with Scotland, and yelled out
> Like syllable of dolour.   IV. 3. 4

> our country sinks beneath the yoke
> It weeps, it bleeds, and each new day a gash
> Is added to her wounds.   IV. 3. 39
>   Not in the legions
> Of horrid hell can come a Devil more damned
> In evils to top Macbeth.
>   I grant him bloody,
> Luxurious, avaricious, false, deceitful,
> Sudden, malicious, smacking of every sin
> That has a name.   IV. 3. 55

With this approach we see the relevance of Malcolm's self-accusation. He has ceased to be a person. His lines repeat and magnify the
evils that have already been attributed to Macbeth, acting as a
mirror wherein the ills of Scotland are reflected. And the statement
of evil is strengthened by contrast with the opposite virtues, 'As
justice, verity, temp'rance, stableness'.

There is no other way in which the scene can be read. And if
dramatic fitness is not sufficient warrant for this approach, we can
refer to the pointers that Shakespeare has provided. Macbeth is
'luxurious' and 'avaricious', and the first sins mentioned by
Malcolm in an expanded statement are lust and avarice. When he
declares,

> Nay, had I power, I should
> Pour the sweet milk of concord into hell,
> Uproar the universal peace, confound
> All unity on earth.   IV. 3. 98

we remember that this is what Macbeth has done. Indeed Macduff is
made to answer:

> These evils thou repeat'st upon thyself
> Hath banished me from Scotland.   IV. 3. 112

Up to this point at least the impersonal function of the speaker is
predominant. And even when Malcolm, once more a person in a
play, announces his innocence, it is impossible not to hear the
impersonal overtone:

> for even now
> I put myself to thy direction, and
> Unspeak mine own detraction, here abjure
> The taints and blames I laid upon myself
> For strangers to my nature.   IV. 3. 121

He speaks for Scotland, and for the forces of order. The 'scotched snake' will 'close and be herself'.

There are only two alternatives; either Shakespeare was a bad dramatist, or his critics have been badly misled by mistaking the *dramatis personae* for real persons in this scene. Unless of course the ubiquitous Interpolator has been at work upon it.

I have called *Macbeth* a statement of evil; but it is a statement not of a philosophy but of ordered emotion. This ordering is of course a continuous process (hence the importance of the scrupulous analysis of each line), it is not merely something that happens in the last Act corresponding to the *dénouement* or unravelling of the plot. All the same, the interests aroused are heightened in the last Act before they are finally 'placed', and we are given a vantage point from which the whole course of the drama may be surveyed in retrospect. There is no formula that will describe this final effect. It is no use saying that we are 'quietened', 'purged' or 'exalted' at the end of *Macbeth* or of any other tragedy. It is no use taking one step nearer the play and saying we are purged, etc., because we see the downfall of a wicked man or because we realize the justice of Macbeth's doom whilst retaining enough sympathy for him or admiration of his potential qualities to be filled with a sense of 'waste'. It is no use discussing the effect in abstract terms at all; we can only discuss it in terms of the poet's concrete realization of certain emotions and attitudes.

At this point it is necessary to return to what I have already said about the importance of images of grace and of the holy supernatural in the play. For the last hundred years or so the critics have not only sentimentalized Macbeth – ignoring the completeness with which Shakespeare shows his final identification with evil – but they have slurred the passages in which the positive good is presented by means of religious symbols. In Act III the banquet scene is immediately followed by a scene in which Lennox and another Lord (both completely impersonal) discuss the situation; the last half of their dialogue is of particular importance. The verse has none of the power of, say, Macbeth's soliloquies, but it would be a mistake to call it undistinguished; it is serenely harmonious, and its tranquillity contrasts with the turbulence of the scenes that immediately precede it and follow it, as its images of grace contrast

with their 'toil and trouble'. Macduff has fled to 'the most pious
Edward', 'the Holy King', who has received Malcolm 'with such
grace'. Lennox prays for the aid of 'some holy Angel',

> that a swift blessing
> May soon return to this our suffering country
> Under a hand accursed!   III. 6. 47

And the 'other Lord' answers, 'I'll send my prayers with him'.
Many of the phrases are general and abstract – 'grace', 'the male-
volence of Fortune', 'his high respect' – but one passage has an
individual particularity that gives it prominence:

> That by the help of these – with Him above
> To ratify the work – we may again
> Give to our tables meat, sleep to our nights,
> Free from our feasts and banquets bloody knives,
> Do faithful homage, and receive free honours –
> All which we pine for now.   III. 6. 32

Food and sleep, society and the political order are here, as before,
represented as supernaturally sanctioned. I have suggested that this
passage is recalled for a moment in Lady Macduff's answer to the
Murderer (IV. 2. 80), and it is certainly this theme which is taken
up when the Doctor enters after the Malcolm Macduff dialogue in
Act IV, Scene 3; the reference to the King's evil may be a compli-
ment to King James, but it is not merely that. We have only to
remember that the unseen Edward stands for the powers that are to
prove 'the Med'cine of the sickly weal' of Scotland to see the
double meaning in

> There are a crew of wretched souls
> That stay his cure. . . .   IV. 3. 141

Their disease is 'called the Evil'. The 'miraculous work', the
'holy prayers', 'the healing benediction', Edward's 'virtue', the
'sundry blessings. . . . that speak him full of grace' are reminders
not only of the evil against which Malcolm is seeking support, but
of the positive qualities against which the evil and disorder must
be measured. Scattered notes ('Gracious England', 'Christendom',
'heaven', 'gentle Heavens') remind us of the theme until the end
of the scene, when we know that Macbeth (the 'hell-kite', 'this
fiend of Scotland')

> Is ripe for shaking, and the powers above
> Put on their instruments.   IV. 3. 238

The words quoted are not mere formalities; they have a positive function, and help to determine the way in which we shall respond to the final scenes.

The description of the King's Evil (IV. 3. 141–59) has a particular relevance; it is directly connected with the disease metaphors of the last Act; and these are strengthened by combining within themselves the ideas of disorder and of the unnatural which run throughout the play. Lady Macbeth's sleep-walking is a 'slumbery agitation', and 'a great perturbation in nature'. Some say Macbeth is 'mad'. We hear of his 'distempered cause', and of his 'pestered senses' which

> recoil and start
> When all that is within him does condemn
> Itself for being there.   V. 2. 23

In the play general impressions are pointed by reference to the individual and particular (cf. Act IV, Scene 3, where 'the general cause' is given precision by the 'Fee-grief due to some single breast'); whilst at the same time particular impressions are reflected and magnified. Not only Macbeth and his wife but the whole land is sick. Caithness says,

> Meet we the medicine of the sickly weal,
> And with him pour we in our country's purge
> Each drop of us.

And Lennox replies,

> Or so much as it needs,
> To dew the sovereign flower and drown the weeds.
>
>   V. 2. 27

– an admirable example, by the way, of the kind of fusion already referred to, since we have not only the weed-flower opposition, but a continuation of the medical metaphor in 'sovereign', which means both 'royal' and 'powerfully remedial'. And the images of health and disease are clearly related to moral good and evil. The Doctor says of Lady Macbeth,

> More needs she the divine than the physician.
> God, God forgive us all!   V. I. 70

Macbeth asks him,

> Canst thou not minister to a mind diseased,
> Pluck from the memory a rooted sorrow,
> Raze out the written troubles of the brain,
> And with some sweet oblivious antidote
> Cleanse the stuffed bosom of that perilous stuff
> Which weighs upon the heart? v. 3. 40

There is terrible irony in his reply to the Doctor's 'Therein the patient must minister to himself': 'Throw physic to the dogs, I'll none of it!'

We have already noticed the association of the ideas of disease and of the unnatural in these final scenes –

> unnatural deeds
> Do breed unnatural troubles, v. 1. 67

and there is propriety in Macbeth's highly charged metaphor,

> My way of life
> Is fallen into the sere, the yellow leaf ... v. 3. 22

But the unnatural has now another part to play, in the peculiar 'reversal' that takes place at the end of *Macbeth*. Hitherto the agent of the unnatural has been Macbeth. Now it is Malcolm who commands Birnam Wood to move, it is 'the good Macduff' who reveals his unnatural birth, and the opponents of Macbeth whose 'dear causes' would 'excite the mortified man'. Hitherto Macbeth has been the deceiver, 'mocking the time with fairest show'; now Malcolm orders.

> Let every soldier hew him down a bough,
> And bear't before him; thereby shall we shadow
> The numbers of our host and make discovery
> Err in report of us. v. 4. 4

Our first reaction is to make some such remark as 'Nature becomes unnatural in order to rid itself of Macbeth'. But this is clearly inadequate; we have to translate it and define our impressions in terms of our response to the play at this point. By associating with the opponents of evil the ideas of deceit and of the unnatural, previously associated solely with Macbeth and the embodiments of evil, Shakespeare emphasizes the disorder and at the same time frees our minds from the burden of the horror. After all, the movement of Birnam Wood and Macduff's unnatural birth have a simple enough explanation.

There is a parallel here with the disorder of the last act. It begins with Lady Macbeth sleep-walking – a 'slumbery agitation' – and the remaining scenes are concerned with marches, stratagems, fighting, suicide, and death in battle. If we merely read the play we are liable to overlook the importance of the sights and sounds which are obvious on the stage. The frequent stage directions should be observed – *Drum and Colours, Enter Malcolm ... and Soldiers Marching, A Cry within of Women* – and there are continuous directions for *Alarums, Flourishes,* and fighting. Macduff orders,

> Make all our trumpets speak, give them all breath,
> Those clamorous harbingers of blood and death.   v. 6. 9

and he traces Macbeth by the noise of fighting:

> That way the noise is. Tyrant, show thy face.
> ... There thou shouldst be:
> By this great clatter one of greatest note
> Seems bruited.   v. 6. 24

There are other suggestions of disorder throughout the Act. Macbeth

> cannot buckle his distempered cause
> Within the belt of rule.   v. 2. 15

He orders, 'Come, put mine armour on', and almost in the same breath, 'Pull't off, I say'. His 'royal preparation' is a noisy confusion. He wishes 'th' estate o' th' world were now undone', though the tone is changed now since he bade the Witches answer him,

> Though bladed cord be lodged and trees blown down;
> Though castles topple on their warders' heads;
> Though palaces and pyramids do slope
> Their heads to their foundations ...   IV. I. 54

But all this disorder has now a positive tendency, towards the good which Macbeth had attempted to destroy, and which he names as 'honour, love, obedience, troops of friends'. At the beginning of the battle Malcolm says,

> Cousins, I hope the days are near at hand
> That chambers will be safe.   v. 4. 2

and Menteith answers, 'We doubt it nothing'. Seyward takes up the theme of certainty as opposed to doubt:

> Thoughts speculative their unsure hopes relate,
> But certain issue strokes must arbitrate
> Towards which, advance the war.   v. 4. 15

And doubt and illusion are finally dispelled:

> Now near enough. Your leavy screens throw down
> And show like those you are.   v. 6. 1

By now there should be no danger of our misinterpreting the greatest of Macbeth's final speeches.

> Tomorrow, and tomorrow, and tomorrow
> Creeps in this petty pace from day to day
> To the last syllable of recorded time,
> And all our yesterdays have lighted fools
> The way to dusty death. Out, out, brief candle!
> Life's but a walking shadow, a poor player
> That struts and frets his hour upon the stage
> And then is heard no more. It is a tale
> Told by an idiot, full of sound and fury,
> Signifying nothing.   v. 5. 19

The theme of the false appearance is revived – with a difference. It is not only that Macbeth sees life as deceitful, but the poetry is so fine that we are almost bullied into accepting an essential ambiguity in the final statement of the play, as though Shakespeare were expressing his own 'philosophy' in the lines. But the lines are 'placed' by the tendency of the last act (order emerging from disorder, truth emerging from behind deceit), culminating in the recognition of the Witches' equivocation ('And be these juggling fiends no more believ'd . . .'), the death of Macbeth, and the last words of Seyward, Macduff, and Malcolm (v. 6. 74–115).

This tendency has behind it the whole weight of the positive values which Shakespeare has already established, and which are evoked in Macbeth's speech –

My way of life
Is fallen into the sere, the yellow leaf;
And that which should accompany old age,
As honour, love, obedience, troops of friends,
I must look to have: but, in their stead,
Curses, not loud, but deep, mouth-honour, breath,
Which the poor heart would fain deny, and dare not.　v. 3. 22

Dr Bradley claims, on the strength of this and the 'Tomorrow, and tomorrow' speech, that Macbeth's 'ruin is never complete. To the end he never totally loses our sympathy. . . . In the very depths a gleam of his native love of goodness, and with it a tinge of tragic grandeur, rests upon him.' But to concentrate attention thus on the *personal* implications of these lines is to obscure the fact that they have an even more important function as the keystone of the system of values that gives emotional coherence to the play. Certainly those values are likely to remain obscured if we concentrate our attention upon 'the two great terrible figures, who dwarf all the remaining characters of the drama', if we ignore the 'unexciting' or 'undramatic' scenes, or if conventional 'sympathy for the hero' is allowed to distort the pattern of the whole.

from 'How Many Children had Lady Macbeth?',
1933. Reprinted in *Explorations*

TWENTY-TWO

Tragic Structure

R. S. CRANE

THE hypotheses of criticism are concerned with the shaping principles, peculiar to the poetic arts, which account in any work for the power of its grammatical materials, in the particular ordering given to these, to move our opinions and feelings in such-and-such a way. They will be of two sorts according as the questions to which they are answers relate to the principles by which poetic works have been constructed as wholes of certain definite kinds or to the reasons which connect a particular part of a given work, directly or indirectly, with such a principle by way of the poetic problems it set for the writer at this point. And there can be no good practical criticism in this mode in which both sorts are not present; for although the primary business of the critic is with the particulars of any work he studies down to its minuter details of diction and rhythm, he can never exhibit the artistic problems involved in these or find other than extra-poetic reasons for their solutions without the guidance of an explicit definition of the formal whole which they have made possible.

A single work will suffice to illustrate both kinds of critical hypotheses as well as the relation between them, and I will begin by considering what idea of the governing form of *Macbeth* appears to accord best with the facts of that play and the sequence of emotions it arouses in us. I shall assume that we have to do, not with a lyric 'statement of evil' or an allegory of the workings of sin in the soul and the state or a metaphysical myth of destruction followed by recreation, or a morality play with individualized characters rather than types, but simply with an imitative tragic drama based on historical materials. To call it an imitative tragic drama, however, does not carry us very far; it merely limits roughly the range of possible forms we have to consider. Among these are the contrasting plot-forms embodied respectively in *Othello* and in *Richard III*: the first a tragic plot-form in the classic sense of Aristotle's analysis in *Poetics* 13; the second a plot-form which Aristotle rejected as non-tragic but which appealed strongly to tragic poets in the Renaissance — a form of serious action designed to arouse moral indignation for the deliberately unjust and seemingly prospering acts of the protagonist and moral satisfaction at his subsequent ruin. The plot-form of *Macbeth* clearly involves elements which assimilate it now to the one and now to the other of both these kinds. The action of the play is twofold, and one of its aspects is the punitive action of Malcolm, Macduff, and their friends which in the end brings about the protagonist's downfall and death. The characters here are all good men, whom Macbeth has unforgivably wronged, and their cause is the unqualifiedly just cause of freeing Scotland from a bloody tyrant and restoring the rightful line of kings. All this is made clear in the representation not only directly through the speeches and acts of the avengers but indirectly by those wonderfully vivid devices of imagery and general thought in which modern critics have found the central value and meaning of the play as a whole; and our responses, when this part of the action is before us, are such as are clearly dictated by the immediate events and the poetic commentary: we desire, that is, the complete success of the counter-action and this as speedily as possible before Macbeth can commit further horrors. We desire this, however — and that is what at once takes the plot-form out of the merely retributive class — not only for the sake of humanity and Scotland but also for the sake of Macbeth himself. For what most sharply distinguishes our view of Macbeth from that of his victims and enemies is that, whereas they see him from the outside only, we see him also, throughout the other action of the play — the major action — from the inside, as he sees himself; and what we see thus is a moral spectacle, the emotional quality of which, for the impartial observer, is not too far removed from the tragic *dynamis* specified in the *Poetics*. This is not to say that the main action of *Macbeth* is not significantly different, in several respects, from the kind of tragic action which Aristotle envisages. The change is not merely from good to bad fortune, but from a good state of character to a state in which the hero is almost, but not quite, transformed into a monster; and the tragic art which initiates the change, and still more the subsequent unjust acts which this entails, are acts done – unlike Othello's killing of Desdemona – in full knowledge of their moral character. We cannot, therefore, state the form of this action in strictly Aristotelian terms, but the form is none the less one that involves, like tragedy in Aristotle's sense, the arousal and catharsis of painful emotions for, and not merely with respect to, the protagonist – emotions for which the terms pity and fear are not entirely inapplicable.

Any adequate hypothesis about the structure of *Macbeth*, then, would have to take both of these sets of facts into account. For both of the views we are given of the hero are true: he is in fact, in terms of the nature and objective consequences of his deeds, what Macduff and Malcolm say he is throughout Acts IV and V, but he is also – and the form of the play is really the interaction of the two views in our opinions and emotions – what we ourselves see him to be as we witness the workings of his mind before the murder of Duncan, then after the murder, and finally when, at the end, all his illusions and hopes gone, he faces Macduff. He is one who commits monstrous deeds without becoming wholly a monster, since his knowledge of the right principle is never altogether obscured, though it is almost in Act IV. We can understand such a person and hence feel fear and pity of a kind for him because he is only doing upon a grander scale and with deeper guilt and more terrifying consequences for himself and others what we can, without too much difficulty, imagine ourselves doing, however less extremely, in circumstances generally similar. For the essential story of *Macbeth* is that of a man, not naturally depraved, who has fallen under the compulsive power of an imagined better state for himself which he can attain only by acting contrary to his normal habits and feelings; who attains this state and then finds that he must continue to act thus, and even worse, in order to hold on to what he has got; who persists and becomes progressively hardened morally in the process; and who then, ultimately, when the once alluring good is about to be taken away from him, faces the loss in terms of what is left of his original character. It is something like this moral universal that underlies, I think, and gives emotional form to the main action of *Macbeth*. It is a form that turns upon the difference between what seemingly advantageous crime appears to be in advance to a basically good but incontinent man and what its moral consequences for such a man inevitably are; and the catharsis is effected not merely by the man's deserved overthrow but by his own inner suffering and by his discovery, before it is too late, of what he had not known before he began to act. If we are normal human beings we must abhor his crimes; yet we cannot completely abhor but must rather pity the man himself, and even when he seems most the monster (as Macbeth does in Act IV) we must still wish for such an outcome as will be best, under the circumstances, not merely for Scotland but for him.

But if this, or something close to it, is indeed the complex emotional structure intended in *Macbeth*, then we have a basis for defining with some precision the various problems of incident, character, thought, imagery, diction, and representation which confronted Shakespeare in writing the play, and hence a starting-point for discussing, in detail, the rationale of its parts. Consider — to take only one instance — the final scene. In the light of the obvious consequences of the form I have attributed to the play as a whole, it is not difficult to state what the main problems at this point are. If the catharsis of the tragedy is to be complete, we must be made to feel both that Macbeth is being killed in a just cause and that his state of mind and the circumstances of his death are such as befit a man who, for all his crimes, has not altogether lost our pity and goodwill. We are of course prepared for this double response by all that has gone before, and, most immediately, in the earlier scenes of Act v, by the fresh glimpses we are given of the motivation of the avengers and by Macbeth's soliloquies. But it will clearly be better if the dual effect can be sustained until the very end; and this requires, on the one hand, that we should be vividly reminded once more of Macbeth's crimes and the justified hatred they have caused and of the prospect of a new and better time which his death holds out for Scotland, and on the other hand, that we should be allowed to take satisfaction, at last, in the manner in which Macbeth himself behaves. The artistic triumph of the scene lies in the completeness with which both problems are solved: the first in the words and actions of Macduff, the speeches about young Seyward, and Malcolm's closing address; the second by a variety of devices, both of invention and of representation, the appropriateness of which to the needed effect can be seen if we ask what we would not want Macbeth to do at this moment. We want him to be killed, as I have said, for his sake no less than that of Scotland; but we would not want him either to seek out Macduff or to flee the encounter when it comes or to 'play the Roman fool'; we would not want him to show no recognition of the wrongs he has done Macduff or, when his last trust in the witches has gone, to continue to show fear or to yield or to fight with savage animosity; and he is made to do none of these things, but rather the contraries of all of them, so that he acts in the end as the Macbeth whose praises we have heard in the second scene of the play. And I would suggest that the cathartic effect of these words and acts is reinforced indirectly, in the representation, by the analogy we can hardly help drawing between his conduct now and the earlier conduct of young Seyward, for of Macbeth too it can be said that 'he parted well and paid his score'; the implication of this analogy is surely one of the functions, though not the only one, which the lines about Seyward are intended to serve.

from *The Languages of Criticism and the Structure of Poetry*, 1953

TWENTY-THREE

The 'Language of Props' in Macbeth

ALAN S. DOWNER

THE drama is a unique form of expression in that it employs living actors to tell its story; its other aspects – setting, characters, dialogue, action, and theme – it shares with other forms of communication. But the fact that the dramatist is not dealing with characters merely, but with three-dimensional persons is paralleled by the fact that he is not dealing with a setting verbally described but three-dimensionally realized, with action that actually occurs in time and space, with dialogue which is spoken by human voices for the human ear: so many tools, so many tribulations. One of the very real problems of the dramatist is just this, that he, unlike the poet, must deal with the thingness of things: to him a mossy stone must be a mossy stone and a ship tossed on an ocean a ship tossed on an ocean, not a synonym for *peace* or *turmoil*. But the point is, surely, that for the poetic dramatist the stone is more than a stone without ever losing its stoniness, and the tempest may be a highly symbolic one without losing its reality. So, although the drama in general makes considerable use of physical objects – 'props' – to tell its story, the higher drama transmutes the physical prop into a symbol, gaining richer meaning without expansion. The poetic drama relates the dramatic symbol to the poetic image, intensifying the unity of the work, and gaining still greater richness without greater bulk, compression being the ever-present necessity of the form.

It is my present purpose to examine the function of imagery in poetic drama, the language of poetry, and its relation to the essentially dramatic devices which might be similarly named the language of props, the language of setting, and the language of action...

There are striking uses of this 'language of props', the realization of the verbal image in dramatic terms, in later Shakespearian tragedy. For example, in *Macbeth* Miss Spurgeon found repeated iteration in the dialogue of the idea of ill-fitting clothes. Mr Cleanth

Brooks has related the image somewhat more closely to the play by seeing it as an interpretation of Macbeth's position as usurper: he is uncomfortable in garments not his own. Actually, the image suggests disguise. Macbeth is an unhappy hypocrite who declares before the murder of Duncan, 'False face must hide what the false heart doth know,' and before the murder of Banquo, 'We must . . . make our faces vizards to our hearts, disguising what they are.'

But the image is more than a mere verbal one. It is *realized*, made visual in the action of the play.

The first four scenes are various moments during and after a battle. In them, Macbeth will naturally be wearing his warrior's costume, his armour, as much a symbol of his nature and achievements as is Duncan's crown. When he defeats Norway, for instance, he is 'lapped in proof', but when Ross and Angus greeted him as Thane of Cawdor, he protests, 'Why do you dress me in borrowed robes?' The image continues, verbally, as Banquo observes, half-jesting,

> New honours come upon him,
> Like our strange garments, cleave not to their mould
> But with the aid of use.   I. 3. 144

Under pressure from his wife, however, he resolves to seize the kingship, to cover his warrior's garments and the golden opinions that went with them with the clothing that was properly Duncan's. The murder is committed with constant reference in the dialogue to the clothing image (skilfully interpreted by Mr Brooks) and the scene as marked in the Folio ends with the flight of Macbeth and his Lady from the crime as she urges him to

> Get on your nightgown, lest occasion call us
> And show us to be watchers.   II. 2. 69

When next Macbeth enters he is wearing his dressing-gown, and if the actor is wise it will be such a gown as calls attention to itself, for at this point the change in costume, the disguising of the armour, dramatizes both the change in Macbeth's nature and the iterated poetic image. From now until nearly the end of the play, Macbeth is cowardly, melancholic, suspicious, and unhappy; the reverse of all the qualities that had made him the admired warrior of the early scenes. He cannot buckle his distempered cause within the belt of rule; and Macduff's fear is prophetic, 'Adieu, lest our old robes sit easier than our new,' prophetic not only for the unhappy Scots, but for Macbeth himself.

One of the achievements of this highly skilful play is the maintaining of interest in, if not sympathy for, the central figure; assassin, evil governor, usurper, and murderer. Shakespeare maintains this interest not merely by portraying Macbeth as a man in the control of wyrd, or too susceptible to uxorial suggestion, but, I think, by making us constantly aware of the armour – the honest warrior's nature – under the loosely hanging robes of a regicide. Until Act II, Scene 3, Macbeth is quite possibly dressed as a warrior. From that point, until Act V, Scene 3, he is dressed in his borrowed robes. But in the latter scene, with his wife eliminated as a motivating force, and with the English army moving against him, he begins to resume some of his former virtues: his courage returns, his forthrightness, his manliness. 'Give me my armour,' he cries, and in a lively passage with the Doctor, he makes grim jests about the power of medicine as Seyton helps him into his warrior's dress. He is all impatience to be back at the business he understands as he does not understand government:

MACBETH: Give me my armour.
SEYTON: 'Tis not needed yet.
MACBETH: I'll put it on.
    Send out more horses, skirr the country round,
    Hang those that talk of fear. Give me mine armour . . .
    Throw physic to the dogs, I'll none of it –
    Come, put mine armour on, give me my staff.
    Seyton, send out. – Doctor, the thanes fly from me. –
    Come, sir, dispatch. – If thou couldst, doctor, cast
    The water of my land, find her disease,
    And purge it to a sound and pristine health,
    I would applaud thee to the very echo,
    That should applaud again. – Pull't off, I say.   v. 3. 33

The tragic fall of this good man is dramatically underlined in his attempts to resume his old way of life. His infirmity of purpose cannot be more strongly presented than in his donning and doffing of the armour, and his bragging exit, with the equally revealing order:

> Bring it after me!   v. 3. 58

This is not an isolated, but only a more complex use of costume as symbol in poetic drama. For subtlety it might be contrasted with the costume changes of Tamburlaine, who, appearing first in his shepherd's weeds, casts them off contemptuously at his first triumph:

> Lie here ye weeds that I disdain to wear!
> This complete armour and this curtle axe
> Are adjuncts more beseeming Tamburlaine;

and who later wears in sequence white, scarlet, and black armour to indicate the stiffening of his attitude towards his victims. This is a simple dramatic device. In *Macbeth* the costume change is related to the iterated image to make concrete Macbeth's state of mind, and related also to the larger problem, the power of evil to corrupt absolutely, with which the play is concerned.

from 'The Life of our Design', in *The Hudson Review*, Vol. 11, No. 2, Summer 1949–50

TWENTY-FOUR

Macbeth and Oedipus

W. H. AUDEN

In 1955 W. H. Auden gave a series of three broadcast talks on poetry in which he developed, with his usual lucid eccentricity, some of his original, far-reaching, and dogmatic distinctions. His comparison of *Macbeth* and *Oedipus* is offered, in the first talk, to illustrate the contrast between the poet and the historian. We are all familiar (or we think we are) with this distinction: but what Auden means by 'poet' and 'historian' turns out to look quite different from what we usually mean. His 'poet' is the man interested only in Being, his 'historian' is the man interested only in Becoming. As we watch him explaining the nature of these two figures, we are meant to realize that this is, after all, something of our familiar distinction. I have not had space for the whole essay, but have tried to include enough of it to make these 'character sketches' clear. His remarks on Shakespeare have been left intact.

*

. . . LET me begin by trying to draw two Theophrastian sort of character sketches – portraits, that is, of fictitious beings from whom every trait except the one they typify has been removed. The first I shall call 'The Poet'. Hearing me call him by a generic term, he will immediately object and give his name, his genealogical tree, his place of birth, and his horoscope, but for which, he says, he would not be a poet, for he believes that every man is fated to be what he is and to act in conformity with his nature. In the rare cases which seem to be exceptions to this law – when, say, a man of honour does something dishonourable – the cause must lie outside himself; for instance, in a fit of madness put on him by a god. There are people whom the poet despises or condemns, but it would never occur to him to think that they could be anything but despicable.

For him mankind are divided into two classes, the gifted few whom he admires because they are really themselves, and the average anonymous mass whom he considers beneath his notice because they are no one in particular. Thus he is interested in well-bred families with ancient titles, great warriors, athletes, beautiful heiresses, wise ancients of both sexes, all who exhibit daring and energy like big-time gangsters and speculators, and monomaniacs of all kinds like pathological misers and spendthrifts.

For him there is little or no difference in kind between the behaviour of men of power and the behaviour of other powerful creatures like the great beasts of prey or of the great forces of nature, the volcano, the ocean tempests, the forest fire. . . .

In any actual writer of poetry born in the west during the last 2,000 years, the poet has had to cohabit with a second type whom, for want of a better term, I shall call 'The Historian'.

The most obvious difference between the historian and the poet is that the historian has no interest in nature, only in human beings, and that he is interested in them precisely because he does not believe that their lives are pre-ordained by fate but that, on the contrary, what their future is to be depends on the choices that they make, for which they are personally responsible. Thus, while the poet, when he meets someone, thinks only in terms of the present moment and asks therefore 'Who is he? What is he like? What does he do?', the historian is interested in the present only as it relates the past to the future and will ask 'Where is he coming from? What is he heading towards?' The poet judges by appearances. For him, therefore, if a man is fortunate, which is an objective fact, he must be good or in favour with the gods, and *vice versa*. The historian will say: 'You never can tell what any appearance is going to mean. This young man who has just inherited £100,000 may before he dies regret it; this other young man who has just lost a leg may later discover that it was the best thing that could have happened to him.' Similarly, while the poet judges the importance of an action by its magnitude, the historian treasures those actions, which may seem quite trivial but which reveal the direction in which the actor is already moving, unknown to himself or others. . . .

If the historian lacks the poet's visual imagination and noble style, he has a better ear for how men who are not actually poets speak. Listening to him, his audience are not under the poet's spell; they remember that they exist as an audience, they remember the part of the story that has already been told and they are conscious of wondering what is going to happen next. The historian's spell is of a different character; he makes his audience believe, not that they are living an experience at this moment but that what they are hearing really happened, because they recognize in what they hear something which they know to be true about themselves. When the poet has finished a tale, everybody remains silent, lost in admiration of the great persons and heroic deeds of which they have just heard: when the historian finishes a tale, everyone jumps to his feet, saying, 'That reminds me of another story'. . . .

Let us compare a work in which the poet has no historian to contend with, and one in which they fight it out between them: for instance, Sophocles's *Oedipus Rex* and Shakespeare's *Macbeth*. I have selected these because in both of them there is a prophecy about the future which comes true. The notion presupposed by the Greek Oracle is that the future is pre-ordained; that is to say, there is no real future because it is already latent in the present. If one asks, therefore, what would have happened if Oedipus had remained in Corinth instead of running away, the only answer can be that, although the actual events would have been different, the results would have been the same; in the end he would have murdered his father and married his mother. What the Oracle says may be put in a riddle form, but, once this is deciphered, what it says is not a promise but a statement of fact like a statement of a scientific law, and there is no question of belief or disbelief. In the Old Testament, God promises that the Land of Canaan shall in the future belong to the Children of Israel, but the fulfilment of this promise depends upon their believing it, and when, as is told in the thirteenth chapter of the Book of Numbers, all but Joshua and Caleb, after spying out the land, say 'We cannot attack such a people as this; they are too strong for us', God postpones the fulfilment of his promise to their children.

In *Macbeth*, the witches prophesy that Macbeth shall become king. If he had listened to them as a Greek would have listened to the Oracle, then he would have been able to sit and wait until by necessity it came to pass. But he takes it as a promise with which he has to co-operate and which, in consequence, brings about his downfall, so that it is legitimate to say that Macbeth should not have listened to them, in which case he would not have become king, and they would have been proved to be what they were, lying voices.

One might say that, though there is a history of Oedipus, Oedipus himself has no history, for there is no relation between his being and his acts. When the play opens he has already committed parricide and incest, but he is still the same person he was before he had done so; it is only when he finds out that the old man whom he killed in a quarrel about precedence, a deed which neither he nor his audience are supposed to think wrong, was, in fact, his father, and that the Queen of Thebes to whom he has been happily married for years is, in fact, his mother, that there is a change, and even then this is a change not in him but in his status. He who formerly was a happy king beloved by his subjects is now a wretched outcast. In *Macbeth*, on the other hand, every action taken by Macbeth has an immediate effect upon him so that, step by step, the brave bold warrior we hear of in the first scene turns before our eyes into the guilt-crazed creature of the 'tomorrow and tomorrow and tomorrow' soliloquy.

At no point during the Greek tragedy is Oedipus faced with a choice so that one could say that he made the wrong one. If, for example, he accepts Tiresias's advice and drops his inquiry into who the criminal is who is responsible for the plague, the plague will continue. But Macbeth not only makes a series of wrong choices which he should not have made, but also, though the past exerts an increasing pressure on the present, at no point does it become necessity; however difficult it might have been, for instance, after the murder of Duncan, to repent and refrain from murdering Banquo, it was not impossible.

The parricide and incest committed by Oedipus are not his acts but things that happen to him without his knowledge and against his desire, presumably as a divine punishment for his *hubris*; for thinking, that is, that he is so fortunate he is a god whom misfortune cannot overtake. Macbeth's acts are his own and not a punishment for, but the outcome of, his pride; of his believing, not that he is a god, but that he can do what he pleases irrespective of God's will.

Watching *Oedipus*, there is no question of the audience identify-

ing themselves with the hero – all psychoanalytical explanations
of the play are nonsense – for what they see is a unique case of
spectacular misfortune. The majority know, like the members of
the chorus, that they will never be great men, so such a thing could
not happen to them: if there is an exceptionally fortunate man in
the audience, the most he will say is, 'I hope nothing like that ever
happens to me', and has quite good grounds for his hope. Watching
Macbeth, every member of the audience knows that the possibility of becoming a Macbeth exists in his nature. One cannot
imagine Sophocles arriving at the idea of a play about Oedipus
except from a knowledge of the myth, but the germ of Macbeth
in Shakespeare's mind could perfectly well have been what Kipling
suggests in his poem, 'The Craftsman'.

> How at Bankside, a boy drowning kittens
> Winced at the business; whereupon his sister
> Lady Macbeth aged seven – thrust 'em under,
> Sombrely scornful.

That is why no one would dream of writing a book about the
characters in Greek tragedy: everything that can be said about them
has been said in the plays themselves, but people have and will continue to write books about Shakespeare's characters and quarrel
furiously about their rival interpretations. The characters in Greek
literature are like Greek statues in which the face is no more significant than any other part of the body. For, like an animal, their
nature is completely expressed in their actions; nothing is left to
the imagination because there is nothing to leave; there is no inner
life of possibilities which are implied in such a phrase as 'I can read
his character in his face'.

It is possible to imagine a Shakespearian type of play using the
premise of Oedipus. If Oedipus is to make certain of not fulfilling
the prophecy, then he must take two vows: never to strike a man
and never to sleep with a woman. Let us imagine, then, a man by
nature highly choleric and passionate, and place him in two
situations in which he is greatly tempted to break these vows; in
the first, some man has done him a mortal injury, some serious
treachery, perhaps; in the second, he falls violently in love with a
woman who reciprocates equally violently. Naturally, he will do

his best to persuade himself that the man could not possibly be his father or the woman his mother, but in this kind of play the author must show us the process of self-deception; that is to say, there must be elements in both situations which would make any impartial observer suspect that the man and the woman could very well be what anger and lust would persuade Oedipus they are not.

Such a treatment demands not only a different plot, but also a different formal structure and a different poetic style. In the original play it is natural that there should be only one place and no breaks in time, for the function of both is external: the action is the revelation of what has already happened, and all that is needed is a place where and a certain length of time in which this can occur.

In our new version such unities are highly unnatural and can be retained, if at all, only by a technical *tour de force,* for the decisive events and choices by which the innocent Oedipus becomes guilty cannot occur all at the same time and it is improbable that they could all occur in the same place. As to style, the unbroken elevation of the Greek version becomes unsuitable and needs to be replaced by something far more mixed, now high, now low like the porter in *Macbeth.* In a world of being, where people are what they are by fate, the more intense the moment and the more magnificent their verbal response to it, the more they manifest their being, and every relaxation weakens the effect and should be eliminated. But in a world where people become by their choices what they previously were not, a moment in which the characters are emotionally relaxed may be just as significant as one in which they are emotionally stirred. . . .

Returning to our imaginary version of *Oedipus,* let us suppose it is written by Shakespeare himself at the height of his powers, equal in poetic splendour to *King Lear* and *Antony and Cleopatra.* Compared with Sophocles it will be a more interesting, possibly more profound, play but it will be a less beautiful and less perfect work of art; for no matter how great the genius of its author, it will lack that exact correspondence of form and content which the Greek play possesses. The modern dramatist is faced with an insoluble problem: how to present a character who by a combination of circumstances and his own free choices becomes different. Becoming and choice are continuous processes, not a series of jumps from one state to another, but it is only as a series of jumps that the dramatist can portray becoming at all, and any answer to the question 'How many different stages do I need to show?' must be arbitrary: there is no Shakespeare play which one cannot imagine either longer or shorter than it is.

From 'The Dyer's Hand', in the *Listener*,
16 June 1955

Suggestions for Further Reading

CLEANTH BROOKS: 'The Naked Babe and the Cloak of Manliness' (in *The Well-Wrought Urn*). Approaches the play through its imagery.

FRANCIS FERGUSSON: '*Macbeth* and the Imitation of an Action' (*English Institute Essays* 1951); reprinted in *The Human Image in Dramatic Literature*.

L. C. KNIGHTS: '*Macbeth*' (in *Some Shakespearean Themes*). Professor Knights's 'second thoughts' on the play, about thirty years after *How Many Children*. The author prefers the later essay as more mature; I prefer the earlier as more incisive. Readers should find it interesting to make the comparison themselves.

F. R. LEAVIS: 'Tragedy and the "Medium"' (in *The Common Pursuit*). Only briefly about *Macbeth*; but if it is read together with George Santayana's 'Tragic Philosophy' (*Scrutiny*, March 1936), to which it is a reply, it should suggest some valuable lines of thought on the play.

ANTONY AND CLEOPATRA

TWENTY-FIVE

The Construction of Antony and Cleopatra

HARLEY GRANVILLE-BARKER

WE should never, probably, think of Shakespeare as sitting down to construct a play as an architect must design a house, in the three dimensions of its building. His theatre did not call for this, as the more rigorous economics of modern staging may be said to do. He was like to a musician, master of an instrument, who takes a theme and, by generally recognized rules, improvises on it; or even to an orator, so accomplished that he can carry a complex subject through a two-hour speech, split it up, run it by divers channels, digress, but never for too long, and at last bring the streams abreast again to blend them in his peroration. Clarity of statement, a sense of proportion, of the value of contrast, justness of emphasis – in these lie the technique involved; and these, it will be found, are the dominant qualities of Shakespeare's stagecraft – of the craft merely, be it understood.

He is apt to lay the main lines of his story very firmly and simply, and to let us see where we are going from the start, to cut the complexities from borrowed plots, and if any side-issue later promises distraction, to make (literally) short work of it. Here he reduces the actual story to simplicity itself. Antony breaks from Cleopatra to patch up an insincere peace with Caesar, since Pompey threatens them both; he marries Octavia, and deserts her to return to Cleopatra; war breaks out, Caesar defeats them and they kill themselves. That is the plot; and every character is concerned with it and hardly a line is spoken that does not relate to it. There is no under-plot, nor any such obvious relief as Falstaff, Nym, Bardolph, Pistol, and Fluellen give to the heroics of the Henriad.

But, for a broad picturesque contrast, Roman and Egyptian are set against each other; and this opposition braces the whole body of the play, even as conflict between character and character will sustain each scene. . . .

*

To begin with we must free the play from act and scene divisions. The Folio gives none. The first five-act division was Rowe's. Johnson thought the first scene of his second act might better be the last scene of his first, but added '. . . it is of small importance, where these unconnected and desultory scenes are interrupted.' Pope made the first scene of Rowe's fifth act into the last scene of Act IV, and after this all the later editors seem to have fallen unquestioningly into line. A five-act division for any play has, of course, its sanctions. The editors of the Folio indulge in it when they think they will. They (they or their printer for them) start out each time with an *Actus Primus, Scaena Prima*; a schoolboy's heading for his copybook. Sometimes they keep this up; once or twice they get half-way through the play and give it up; sometimes, as with *Antony and Cleopatra*, they just leave it at that. Now, whatever other dramatists may have done, whatever Shakespeare may have done in other plays, whatever may have been the custom of the public and private theatre for which he wrote – and it was probably a differing and a changing one – in the matter of making pauses during a performance, and whether those pauses were formal or prolonged, in this play there is no *dramatically* indicated act-division at all. There is, that is to say (as far as I can discover) no juncture where the play's acting will be made more effective by a pause. On the contrary, each scene has an effective relation to the next, which a pause between them will weaken or destroy. There may have been four pauses in the original performing, or three, two, or one; there may have been none at all, though that is hardly likely. But it would always (again, as far as I can discern) be a question of custom or convenience, not of dramatic effect. . . .

*

But . . . the medium that he worked in so spontaneously is alien to us. Even the nomenclature under which we discuss it betrays us to error. Setting disputable act-division aside, what do we mean by scene-division and by 'scene'? . . .

The layman must remember that he is reading a play, and should be imaginatively translating it into performance as he reads. Into what sort of performance do the editors help him to translate this, and the whole stretch of action from the eve of the first battle with

Caesar to the carrying of Antony dying to the Monument? They parcel it into twenty-two scenes, two of four lines each, one of six, one of nine, one of ten, three of sixteen lines and two of twenty-two; the rest are of more normal length. Scenes, as the editors of the Folio understood the word, they may be; as localized scenes they make dramatic nonsense.

Do the modern editors mean us to envisage the play in performance with painted scenery shifting every minute or so, transporting us round Actium, from one camp to another, to Alexandria and back again? Apparently. They know that Shakespeare's theatre provided for nothing of the sort; do they never stop to think what the effect of this cinematographic patchwork of their devising must be? . . .

*

Shakespeare will always have, of course, as the novelist has, the whereabouts of his characters in mind, and casual allusion to it will crop out. There may also be the demands of the action for a house-door, a balcony, a tree, or a cavern to be satisfied; but these things will have rather the utility of furniture than the value of scenery. And – this is the point – he need never give more atention to his play's background than he feels will be dramatically profitable. Moreover, he can give it – yet again as does the novelist – the exact sort of attention he chooses. . . .

*

In *Antony and Cleopatra* we find, except for the one episode of the sentries on guard listening to the mysterious music, no verbal scene-painting of any sort, direct or subtle; nor, as we have noted, more than the very minimum of reference to the locality of the scenes. The reason is plain. It is a play of action and of multiplied incident. The story is simple, but the tributary threads of it are manifold, and the interweaving conflicts of purpose complex enough. Its theme (once again) is not merely Antony's love for Cleopatra, but his ruin as general and statesman, the final ascension of Octavius, and the true end of

> . . . that work the ides of March begun.

Therefore the dead Fulvia's doings, Pompey's grievances, Caesar's policy, Lepidus and his time-serving, Ventidius baulked of a bigger victory – these things and their like are of first importance, and we must be kept alive to them. But an audience has only a certain amount of attention to bestow, and it must be economized. It does not matter much where Caesar and Lepidus, Pompey and Mene- crates and Menas have their talks, nor whether the bargaining with Antony takes place indoors or out; so Shakespeare spends hardly a thought or a line upon it. Nor upon the beauties of the prospect – nor the weather! Antony and Caesar, we feel, would take a prosaic view of such things; and, for our part, we shall know them no better for viewing them against a picturesque background. But that each turn in the battle of their quick, ruthless Roman minds should be made clear to us – this matters a great deal, and to this all else, if need be, is sacrificed. Emotion, and at full pitch, is in store; but it will not be freed till the issues of the action are narrowing to the point of solution. Meanwhile, we have clarity, the clarity of a desert landscape, the theme in its stark integrity. *Antony and Cleopatra* is, among other things, the most business-like of plays. . . .

*

To give anything of the spaciousness of a true scene to the four or five verse lines, by which now Caesar, now Antony show us the quality of their generalship, they would need to be multiplied by four; and this would weaken the present effect even in magnifying it. The larger episodes could easily be localized; but the others would then lose substance by comparison; what is more, the unity of the whole complex event would be destroyed. And it is in this unity that its dramatic strength lies. It is by the welding of the mixed mass of incident and character into a consistent whole, freed from all irrelevant circumstance, that its value is isolated and made clear. Obliterate scenic locality, we have still the stage itself left, certainly. But make-believe makes short work of those familiar features; and, once we are enthralled and they vanish, there is nothing left to stand between us and the essential drama; we are at one with its realities. Here, surely, is a technical achievement of some account.

Why show us this long panorama of detail? Why not (as a Greek and probably a modern dramatist would) plan a few full-charged organic, significant scenes, and compress the story to fit them? Again (if we could imagine Shakespeare putting himself the question) the answer is plain. Antony's is a great captain's downfall, the end of a man who has ruled half the Roman world, and we are to see both why he ends and how; and to see, as near as may be, the very process of it. The poor strategy, the weak will, the useless bargaining, set against Caesar's steady mind; these are as significant every whit as the passion that wreaks vengeance on the wretched Thidias and storms at Cleopatra. And the strung-out sequence of events, that are tense often and feverish while they matter little, slackened to triteness though they matter much, now catching up, now shedding their actors as they pass, time and place apt to seem the most fortuitous things about them – does not this both show us the true process of the matter, and give us, besides, just the impression that in life will belong to our share in such a crisis? Bouts of noisy fighting with heart-rent love-scenes in between would doubtless make a good show. But here, if Plutarch tells true, is a picture of the business of war as these Roman realists waged it, with luck and cunning, passion and judgement and interest all at odds in leaders and followers too. It is history directly dramatized.

from *Prefaces to Shakespeare II*,
1930

TWENTY-SIX

The Style of Antony and Cleopatra

J. MIDDLETON MURRY

GREAT work simply will not yield up its full significance, its essential beauty, at the first reading; not until you have patiently worked your way into the creative centre can you truly say that you apprehend it; and only when you have truly apprehended a work of literature are you in a position to make positive declarations about its style.

For the highest style is that wherein the two current meanings of the word blend; it is a combination of the maximum of personality with the maximum of impersonality; on the one hand it is a concentration of peculiar and personal emotion, on the other it is a complete projection of this personal emotion into the created thing. I hope that my attempted anatomy of the process by which objective literature is created will have given this apparent paradox some meaning. The manifest dangers of talking about style are two: the danger of talking about the accidents and not the essentials; and, in the endeavour to avoid this, the danger of vague generalization. Style is many things; but the more definable these are, the more capable of being pointed at with the finger, the more remote are they from the central meaning hidden in the word; the expression that is inevitable and organic to an individual mode of experience, an expression which, even when this exact relation has been achieved, rises or falls in the scale of absolute perfection according as the mode of experience expressed is more or less significant and universal – more or less completely embraces, is more or less adequate to, the whole of our human universe. In comparison with this meaning of the word Style, others seem to fade away almost into triviality; for this is the style that is the very pinnacle of the pyramid of art, the end that is the greatest of all as Aristotle would say, at once the supreme achievement and the vital principle of all that is enduring in literature, the surpassing virtue that makes for many of us some few dozen lines in Shakespeare the most splendid conquest of the human mind.

The culmination of *Anthony and Cleopatra* is such a passage: in the scene of the death of Cleopatra style reaches an absolute perfection:

CLEOPATRA: Give me my robe, put on my crown, I have
Immortal longings in me. Now no more
The juice of Egypt's grape shall moist this lip.
Yare, yare, good Iras; quick. Methinks I hear
Antony call. I see him rouse himself
To praise my noble act. I hear him mock
The luck of Caesar, which the gods give men
To excuse their after wrath. Husband, I come.
Now to that name my courage prove my title!
I am fire, and air; my other elements
I give to baser life. So, have you done?
Come then, and take the last warmth of my lips.
Farewell, kind Charmian, Iras, long farewell.
Have I the aspic in my lips? Dost fall?
If thou and nature can so gently part,
The stroke of death is as a lover's pinch,
Which hurts, and is desired. Dost thou lie still?
If thus thou vanishest, thou tell'st the world
It is not worth leave-taking.

CHARMIAN: Dissolve, thick cloud, and rain, that I may say,
The gods themselves do weep.

CLEOPATRA: This proves me base:
If she first meet the curlèd Antony,
He'll make demand of her, and spend that kiss
Which is my heaven to have. Come, thou mortal
    wretch,
With thy sharp teeth this knot intrinsicate
Of life at once untie. Poor venomous fool,
Be angry and dispatch. O, couldst thou speak,
That I might hear thee call great Caesar ass
Unpolicied!

CHARMIAN: O Eastern star!

CLEOPATRA: _   Peace, peace!
Dost thou not see my baby at my breast,
That sucks the nurse asleep?

CHARMIAN: O, break! O break!

233

CLEOPATRA: As sweet as balm, as soft as air, as gentle –
O Antony! Nay, I will take thee too.
What should I stay –   *Dies.*
CHARMIAN: In this vile world? So, fare thee well.
Now boast thee, death, in thy possession lies
A lass unparallel'd. Downy windows, close;
And golden Phoebus never be beheld
Of eyes again so royal! Your crown's awry;
I'll mend it, and then play –   v. 2. 278

After all, one can say little of such a passage that is not impertinent: one may point to the extreme subtlety of the orchestration, show how Cleopatra begins with three lines in the grand style 'fitting for a princess descended of so many royal kings' and steps, as it were down from the throne, to more and more intimate emotion – 'Husband, I come' – then, by way of a simile that is dramatically perfect, bearing an essential part in the process of the emotional change – 'the stroke of death is as a lover's pinch Which hurts and is desired' – to the divine jealousy of passionate love – 'If she first meet the curlèd Antony, He'll make demand of her, and spend that kiss Which is my heaven to have' – there is more true style in that simple adjective, the *curlèd* Antony, than in many pages of the best our moderns can do – thence through a perfect metaphor, perhaps the most wonderful dramatic metaphor ever used, which in a moment of time consummates the passion of love with a heart-rending irony – 'Dost thou not see my baby at my breast, That sucks the nurse asleep?' – to the final rest of the absolute intimacy of love, and death ('As sweet as balm, as soft as air, as gentle – O Antony!').

And while Cleopatra is making this swift and breathless passage from the dignity of a queen to the perfect intimacy of the lover, Charmian's voice reminds us that a great queen is dying; reminds us most magically of Cleopatra's power and beauty – 'O Eastern star' – when the queen herself for a moment rallies into the scornful, careless violence that is part of her. One can hardly speak of an art so mysterious and masterly in such cold terms as contrast; it is a crude anatomizing of the effect to say that it is based on the double contrast of Cleopatra the queen changing into Cleopatra the woman, while Charmian lifts her into the queen again. But if we try to isolate the points at which the style of this perfect and complex passage is concentrated into a single phrase, we must choose first the simile and then the metaphor. Both are crucial; both are extremely simple:

> The stroke of death is as a lover's pinch,
> Which hurts, and is desired.   v. 2. 293

> Dost thou not see my baby at my breast,
> That sucks the nurse asleep?   v. 2. 307

There is nothing of the grand style here; and if it be said that the grand style is inappropriate in such a moment of dramatic emotion, surely, if ever there was a moment which might be said to demand the grand style, it was the setting of the Eastern star. Moreover, Shakespeare deliberately opened the movement in the grand style. There is no mistaking

> Give me my robe, put on my crown, I have
> Immortal longings in me. Now no more
> The juice of Egypt's grape shall moist this lip.   v. 2. 278

The technical basis of the whole passage is the passing from the grand style; the leaving the royal note to be sounded by Charmian alone, while Cleopatra becomes pure woman. But the simplicity into which it passes is of a different kind from the simplicity of Lear's

> Thou'lt come no more
> Never, never, never, never, never.
> Pray you undo this button.   v. 3. 308

Those are the simple words that a great king might actually have said: Cleopatra's are not those of a queen, nor are they, in reality, those of a lover. A dying woman does not use such figures of speech; and at the pinnacle of her complex emotion, a Cleopatra would have no language to express it. This very discrepancy between emotion and the actual language of emotion is deliberately and triumphantly used by Shakespeare in the final scene of *Lear*; in the death scene of Cleopatra he achieves the miracle: he makes the language completely adequate to the emotion and yet keeps it simple. The emotion is, to the last drop, *expressed*. And this is chiefly done, as I have said, by using a simile and a metaphor; the secret of them both is that they bring death, the outward and visible sign of the scene, under the sovereignty of love, which is the inward and spiritual grace.

from *The Problem of Style*, Lecture II, 1921

TWENTY-SEVEN

The Morality of Antony and Cleopatra

W. K. WIMSATT, JR

This piece should perhaps be called 'The Immorality of *Antony and Cleopatra*'. The essay from which it is taken deals with a point in literary theory, and uses the play simply as an illustration; I think Mr Wimsatt's interpretation can stand on its own merits, but in justice to his presentation it seems best to indicate what point he is making.

The essay begins by examining Plato's attempt to subject poets to a non-literary, a moral censorship. Wimsatt shows that the business of literary criticism is not to argue about Plato's decision that poetry is less important than morality, but to examine the premise on which it is based: that 'the poetic value of poetry is not the same as, or even strictly determined by its truth or morality.' This is not obviously true: since words have meanings and are expressive of ideas, it seems much less true of poetry than of the other arts. Yet if the premise is rejected, we find ourselves driven to one of two extreme positions. 'Either (1) morals reaches over and claims poetry – not simply as superior to poetry but as defining poetry; or (2) poetry reaches over and claims to define morals.' Wimsatt's essay 'is an attempt to express the point of view of one who accepting a moral code would yet save poetic value – not as superior to moral value, but as different from it.'

*

... IF the Platonic proposition, asserting the separability of poetry and morals, is not true, then one of two extremely unified and simplified views or claims will follow – or have followed at various times. Either (1) morals reaches over and claims poetry – not simply as superior to poetry but as defining poetry; or (2) poetry reaches over and claims to define morals. We have seen the second view in such romantic and post-romantic statements as that of Shelley, 'Poets are the unacknowledged legislators of the world', or in the system of Matthew Arnold, where poetry is a 'criticism of life'. 'More and more mankind will discover that we have to turn to poetry to interpret life for us, to console us, to sustain us. Without poetry, our science will appear incomplete; and most of what now passes with us for religion and philosophy will be replaced by poetry.' More recent psychological and anthropological theories of poetry have tended to continue in this direction. It is easy to see that a morality of this sort, determined by poetry, is not really a morality in the sense of a code, but a relative morality of almost indefinite diversity and flexibility – for such is poetry – and that hence what theorists of this school mean in the end is that they do not subscribe to a code. For these we may say that in the large sense the problem to be discussed in this essay does not exist, since there is no distinction between, and hence no need of explaining the relation between, poetry and morals.

Nor does the problem really exist for those of the other school, who make poetic value depend upon moral value: Sir Philip Sidney, for instance, when he answers Gosson with the argument that poetry is a 'feigning notable images of virtues [and] vices', or Rymer and Dennis a century later, the school of 'poetic justice', or the Earl of Roscommon in his couplet:

> Immodest words admit of no Defence,
> For want of Decency is want of Sense.

Among recent statements of the moral view the most extreme is perhaps that of Arthur Machen: 'Literature is the expression, through the aesthetic medium of words, of the dogmas of the Catholic Church, and that which is out of harmony with these dogmas is not literature.' More moderately the late Irving Babbitt and other neohumanists have said that poetry gives ethical insight.

If the Arnoldian view, as we have seen, leaves morals in a bad way, it should be equally clear that the rigorous moral view not only leaves little to the critic of poetry in his own right (a loss which might perhaps have to be overlooked) but also makes a vast invasion into the usually recognized canon of the world's poetry – so much of it is in one way or another immoral. Or to put this more moderately and without the unhappy implication that a great part of the world's best literature is substantially evil, let us say that a moral code must be by its nature too rigid to accommodate, or at least too rigid to account for or specifically sanction, the widely heterogeneous concreteness of the world's recognized poetry. There is no religion or philosophy that will embrace Homer's heroes and gods, the fatalism of Greek tragedy, the atomism of Lucretius, the Heaven, Purgatory, and Hell of Dante, the Senecan Stoicism of Shakespeare, the occultism – what has seemed to many the diabolism – of Milton, the world soul of Wordsworth, the flowers of evil of Baudelaire. The choice between poetry and morals is not specifically a Christian one – though today in the Western world it may be felt most acutely by a serious Christian. It is the choice which appears for any moralist – for Plato banishing the poets from the city, for Tolstoy in his old age repudiating all of his own work except two of his simplest short stories, for the totalitarian Marxist – except that for the Marxist there is no nice problem. He simply rejects – almost everything.

This essay is an attempt to express the point of view of one who accepting a moral code would yet save poetic value – not as superior to moral value but as different from it. . . .

We may first of all make short work of a case often described with approval by the moralist, where evil is represented *as* evil – in the novels, for example, of Graham Greene (if so simple a statement does them justice, or if so simple a case ever really occurs). Here, of course, there is no moral evil, and no problem. The effects of the presentation may be unhappy for this or that reader (a moral, not an artistic, issue), but the meaning itself, the interpretation, is moral. Whatever literary quality is present, it has its moral basis. . . . If our theory is to be different from a moral theory, vileness must be vileness represented as attractive, vileness with an apology, or vileness recommended. In short, the poem must be vile.

There are two main ways in which a poem may approach vileness – that is, in which it may be ethically defective: (1) by asserting an unacceptable philosophy; (2) by approving, commending, or inviting an immoral choice or passion. It is perhaps easier to see that the first way will rarely of itself be incompatible with some wisdom and with some or even a great deal of poetic value. One may agree with T. S. Eliot that poetry does not characteristically state philosophies. 'In truth,' says Eliot, 'neither Shakespeare nor Dante did any real thinking – that was not their job.' Poetry does not think, but presents the feelings connected with thinking, or thoughts as the grounds of feeling. It is perhaps true that, as Professor Norman Foerster says, Wordsworth's 'Tintern Abbey' expresses a degree of 'unwisdom'. But then this unwisdom – the fusion of teleological naturalism, associationism, and pantheism which pervades the poem and without which indeed the poem would not be – is unwise simply in that it is not enough, it comes short of being an acceptable philosophy. Indeed we know this deficiency not so much through the poem itself as through our knowledge of its philosophic antecedents in Hartley or in Cudworth. As a philosophy it is better than no philosophy, or better, say, than dialectical materialism – because it contains much larger elements of truth. As an idea in a poem, a semi-metaphoric notion of a spirit pervading a landscape, it need be no more of a philosophy than one chooses to make it. It is one way of being inspired by a landscape, one approach, we may easily say, toward God. Poems, on the whole, as dramatic and specific utterances, here and now, tend to escape the defect of philosophic incompleteness. The philosophy need only be adequate to the situation in hand – or reach beyond that by symbolic extension.

A harder case is the second of the two named above, that of a poem which embodies a clear approval of an evil choice and its evil emotion. An answer to the question how we are to find poetic value in such a poem may be suggested in the statement that on the assumption of a Socratic ethic we might have more difficulty in doing so. On the Christian grounds of an ethic of will, we may find the distinction easier. The fact indeed that it seems to us possible to distinguish this class, the simply immoral, from the other, the philosophically wrong, marks the great difference between an ethic where the virtuous man is he who resists temptation and that where the virtuous man is he who is never tempted. But once admit temptation, and much is open to us – a wide realm of motives which may be profoundly moving and sympathetic though falling short of the morally acceptable. We have a question of how much good can be the cause of sin. Here I would be strictly Thomistic and would accept Maritain and Adler for a certain distance as my guides. The human sinner, so we are instructed in the classic explanation, does not choose evil *qua* evil – a contradiction, since *bonum* is defined as *terminus appetitus*. He chooses a lower good or one inappropriate to the moment – *quod non est vel nunc vel hoc modo bonum*. But of lower and inappropriate goods there are many levels, lower and higher, and in the gamut of human goods which in some situations the virtuous man forgoes, there is room for an indefinite range of complexity, richness, and sympathy.

As a ground on which to explore this principle I choose the *Antony and Cleopatra* of Shakespeare. 'The tragedy of *Antony and Cleopatra*,' says Benedetto Croce, 'is composed of the violent sense of pleasure, in its power to bind and to dominate, coupled with a shudder at its abject effects of dissolution and of death.' If this is so, then of course there is no problem. *Antony and Cleopatra* is simply one of the easy cases, already alluded to, in which evil is represented as evil: the implications are basically moral. Again, there is the explanation of the theologically minded critic S. L. Bethell, according to which *Antony and Cleopatra* celebrates 'affections rooted deep in the sensual nature', intuitive, spontaneous, and positive, with all their 'moral and aesthetic corollaries'. The antitype is Caesar, the cold politician whose heart is set entirely on the passing world. In the tragic *dénouement* the 'element of self-giving inherent in the sensual nature' is 'purged of selfish fear' and 'revealed in its eternal significance'. It is not my purpose to deny the availability of such views to the interpretation of *Antony and Cleopatra* or in general of other poems which present similar moral problems. The solution of Bethell may, in fact, appear to differ only by a twist of emphasis from what I myself propose. The difference is that I seek a formulation which will enable us to say frankly that a poem is a great poem, yet immoral.

What is celebrated in *Antony and Cleopatra* is the passionate surrender of an illicit love, the victory of this love over practical, political, and moral concerns, and the final superiority of the suicide lovers over circumstance. That is a crudely one-sided statement which makes the play as plainly immoral as it can be made. There is of course far more – the complex, wanton, and subtle wiles of the voluptuary queen, her infinite variety which age cannot wither nor custom stale, the grizzled and generous manhood and the military bravery of Antony – the whole opulent and burnished panorama of empire and its corruptions. Such intricacies and depths surely at least add to the interest of immorality and – without making it any more moral – yet make it more understandable, more than a mere barren vileness, a filthy negation. It is to be noted that the reasons on the side of morality are so far as possible undercut, diminished, or removed from the play. The politics from which Antony secedes are not a noble Roman republicanism, the ideals of a Brutus or a Cato, but the treacheries and back-stabbing of a drunken party on a pirate's barge. The victimized Octavia is a pallid and remote figure, never (as in Dryden's version) made to appear as a rival motive to the Egyptian seductions. The suicides which provide the catastrophe have at least the subjective palliation that they are within the Stoic code which is the standard of the whole scene.

> Give me my robe, put on my crown, I have
> Immortal longings in me. Now no more
> The juice of Egypt's grape shall moist this lip.
> Yare, yare, good Iras; quick. Methinks I hear
> Antony call. I see him rouse himself
> To praise my noble act. I hear him mock
> The luck of Caesar, which the gods give men
> To excuse their after wrath. Husband, I come.
> Now to that name my courage prove my title!
> I am fire, and air; my other elements
> I give to baser life.   v. 2. 278

There is no escaping the fact that the poetic splendour of this play, and in particular of its concluding scenes, is something which exists in closest juncture with the acts of suicide and with the whole glorified story of passion. The poetic values are strictly dependent – if not upon the immorality as such – yet upon the immoral acts. Even though, or rather because, the play pleads for certain evil choices, it presents these choices in all their mature interest and capacity to arouse human sympathy. The motives are wrong, but they are not base, silly, or degenerate. They are not lacking in the positive being of deep and complex human desire. It is not possible to despise Antony and Cleopatra. If one will employ the classic concept of 'imitation', the play imitates or presents the reasons for sin, a mature and richly human state of sin. Imitation, on this understanding, is not prior to and exclusive of interpretation, but follows it. The interpretation and judgement are taken as presented objects. This is the meaning of the defence repeated in every generation by the poet. 'I moot,' says Chaucer, 'reherce Hir tales alle

.... Or elles falsen some of my mateere.' 'Art,' says William Butler Yeats, 'is a revelation, and not a criticism.'....

One of the faults which Plato found with poetry was that in imitating the actions and feelings of men, poetry discovered the lack of unity in their lives, the strife and inconsistency. Recent schools of criticism, as we have said, have likewise noted the importance to poetry of the elements of variety and strife in human living and have seen the poem as a report made under tension or an ironically suspended judgement rather than a commitment to solutions. And this view would seem to put the poem clearly in the realm of the amoral or premoral. But again, recent criticism has noted with approval the Coleridgean doctrine of a resolution or *reconciliation* of opposites, a doctrine which may not read so well with the ironic. To the present writer it would seem that though poetry is inclusive, it is also exclusive in the sense that a poem has a presiding idea, attitude, and coherence and thus at least a tendency to an assertion. As certain critics of a theological leaning have recently been saying, poetry, though it is not dogma and cannot take the place of dogma, yet finds in a frame of beliefs its 'ultimate character' and 'latent pre-suppositions'. If it is possible, as it has been the main burden of this essay to insist, that a poem, even a great poem, may fall short of being moral – or to put it another way, if it is true that starting with the fixity of dogma we cannot hope to define the content of poems – it is yet true that poems as empirically discovered and tested do tend, within their limits and given the peculiar *données* or presuppositions of each, to point toward the higher integration of dogma. The Christian critic, if he cares to insist to the full at all moments on his Christianity, as well as on his critical discernment, may without doing violence to the latter follow the direction recently pointed out to the poet: 'Christian dogma will aid the artist not by giving him a privileged and special subject-matter but rather by defining for him a perspective from which "full light" can be had on all subject matters.' Perhaps it follows that in this light the greatest poems for the Christian will never be that kind, the great though immoral, which it has been our labour to describe. *Antony and Cleopatra* will not be so great as *King Lear*. The testimony of the critical tradition would seem to confirm this. The greatest poetry will be morally right, even though perhaps obscurely so, in groping confusions of will and knowledge – as *Oedipus the King* foreshadows *Lear*. All this is but the consistent capstone which completes but does not contradict a system of values in which poetic is distinguished from moral and both are understood in relation to the master ideas of evil as negation or not-being, a gap in order, and of good as positive, or being – in the natural order the designed complexity of what is most truly one or most has being.

from 'Poetry and Morals: a Relation Reargued', in *The Verbal Icon*, 1954

ANTONY AND CLEOPATRA

Suggestions for Further Reading

A. C. BRADLEY: '*Antony and Cleopatra*' (in *Oxford Lectures on Poetry*).

LORD DAVID CECIL: '*Antony and Cleopatra*' (in *Poets and Storytellers*). 'The play is a panorama, not a tragedy: its central theme is success, not love.' The conclusion may seem eccentric, but it is arrived at through a warm and genuine response.

DAVID DAICHES: 'Imagery and Meaning in *Antony and Cleopatra*' (in *English Studies*, October 1962).

F. R. LEAVIS: '*Antony and Cleopatra* and *All for Love*: A Critical Exercise' (*Scrutiny*, v, 1937).

D. A. TRAVERSI: *An Approach to Shakespeare*. The discussion of *Antony and Cleopatra* offers a very subtle account of the poetry of the play, and of the balance it strikes between realistic and lyrical attitudes to love. Its aim is to 'evolve a certain tragic greatness for Cleopatra's passion out of its very stressed imperfections, out of the impermanence of the flesh and the corrupt world with which it is organically connected'.

CORIOLANUS

TWENTY-EIGHT

Coriolanus as Political Character

JOHN PALMER

The first part of this extract is a discussion of the opening scene of *Coriolanus*. It is profusely illustrated with quotations which (to save space) I have omitted. Since Palmer moves through the scene from beginning to end, the passages are quoted more or less in the order in which they occur; so the reader who has a text of the play in front of him will have no difficulty in seeing which speech is being referred to at any moment.

*

SHAKESPEARE in *Coriolanus* takes for his theme a recurrent political problem of all times and places. A representative group of Roman patricians, whose attitudes and dispositions are embodied at a maximum in a heroically proud member of their class, is confronted with a representative group of Roman plebeians, whose grievances call for a limitation of the rights conferred by birth and privilege upon their rulers. Politics are a predominating interest in scene after scene of the play. It is true that Shakespeare's imagination, as always, is concentrated rather upon the individual men and women who play their parts in a public contention than upon the social implications of their behaviour, but in this particular tragedy the individual men and women are passionately concerned with their rights and wrongs as citizens in a community. The ultimate climax of the tragedy is a conflict between personal pride and family affection rather than a conflict between the principles of aristocratic and popular government. But the virtues and vices of the principal characters are all related to their place and function in commonwealth; their actions and passions are almost wholly governed by their conceptions of what is due to them or expected of them as belonging to an estate of the nation.

Coriolanus, being the most exclusively political play by Shakespeare, has naturally raised in its most acute form the question whether and, if so, to what extent the author's personal political sympathies are engaged. Careful critics and casual audiences alike, feeling the immediate impact of the play, have, according to their considered opinions or momentary prejudice, variously regarded it as an impartial presentation of the secular struggle between the few and the many, a whole-hearted indictment of democracy, or an ardent profession of faith in the aristocratic principle. Much eloquent and persuasive comment has been written in the conviction that Shakespeare definitely reveals himself as temperamentally hostile to the mutable, rank-scented many. The view has also its champions that Shakespeare, in his portrait of Coriolanus and of the ruin that overtakes him, is rebuking the insolence of caste and exposing the stupidity and selfishness of a typical autocrat. Such speculations are better left for consideration at a later stage. It will be easier – it may even be unnecessary – to discuss Shakespeare's political intentions when we have watched the drama unfold itself episode by episode to its conclusion.

The origin and merits of the political dispute which determines the action of the play are clearly stated in the opening scene. The grievances of the people, the quality of mind and temper in which they are approached alike by the patricians and the plebeians, the attitude of Marcius himself, the watchful sagacity of the popular leaders are in turn disclosed. Shakespeare states at once the principal themes of his composition, each to be further developed in its appropriate setting, and he states them with a careful precision which calls for an equally careful precision in their analysis.

It is to be noted that these citizens of Rome, who enter with clubs, staves, and other weapons, have good and sufficient reason for mutiny. They are resolved to 'die rather than famish'. Caius Marcius is their enemy-in-chief, a 'very dog to the commonalty'. First Citizen, who is the most violently inclined of them all, calls God to witness that he speaks 'in hunger for bread, not in thirst for revenge', and his indictment is well-founded.

Menenius Agrippa now comes upon the stage. He is a patrician, but 'one that hath always loved the people'. With him the citizens are ready to discuss matters in good faith. They have no quarrel with a noble Roman who has a decent regard for their interests. Menenius retorts with his celebrated fable of the belly and its members. This passage, apart from its quality as a lively specimen of dramatic dialogue, helps indirectly to establish Shakespeare's general attitude to the citizens of Rome. First Citizen is ready to hear the fable, though he honestly warns Menenius: 'you must not think to fob off our disgrace with a tale'. He is intrigued by the story and alert to seize its drift. The genial, conversable style of the senator is contrasted with the more serious, emotional approach of the man of the people who, though his fancy is caught by the narrative and though he contributes picturesque touches of his own, presses inexorably for a conclusion. Menenius is entirely at ease with these people and they with him. There is good-natured chaff on both sides. The senator twits the citizen with his eloquence ('Fore me, this fellow speaks!) the citizen comments gruffly on the senator's prolixity (You're long about it). There is no bad blood between them and, on the popular side, a readiness to consider the other fellow's point of view.

There is another point to be noted. Menenius is popular. The citizens like him for his good humour and his honesty. But Shakespeare insists from the outset that he has no understanding of the people's grievances, no real respect for their rights or opinions, no grasp of the social issues involved. Menenius maintains to the last his attitude of familiarity, man to man, with the citizens, but concludes with the monstrous assertion that all good derives from the nobility and that none can come of the commons. Menenius is Shakespeare's portrait of an average member of the privileged class in any community, the speaking likeness of an English squire removed to a Roman setting. He can talk to the people as one man to another because he is entirely assured of his position. For him it is an axiom that his class is supreme in the nation by a benevolent and wholly natural dispensation of providence. He is disposed to regard these citizens with an affectionate tolerance, provided they know their place and are content to ascribe their misfortunes to heaven and not to the government of which he is a member.

That is how Shakespeare sees the good-natured aristocrat, who can be tolerant because it never occurs to him to question his own status or that of the masses. But we are now to behold an aristocrat for whom the masses have no status at all, who has a blind contempt for the common man and is impatient of any claim to consideration or fair dealing put forward by persons not of his own class.

Caius Marcius comes upon the scene as Menenius concludes his fable. Shakespeare presents his hero at once in all his superbity. He returns the greeting of Menenius with a single word and turns at once upon the citizens. Marcius is not prepared to argue the matter. The question, for him, is not whether the demand of the citizens is just or their contention well founded. For him it is an outrage that these men should presume to have any opinion at all and his remedy for their grievances is a general massacre.

Menenius asks Marcius what has happened on the other side of the city, where the main body of the rebels has met the representatives of the senate. Marcius tells his story in a fashion that stresses in every line his indifference to the people's hardships and his indignation that any concessions should be accorded them. The senate, it seems, have decided to allow them representatives to defend their interests. This, in his view, is that thin end of the wedge which is the eternal bugbear of privilege.

Shakespeare, in this opening scene, clearly indicates the reasons on which Caius Marcius bases his contempt for the people of Rome. They have no liking for war and they fall short of his own high standard of valour. Then, too, they are fickle and not to be trusted. A born soldier, who is never so happy as on the field of battle, may perhaps be excused for feeling that he is a braver and better man than persons of a less martial disposition. The accusation that the citizens of Rome are uncertain in their allegiance comes less appropriately from a Roman general who, under the influence of private passion, is shortly to lead a hostile army against his countrymen.

Shakespeare, while according to Marcius the palm for valour, is careful to indicate that his hero's bravery is inspired by family feeling and love of fame rather than any desire to serve the commonwealth. First Citizen has shrewdly affirmed that 'what he hath done famously, he did it to that end. Though soft-conscienced men can be content to say it was for his country, he did it to please his mother and to be partly proud'; and, lest we should take this to be a partisan conclusion, Shakespeare, towards the end of the scene, drives the point firmly home in a speech delivered by Marcius himself when he learns that the Volsces are in arms under Tullus Aufidius. First he exclaims that, if he were not Caius Marcius, he would wish to be Aufidius. Next he declares that, if

Aufidius were on *his* side in the war, he would go over to the enemy for the sheer pleasure of fighting so excellent a soldier. That the Volsces are preparing to attack his native land is meat and drink to Marcius. Here is not only a heaven-sent opportunity to increase his glory, but a chance to get even with the rabble of Rome.

This opening scene concludes with a dialogue between Sicinius and Brutus, the newly-elected tribunes of the people. Shakespeare's presentation of these two men completes his statement of the major theme of the tragedy. No two characters in Shakespeare have been more severely handled by the critics. Since Dr Johnson referred to their 'plebeian malignity and tribunitian insolence', they have been repeatedly held up to obloquy as a brace of intriguing, mean-spirited rascals whose base manoeuvres precipitate the tragedy and utterly discredit the popular cause. On that issue let us again reserve judgement till we have carefully examined their purposes and proceedings. For better or worse, these tribunes are Shakespeare's counterfeit presentment of two labour leaders. They are the natural products of a class war in the commonwealth. They use their wits to defend the interests of the popular party and to remove from power a declared enemy of the people. They have neither the wish, training, nor ability to disguise the quality or intention of their activities. In working for their party they do not claim to be working disinterestedly for the nation. In resorting to the lawful and customary tricks of the political trade they neglect the noble postures and impressive mimicries adopted by persons with a longer experience of public life and of the deportment which public life requires. Whether their conduct be better or worse than that of their political opponents will appear in due course. Meanwhile it is worth noting that Shakespeare, in introducing them to the audience, draws special attention to the quality which will be found throughout the play to distinguish them from their rivals. They are discussing the appointment of Marcius to be second-in-command, under Cominius, of the Roman forces. They comment on his pride, on his contempt for the people and for themselves. Then comes the important message:

SICINIUS: I do wonder
        His insolence can brook to be commanded
        Under Cominius.

BRUTUS:　　　　　　Fame, at the which he aims –
In whom already he is well grac'd – cannot
Better be held nor more attain'd than by
A place below the first; for what miscarries
Shall be the general's fault, though he perform
To th' utmost of a man, and giddy censure
Will then cry out of Marcius, 'O, if he
Had borne the business!'

SICINIUS:　　　　　　Besides, if things go well,
Opinion, that so sticks on Marcius, shall
Of his demerits rob Cominius.

BRUTUS:　　　　　　　　　　　Come.
Half all Cominius' honours are to Marcius,
Though Marcius earned them not; and all his faults
To Marcius shall be honours, though indeed
In aught he merit not.　　　　　　　　　I. I. 259

It is not, admittedly, a generous diagnosis. It suggests that
Marcius, in agreeing to serve under Cominius, is displaying a
political sagacity which as a matter of fact is foreign to his nature.
But, essentially, the tribunes are right and they are giving proof of
precisely that 'realism' and precisely that suspicion of their political
rulers which are characteristic of popular leaders in all times and
places. Tribunes of the people have notoriously little respect for
professions of altruism and of stainless regard for the public welfare
uttered by their social superiors. Marcius did not accept the post of
second-in-command with the deliberate design of advancing himself at the expense of his commander. But, in accepting a subordinate position, he certainly expected that, whatever happened, his
own reputation would not be diminished by the arrangement. These
tribunes are not concerned with the *motives* of Marcius in the particular case, but with the dangers inherent in his character. They are
diagnosing not the man but the situation, and in their reading of
the situation they are, as the event will show, entirely right. They
regard themselves as watch-dogs of the people, and Shakespeare,
in this opening scene, is at some pains to show that they are well
qualified for their office and that they intend to be alert and vigilant
in its exercise.

*

In *Coriolanus* the citizens of Rome are with difficulty goaded into becoming a mob by the provocation of their leaders and the insufferable behaviour of Marcius himself. Nor does their behaviour, even as a mob, compare at all unfavourably with that of the senatorial party. There is no evidence in this play that Shakespeare hated the people unless we fall into the strange assumption that Caius Marcius Coriolanus speaks for the author. Marcius certainly hated the people and that was why he came to a bad end. To quote the speeches in which he expresses an immeasurable contempt for plebeians – and thereby reveals a conspicuous lack of judgement and humanity – as though they sprang from Shakespeare's heart of hearts is almost to deny that Shakespeare had the capacity to be a dramatist. There is, it is true, a gusto in those speeches which, to a critic who leans to the arbitrary side, is irresistibly pleasing. But there is an equal gusto in Iago's scorn of Othello's simplicity and in Richard of Gloucester's contempt of Lady Anne. Yet no one has ever sought to identify Shakespeare with Iago or with Richard.

The contention that Shakespeare hated the common people has found much comfort and support in the fact that he never loses an opportunity of reminding us that they smell. Poor suitors have strong breaths. The many are not only mutable but rank-scented. The citizens on the Capitol uttered such a deal of stinking breath that it almost choked Caesar. The laws that are to come from the mouth of Jack Cade will be 'stinking law, for his breath stinks with eating toasted cheese'. Brutus, the tribune, heard Marcius declare that he would never show his wounds to the people or 'beg their stinking breaths'. Marcius hated their breath as 'reek of the rotten fens'. The citizens who banished him threw up their 'stinking greasy caps'.

This would seem to prove not that Shakespeare hated the people, but that he had a sensitive nose. It was a nose, moreover, that was not offended only by odours of low degree. The offence of Claudius, King of Denmark, was rank; it smelled to heaven. Not all the perfumes of Arabia could wash the smell of blood from the patrician hand of Lady Macbeth. The hand of Lear smelled of mortality and he called for an ounce of civet to sweeten an imagination that reeked with the proud iniquities of man. Hamlet's last gesture over the skull of poor Yorick was to stop his nose. Shakespeare's world was as full of smells, good and bad, as Prospero's island was full of noises.

The people smell worse in *Coriolanus* than anywhere else and it is not therefore surprising that this play has been most often called in evidence for Shakespeare's dislike of the masses. It should therefore be noted that, in writing *Coriolanus*, he went out of his way to exonerate the citizens of Rome from the worst charges brought against them by the historian from whom he adapted his material. Shakespeare deliberately amended Plutarch in two important particulars, on both occasions in favour of the people and to the detriment of the right-hand file. One of his amendments, as we noted in reading the play, was to attribute to Marcius the terrible design of destroying Rome, whereas in Plutarch his plan was more in the nature of a project to secure success for the aristocratic Roman party with the help of the corresponding party in Antium. The second emendation is even more significant. The Roman citizens in Plutarch are not flouted by Marcius when he stands for the consulship. Their behaviour, as reported by the historian, has none of the somewhat bewildered generosity in the face of menace and strikingly magnanimous forbearance in the face of insult on which Shakespeare so vividly insists. Shakespeare, who follows Plutarch with remarkable fidelity in all other respects, here departs from his authority in order to put the conduct of the citizens in a better light. Their behaviour in the play is more reasonable than in Plutarch, more comprehensible, more calculated to secure the sympathy of the spectator, while the behaviour of Marcius is correspondingly less reasonable, less comprehensible and less likely to obtain indulgence. Whoever is bent on identifying Shakespeare with his characters, and thereby detecting his political inclinations, would be driven to conclude, upon a careful comparison of his play with its historical source, that he had a bias, not towards authority, but towards the popular principle. No such bias need, however, be presumed. Shakespeare deliberately weighted the scales against Marcius and in favour of the people because his dramatic intention made it essential for him to do so. He was writing the tragedy of a man whose contempt for the people was beyond all reason, whose pride offended natural justice and fair dealing. The audience must accordingly be made to understand that the speeches in which

Marcius condemns the people are intended to reveal the senseless arrogance of the speaker, and not to be read as statements of political truth. Shakespeare, in his deviations from Plutarch, tried to make this plain to the simplest spectator. He did not succeed with some of his commentators, whose own bias in favour of authority has tempted them to receive those speeches as Shakespeare's political testament.

from *Political Characters of Shakespeare,*
1945

TWENTY-NINE

Shakespeare's Politics

ERIC BENTLEY

MELODRAMA presents the struggle of right and wrong; tragedy –
on one famous view of it – the struggle of right and right; Shakespeare's *Coriolanus* the struggle of wrong and wrong. That's what
makes the play so hard to take. As one of Henry Luce's anonymous
spokesmen recently indicated, the American theatre public insists
on some characters being simply right and others simply wrong. He
might have said the same of any other public, American or un-
American, in the theatre or out of it. We all view life as melodrama,
insofar as we are fools. Only to the extent that we are men can we
see it as tragedy or comedy.

Now, though our folly is by no means confined inside theatre
walls, our humanity is very easily left outside them. For we are
wholly foolish when our individuality is lost in mob emotion, and
any crowd of people – including an audience – can become a mob.
Tragedy and comedy always tend, in the theatre, to decline into
melodrama and farce; those critics who are the mob's representatives praise tragedy and comedy precisely in the degree that they do
so decline: *Hamlet* is 'as exciting as a who-done-it', *The Would-Be
Gentleman* is 'as funny as *Room Service*'. Etcetera.

If it is hard, then, for a producer to put across a tragedy or a
comedy, how much harder for him to put across a play that combines the more forbidding features of both to the exclusion of every
melodramatic and farcical possibility! Such a play is *Coriolanus*; it
is absolutely nothing but a masterpiece; we almost have to feel
sorry for it.

Except that it hurts our feelings, gets under our skin, affronts
our prejudices, and corrects our convictions. It is the most modern
of Shakespeare's works in the sense that modern writers have been
trying to write it: no wonder that our greatest comedian, Shaw,
called it the greatest of Shakespeare's comedies! Those who have
attempted political tragedy in our time have achieved, at best,

brilliant political melodramas like *Darkness at Noon*. At worst, they have excitedly informed us that fascism or communism or capitalism is wicked and that common folk (like you and me in the $7.80 orchestra) are models of heroic virtue and good sense.

It is true that you can't fully identify yourself with anyone in *Coriolanus*. From the Broadway viewpoint, that is bad. From the human viewpoint, it is good – because you are prevented from dissociating yourself from evil, from pushing evil away, from locating it exclusively in the other fellow, the other place, Moscow or Corioli. The evil is here in Rome, in Washington, in Coriolanus, in our classmate Alger Hiss, in me, and in you – *hypocrite lecteur*. The reference to Hiss will seem pretty callow to our Marxist friends, not only because he was quite right to be a spy for Moscow (or is it that he *wasn't* a spy? I forget), but also because they acknowledge no continuity between personal character and political action. The rest of us have been coming round from the Marxist position (if we ever held it) to the Shakespearian one and are willing to see treason – that of Alger Hiss or Benedict Arnold – as the other face of pride, first of the deadly sins. Some degree of identification with Coriolanus we have, perforce, to permit ourselves.

The dignity of John Houseman's production derives from taste, intelligence, and discretion – most of all, discretion. Mr Houseman is a man of integrity, and has resisted the temptation to slant a masterpiece whose greatness is all vertical. The People – about whom Shakespeare is so 'undemocratic' – are presented in all their moral ambiguity. No attempt is made to whitewash the enemy leader, Aufidius. If Mr Houseman tips the scales at all, it is to overweight the badness of his hero. Perhaps this was the inevitable result of casting Robert Ryan for the role. Unable to suggest caste and the pride of caste, Mr Ryan seems too simply a boor (and, hence, a bore). Not that one suspects this actor to be boorish by nature: he works all too hard and too obviously at it. It is only that, if Coriolanus is not an aristocrat, he is just a disgruntled gladiator. . . .

Mr Houseman's method yields results, both general and of detail. The chief general merit of the production – beyond the competence we can happily take for granted – is the peculiar sense of movement it conveys. This is a play that – for all the Elizabethan bustle of the scenes taken separately – remains stationary for whole sequences; then, of a sudden, it turns, as on a hinge or pivot, like some majestic old door. The alteration of stillness and tremendous reversal is Greek and awe-inspiring in its majesty. I would say that Mr Houseman's largest achievement is to communicate a sense of this ancient and alien grandeur. . . .

from *The Dramatic Event*,
1956

Suggestions for Further Reading

H. GRANVILLE-BARKER: *Prefaces to Shakespeare V*.

A. C. BRADLEY: '*Coriolanus*' (in *A Miscellany*).

I. R. BROWNING: 'Boy of Tears' (*Essays in Criticism*, January 1955). Gives central place to Coriolanus' relationship with his mother. 'His desire has ever been to please her, and now (Act V, Scene 3), most cruelly, she condemns a course of action to which everything she has done in the past has rigidly conduced.'

WILLIAM ROSEN: '*Coriolanus*' (in *Shakespeare and the Craft of Tragedy*).

T.J.B. SPENCER: 'Shakespeare and the Elizabethan Romans' (in *Shakespeare Survey 10*). Though the reading lists are concerned with criticism and not scholarship, I must mention this valuable account of Elizabethan attitudes to Roman history, since it throws so much light on Shakespeare's political purposes in *Coriolanus*.

D. A. TRAVERSI: *An Approach to Shakespeare*. Contains a discussion of *Coriolanus* among *The Last Plays*. Traversi approaches a play's themes (in this case the ruthlessness of the social critique, and the 'tragic futility' of the hero's career) through analysis of the quality of the verse.

J. MIDDLETON MURRY: 'A Neglected Heroine of Shakespeare' (in *Countries of the Mind*).

T. S. ELIOT: 'Coriolan' (in *Collected Poems*). These two 'unfinished poems' are not about Shakespeare's play, but the title is no doubt a hint that they are expressing a political attitude similar to Shakespeare's (or to his hero's?).

TIMON OF ATHENS

THIRTY

Introduction to Timon of Athens

J. C. MAXWELL

... How does Shakespeare set about presenting us with a play that shall combine some of the qualities of a moral apologue with an adequate degree of realism? The opening scene is effective from this point of view in that it plunges us into the bright but unstable world of Timon's bounty, and at the same time isolates the 'morality' aspect of the situation in the poet's account of his 'rough work' (I. I. 46–52). Already we are being brought to realize how precarious Timon's prosperity is. It is customary to contrast Timon in his prosperity with Timon after his fall, and I do not think sufficient stress has been laid on the fact that when the play opens he is already ruined. It is true that we do not know this for certain at the very start, but there is an ominous atmosphere about even the first scene that makes it only the fulfilment of what we have expected when Timon's ruin is first announced by Flavius in I. 2. We have had the well-worn apologue of the hill of Fortune, and the hope, after a vivid description of Timon's prodigality, 'Long may he live in fortunes!' (I. I. 285). No audience could doubt what that foreshadowed. The insubstantiality of the glittering pageant is suggested in the opening lines, 'Magic of bounty, all these spirits thy power Hath conjured to attend' (I. I. 6–7). The picture of Fortune which the Poet presents is almost like a challenge on Shakespeare's part – he announces that he is going to deal with one of the most familiar of commonplaces, and prompts our interest in the question how he is going to give an individual turn to it; as the painter says:

> 'Tis common:
> A thousand moral paintings I can show,
> That shall demonstrate these quick blows of Fortune's
> More pregnantly than words.   I. I. 92

This crucial opening scene holds the balance delicately between the two extremes to be avoided in our attitude towards Timon. It is the only scene in which there is clear indication of genuine personal feeling in his generosity, and it is shown in contrast with a typical representative of the spirit of Athens, the 'old Athenian'. Timon as shown here is not adequately described by the more rigorous critics, such as Warwick Bond (*Modern Language Review*, XXVI (1931), p. 53) 'the great spendthrift, avoiding all that is unpleasant, allowing himself to expand in a foolish glow of lazy benevolence, and prompted as much by love of admiration and flattery as by a real charity', and O. J. Campbell (*Shakespeare's Satire* (1943), p. 187) 'The similarity of his response to each one of these adulators in turn makes his generosity seem automatic and therefore ridiculous.' This episode is an exception to that 'similarity', but at the same time it does show the subtle corruption exercised by the materialistic spirit of Athens. Timon cannot really overcome it; he can only outbid it in its own currency of gold – and it is a further irony that he cannot, by now, even do that: the audience is already conscious that his 'to build his fortune I will strain a little' is a grim understatement of his financial embarrassments. This theme of the impossibility of genuinely defeating the ethos of Athens is perhaps most clearly expressed in a passage of detached comment at the end of the scene, where one of the Lords remarks, 'no gift to him But breeds the giver a return exceeding All use of quittance' (I. I. 280–82). We are soon to learn that Timon has been having recourse to usurers in the literal sense, but the implications of these lines are more profound: by his habit of lavish recompense, Timon is turning even those who ostensibly give him free gifts into usurers, more successful usurers than the real ones: the word 'breeds' recalls the traditional doctrine about 'barren metal'. In this sense of the guilt shared both by lender and borrower, and infecting all transactions in a usurious society, lies the advance in complexity in Shakespeare's treatment of usury since *The Merchant of Venice*.

This first scene has foreshadowed the approaching fall, and has shown us in some measure how even the more genuinely fine sides of Timon's nature are corrupted by the spirit of his society, but on the whole we have so far seen him at his best. In the second scene the conceptions of 'bounty' and 'goodness' begin to receive penetrating criticism. Already in I. I, the merchant's obviously interested reference to Timon's 'untirable and continuate goodness' has caught our attention. Perhaps we are already meant to have a sense of its being too much 'on tap' – 'automatic' in Campbell's phrase already quoted – and when Lucilius says

> never may
> That state or fortune fall into my keeping
> Which is not owed to you!   I. I. 152

it is clear that Timon is in danger of complacently accepting superhuman honours. In I. 2, Timon in the opening exchanges with Ventidius brushes aside all idea of return of favours, but he later (I. 2. 84–103) expresses his ideal of friendship – 'so many like brothers commanding one another's fortunes!' By doing so, he makes us realize how his whole mode of life has cut him off from the possibility of really entering into the relationship of reciprocity which he here describes so feelingly, if with a touch of sentimentality.

It will be best at this point to interrupt the chronological order and to trace this theme through the subsequent acts. For some time the spotlight is upon the baseness of Timon's beneficiaries rather than on his own feelings, and this part of the play culminates in the choric comment of the Stranger in III. 2. 75–86. It makes an appearance in Flavius's speech in II. 2, where there is the usual reference to bounty (l. 170), and the flatterers are quoted as saying, 'Great Timon, noble, worthy, royal Timon'. We accept the claim, 'Unwisely, not ignobly, have I given' (l. 180), but the whole context forbids us to forget that wisdom, prudence, is a considerable part of human virtue in its widest sense, and it is at his own risk that a private citizen displays 'royal' qualities.

The critical attitude towards this sort of 'goodness' is firmly established by the time we come, after the fall, to Flavius's paradoxical summing-up of Timon's fate:

> Undone by goodness! Strange, unusual blood,
> When man's worst sin is, he does too much good!
> Who then dares to be half so kind again?
> For bounty, that makes gods, does still mar men.   IV. 2. 38

Shakespeare is here using his gnomic technique with a good deal of subtlety. We are meant to accept what Flavius says, but not to regard him as having adequate insight into Timon's nature, and the special connotations that the play has given to 'goodness' and 'bounty' enable us to achieve both these ends at once. For Flavius, his old master is in a straightforward sense 'too good for this world', but the audience is meant to take his comments, which for the speaker are really a confession of inability to understand the ways of the universe, as literal truth. The audience can see, if Flavius – his heart stronger than his head – cannot, that an attempt on the part of man to ape divine bounty, ever spontaneously giving without receiving anything in return, is presumptuous and must inevitably be frustrated. Timon cannot grasp the notion of the necessary reciprocity of creation. This is the point of the curious lines IV. 3. 437–44. Since for Timon giving must be only giving, receiving only receiving, even if he has in his adversity expected a reversal of the roles, the normal processes of give-and-take in nature appear as thievery, on the analogy of the corrupted society of Athens, which has also lost the notion of reciprocity; which has, indeed, destroyed it in Timon's mind. Flavius's own goodness, in contrast, is the genuine, human thing: his determination to seek out Timon and serve him is immediately and ironically followed by Timon's soliloquy, 'O blessed breeding sun'. And human, *costing* generosity has already been presented in III. 5, a scene introducing a *motif* which I suspect Shakespeare would have exploited more fully if he had completed the play. Alcibiades, who pleads for his friend's life, and has kept back the state's foes, is 'rich only in large hurts' (l. 111), and it is he who most explicitly denounces the 'usuring senate' (l. 112).

Like 'bounty' and 'goodness', 'free' is a word which meets with keen criticism in the course of the play. The words are linked directly in Flavius's gnomic lines which close Act II:

> I would I could not think it.
> That thought is bounty's foe;
> Being free itself, it thinks all others so. II. 2. 332

And 'free' occurs with a subtle gradation of senses in various passages. The very first time it occurs is at I. 1. 48, where there is something ominous about the 'free drift' that 'moves itself In a wide sea of wax'. The next two occurrences have a sense of paradox about them: the 'slaves and servants' of the Poet's representation of Timon 'through him Drink the free air' (I. I. 85–6); and the implication that Timon's 'freeness' is oppressive to its recipients is even more directly expressed when to his 'I'll pay the debt and free him', the messenger rejoins 'your lordship ever binds him' (ll. 106–7). It adds to the irony that Ventidius does not in fact consider himself bound when Timon really needs him, but Timon's bounty is of the kind that offers a temptation to throw off the rather stifling burden it imposes. We are ready by this time to let any passing allusions have their effect. Ventidius makes an attempt to restore Timon's gift to his 'free heart' (I. 2. 6), but it is refused – Timon 'gave it freely ever', and it turns out that this time Ventidius takes him at his word for good. Another, more humdrum sense of the word is introduced when Apemantus prays never to trust 'a keeper with my freedom' (l. 67). The 'five best senses . . . come freely To gratulate thy plenteous bosom' (ll. 188–20); and an interested donor claims to be making his gift 'out of his free love' (l. 186). The theme naturally becomes less prominent as the play advances. Lucullus, in his greedy expectation of further gifts, refers to 'that honourable, complete, free-hearted gentleman of Athens, thy very bountiful good lord and master' (III. I. 9–11), combining all the words I have been discussing; and in the last reference before his ruin, Timon ironically combines the play's primary sense for the word 'generous' with the more prosaic, Apemantean sense of mere freedom from restraint:

> Have I been ever free, and must my house
> Be my retentive enemy, my gaol?   III. 4. 81

In the last two acts we have one concentrated use, where Timon looks back on the past, and talks of

> The sweet degrees that this brief world affords
> To such as may the passive drugs of it
> Freely command.   IV. 3. 252

Whether 'drugs' or 'drudges', or a pun on both, is intended, the notion is conveyed that Timon's liberality has been something that involves subservience on the part of its instruments, human or material. Act IV, like Act II, ends with a gnomic couplet in which the word 'free' occurs, though in a less pregnant sense, 'fly, whilst thou are blest and free', and Act V has only one unremarkable instance of the word (v. 1. 44). Although the dangers of reading profound significance into recurrent words is obvious, I think that 'free' does run through this play in such a way as to constitute a comment on what Timon's situation and behaviour involve in terms of human relationships.

The other topics I should like to discuss are the relation between Timon and Lear, and the parts played by Alcibiades and Apemantus.

Timon's invective has often been compared with that of Lear. Biographically-minded critics have even suggested that the emotion which Shakespeare has just been able to keep in check and express in the form of art in *Lear* has got the better of him in *Timon*, but I think that both the similarity and the differences can readily be explained on artistic grounds. Timon like Lear 'hath ever but slenderly known himself'. He will not listen to the truth – 'he will not hear till feel', says Flavius (II. 2. 7) – and when Flavius tries to enlighten him he retorts 'Come, sermon me no further' (II. 2. 178). The difference between him and Lear after their falls is that Lear learns by his misfortune as Timon does not. That does not mean that there is no substance in his tirades – much of them consists of the stock-in-trade of the traditional moral satirist – but there is no hint of insight or wisdom behind them. One might express the difference between Lear and Timon by saying that Lear in affliction comes to *see* as he never did before; Timon does not undergo the ultimate ordeal of madness, and the utmost he attains to is to *see* through particular shams and injustices. Unlike Lear, who finally welcomes and values love, he grudges it when the disinterested affection of Flavius forces him to modify his wholesale condemnation of mankind (IV. 3. 491–503). When, a few lines earlier, he has said, 'I never had an honest man about me, I; all I kept were knaves, to serve in meat to villains' (ll. 476–7), he has not merely exaggerated, he has been utterly wrong, since at the risk of undue simplification Shakespeare has insisted that all

Timon's servants, in contrast to his flatterers, are faithful to him and have a genuine affection for him (IV. 2). This picture is perhaps modified by the curious incomplete suggestions of a wisdom by withdrawal to be achieved only in death, but there is no direct connexion between that and his sufferings – it is *nothing* that brings him 'all things' (V. I. 186). Even here, the effect is partly counteracted by the more satiric and less mysteriously resonant lines (ll. 219–22) which are appended to Timon's description of his choice of a grave, and whose tone recurs in the epitaphs from Plutarch used in the final scene. In the last instance, it is perhaps the possibility of taking these over unchanged, and so remaining within the stock-character framework of 'Timon Misanthropus', that best shows how Shakespeare has stopped short of a genuinely tragic remoulding of the traditional figure.

Shakespeare has evidently relied on the contrast between Timon and Alcibiades and between Timon and Apemantus to convey much of his meaning, and it is perhaps here that we are most conscious of the incompleteness of the draft. Most critics have seen the importance of the contrast between Timon and Alcibiades and their respective responses to Athenian baseness. Collins (*Review of English Studies*, XXII (1946), 104) has given perhaps the best account of what Alcibiades means for the play, in stressing how in III. 5, 'a real man has pleaded for his friend', and how, at the end of the play with Alcibiades's return to Athens, 'sanity, with common decency is restored; there shall be human-heartedness again'; but he destroys some of the effect of his criticism by exaggerating the contrast in technique between the handling of Timon and that of Alcibiades – the criticism of Timon that is implied in the figure of Alcibiades is much more telling than it would be if Timon were, as Collins writes, an 'abstract Virtue almost ready to be transformed to a similarly abstract Vice'. In fact it is hard to see how a play could successfully work simultaneously on those two levels. The contrast is not, as Collins holds, between idealism and realism, but between an inhuman excess and a balanced humanity. Alcibiades can see what is wrong with Athens – 'banish usury' (III. 5. 99), and he is not provoked to indiscriminate hatred, 'I will use the olive with my sword' (V. 4. 82). Only the outlines of the theme are indicated, but the intention is clear. The other exemplar of human-heartedness in the play, the steward Flavius, is treated in more detail, in several of Shakespeare's most tenderly beautiful scenes. (I find it significant that Campbell, in making out the treatment to be satirical throughout, is led to ignore the roles of both Flavius and Alcibiades in the play.) In him, and in Timon's other servants, we see genuine personal affection, contrasting strongly with Timon's more equivocal 'bounty'. It is noteworthy that Shakespeare seems to have been much more certain what the most significant scene involving Alcibiades, III. 5, was to represent in the play's system of values than what its place in the action was to be. Its main function in the plot is, of course, to give the occasion for Alcibiades's banishment, but it would surely have been more closely integrated into the action in a final version. To me, as to Ellis-Fermor (*Review of English Studies*, XVIII, 1942) the scene reads like a vigorous roughing-out, of particular interest for the study of a theme taking shape under Shakespeare's hands. The lack of final shaping is perhaps even more to be regretted in IV. 3, when Timon and Alcibiades meet for the last time. As the scene stands, the presence of Phyrnia and Timandra provides an occasion for Timon's invective, but scarcely helps to elucidate the Alcibiades theme. I should be reluctant to regard it as intended to indicate that the claims of Alcibiades in the final scene to regenerate Athens are to be taken cynically.

In the absence of a full development of the Alcibiades theme, the other main contrast of the play, that between Timon and Apemantus, perhaps assumes undue prominence. Here there is no doubt that, especially in Act IV, this part of the play is relatively near completion. There is less of Apemantus in the first three acts, but perhaps about as much as Shakespeare meant there to be. In the earlier scenes, Apemantus falls easily enough under the type of 'scurrilous and profane jester' first introduced by Jonson in *Every Man out of his Humour* in the person of Carlo Buffone. No radical criticism of a specific kind is conveyed by his railing. In Act IV he is able to argue with Timon on equal terms, and is given some of the most impressive poetry of the play. In spite of this, and in spite of the superficially keen play of dialectic, he seems even more ineffective than before. The audience knows that he is arguing on false premisses, since Timon has discovered his new store of gold, and does not act the misanthrope 'enforcedly' (IV. 3. 240). But even if this were not so, we can see that Timon would still be right in saying 'thou flatter'st misery' (l. 233). Apemantus's speech beginning 'Thou hast cast away thyself' (l. 220) is such a characteristic piece of Shakespeare's mature verse that we tend to overlook how unnecessary it is for Timon to have all this pointed out to him. It is not only unnecessary, it becomes clear as the scene proceeds that from Timon's point of view it is a falsely romantic picture. Apemantus for all his cynicism has a picture of a finely incorruptible 'Nature' refusing to flatter man – a picture made in his own image, and one to which, in turn, he strives to approximate even more closely. The core of Timon's criticism of cynicism is in the long speech beginning at l. 324, 'A beastly ambition'. The real animal world, in contrast to Apemantus's idealized picture, is just as full of conflict and inequality as the human – 'what beast couldst thou be that were not subject to a beast?' If Timon himself later wishes 'that beasts may have the world in empire', it is from pure hatred of mankind, not from any idealization of beasts. All this does not mean that we are asked to share Timon's total vision – I have already commented on the failure of insight shown in the speech, 'The sun's a thief' – but it does dispose of Apemantus's essentially sentimental and self-indulgent cynicism. One could have prophesied Shakespeare's attitude towards a philosophy of life that took the dog as its ideal.

It would be natural to hope to follow up a piecemeal treatment of themes by an attempt to see them together in a coherent picture, and it is the radical criticism to be made of the play that, unless I have badly failed to read it aright, this is not possible. At a highly abstract level, it is easier to summarize without serious distortion than any other of the plays. To say that it is a study of a potentially noble but unbalanced and prodigal nature, corrupted by a usurious and materialistic society with its flattery, and thrown off his balance and plunged into an equally extreme and indiscriminate misanthropy when the loss of his wealth discovers the falsehood of his friends – to say this is probably a less hopelessly inadequate account of 'what the play is about' than could be given for any other important play of Shakespeare. But once we descend from such generalities, and attempt an analysis in terms of individual themes, there seems to be less over and above, or rather encompassing, those themes than in the greatest works. Each is worked out with passion and brilliance, though to different degrees of completeness: the interviews with the false friends – variations on a single theme, but wittily differentiated – are, I think, often underrated. Their merits were recognized by P. Stapfer, *Shakespeare and Classical Antiquity* (1880), p. 238, who found in them some of the spirit of Molière. Yet whole-hearted encomiums of the play always give the impression of special pleading, and attempts to make it out to be all of a piece are unduly schematic and incomplete. Nor does this mean simply that the play is too rich and varied to be brought under a systematic description. On the contrary one feels that it is a play that ought to have been neat and shapely – it aims more at the formal qualities of *Coriolanus* than at those of *Antony and Cleopatra* or of *King Lear*. It is easy to be wise after the event, and to say that Shakespeare chose a theme that was too exaggerated or too monotonous or what you will. There is no harm in such conjecture. All we can say for certain – a few critics would deny even this – is that Shakespeare did not bring his work on the play to a satisfying stage of completion. That he could not have done so, who would venture to say?

from the Introduction to the New Shakespeare edition of *Timon of Athens* (first published in *Scrutiny*, 1948)

ON TRAGEDY:
AND ON
SHAKESPEARIAN
TRAGEDY

The aim of this last section is to invite the reader to generalize from his reactions to the plays, and to think about the nature of tragedy – of tragedy in general, of Elizabethan and of Shakespearian tragedy in particular.

It is possible to discuss this at great length, or at very short length – in a book, or in an aphorism. The more general the subject, the more revealing an aphorism can be – if it is taken slowly, and reflected·on. *The Birth of Tragedy*, for instance, is not Nietzsche's only account of the subject. One of the aphorisms in *Beyond Good and Evil* runs: 'the sense for tragedy increases and decreases with sensuality.' This puzzling remark is perhaps explained later in the book, when he says that tragedy, like 'practically everything that we call "superior culture"' rests on the intellectualization and deepening of *cruelty*. . . . Naturally we must get rid of the old ridiculous psychology which knew no better than to teach that cruelty only arises at the sight of *someone else's* suffering. There is a rich, an over-rich pleasure in one's own suffering, in making oneself suffer.'

One view of tragedy holds that its essence lies not in the hero's responsibility (as some say) nor in his redemption (as others say), but simply in the quality of his defiance when the inevitable happens to him. This can be stated in a book, or in a sentence – as by Lawrence, when he writes (criticizing Arnold Bennett) 'I hate Bennett's resignation. Tragedy ought really to be a great kick at misery'. And against this we can set another version of what the tragic attitude is, a claim that it is something more restrained, more controlled, more dignified, than Lawrence's 'kick', or the 'shout' recommended by Jean Anouilh. This is the version of Joseph Conrad, perhaps the most purely tragic of modern novelists, and it too can be stated in a sentence or so:

The sight of human affairs deserves admiration and pity. They are worthy of respect, too. And he is not insensible who pays them the undemonstrative tribute of a sigh which is not a sob, and of a smile which is not a grin.

(Preface to *A Personal Record*)

But a series of aphorisms, or classified opinions, though one could make it satisfying and systematic, does not seem to me the most useful form to give this section. I have preferred to let a few writers develop their views at length, even though the price is an even greater incompleteness than in the other sections of the book. Many theories of tragedy are not represented at all here (though some of these, of course, were implied in earlier essays – the Aristotelian in Professor Crane's piece on *Macbeth*, the Freudian in Ernest Jones's on *Hamlet*, something between the two in Professor Stampfer's on *Lear*, and so on). I have chosen two general essays on tragedy, both of which I admire greatly, both from longer books that I hope the reader will turn up, and by two strongly contrasting authors: a turgid reckless genius of the high Germanic order, and a clear-headed, scholarly English professor. The short piece from Donatus's commentary on Terence is intended to jolt the reader out of his modern assumptions. Mr Eliot's essay is partly concerned with certain universal tragic attitudes, and partly with what is specifically Elizabethan; and it exhibits that mixture of the historical and the absolutist which gives Mr Eliot's mind its peculiar and fascinating quality. Finally Mr Schwartz confronts Shakespeare's plays with nothing but his naked response and his own observation of life. I am glad to end with a poem: for Shakespeare is a part of our life (and so of poetic material) as well as of our literature.

THIRTY-ONE

The Dionysiac Greek

FRIEDRICH NIETZSCHE

The following extracts are from *The Birth of Tragedy*, Nietzsche's murky, brilliant, and influential essay on Greek drama. Much of this essay can be generalized, and many of its insights seem to unfold further in our minds if we apply them to Shakespeare. 'Wisdom is a crime committed on Nature' might serve for an epigraph on *Hamlet.*

The extracts I have chosen follow after Nietzsche's famous contrast between the Apollonian and the Dionysiac: dream and intoxication, individuation and communal merging. The dream clarity of the Apollonian artist, claims Nietzsche, is the obverse of the 'wisdom of Silenus', that it is best not to be, and the second best is to die soon. As a reaction against this, Homeric or Apollonian art (what Schiller calls naïve art) maintains itself in a perpetual state of military encampment. The Apollonian element in Greek Tragedy is the dialogue.

The oldest element of such tragedy, however, is the chorus. The life force which it represents rescues from that paralysing of the will which occurs when understanding kills action. The Dionysiac rite reforges the bond between man and man, and between man and nature. And Greek Tragedy is a Dionysiac chorus which again and again discharges itself in Apollonian images.

The following passages continue the discussion from this point.

*

IT is certainly true, as Schiller saw, that the Greek chorus of satyrs, the chorus of primitive tragedy, moved on ideal ground, a ground raised high above the common path of mortals. The Greek has built for his chorus the scaffolding of a fictive chthonic realm and placed thereon fictive nature spirits. Tragedy developed on this foundation, and so has been exempt since its beginning from the embarrassing task of copying actuality. All the same, the world of tragedy is by no means a world arbitrarily projected between heaven and earth; rather it is a world having the same reality and credibility as Olympus possessed for the devout Greek. The satyr, as the Dionysiac chorist, dwells in a reality sanctioned by myth and ritual. That tragedy should begin with him, that the Dionysiac wisdom of tragedy should speak through him, is as puzzling a phenomenon as, more generally, the origin of tragedy from the chorus. Perhaps we can gain a starting point for this inquiry by claiming that the satyr, that fictive nature sprite, stands to cultured man in the same relation as Dionysiac music does to civilization. Richard Wagner has said of the latter that it is absorbed by music as lamplight by daylight. In the same manner, I believe, the cultured Greek felt himself absorbed into the satyr chorus, and in the next development of Greek tragedy state and society, in fact all that separated man from man, gave way before an overwhelming sense of unity which led back into the heart of nature. The metaphysical solace (with which, I wish to say at once, all true tragedy sends us away) that, despite every phenomenal change, life is at bottom indestructibly joyful and powerful, was expressed most concretely in the chorus of satyrs, nature beings who dwell behind all civilization and preserve their identity through every change of generation and historical movement.

With this chorus the profound Greek, so uniquely susceptible to the subtlest and deepest suffering, who had penetrated the destructive agencies of both nature and history, solaced himself. Though he had been in danger of craving a Buddhistic denial of the will, he was saved by art, and through art life reclaimed him.

While the transport of the Dionysiac state, with its suspension of all the ordinary barriers of existence, lasts, it carries with it a Lethean element in which everything that has been experienced by the individual is drowned. This chasm of oblivion separates the quotidian reality from the Dionysiac. But as soon as that quotidian reality enters consciousness once more it is viewed with loathing, and the consequence is an ascetic, aboulic state of mind. In this sense Dionysiac man might be said to resemble Hamlet: both have looked deeply into the true nature of things, they have *understood* and are now loath to act. They realize that no action of theirs can work any change in the eternal condition of things, and they regard the imputation as ludicrous or debasing that they should set right the time which is out of joint. Understanding kills action, for in order to act we require the veil of illusion; such is Hamlet's doctrine, not to be confounded with the cheap wisdom of John-a-

Dreams, who through too much reflection, as it were a surplus of possibilities, never arrives at action. What, both in the case of Hamlet and of Dionysiac man, overbalances any motive leading to action, is not reflection but understanding, the apprehension of truth and its terror. Now no comfort any longer avails, desire reaches beyond the transcendental world, beyond the gods themselves, and existence, together with its gulling reflection in the gods and an immortal Beyond, is denied. The truth once seen, man is aware everywhere of the ghastly absurdity of existence, comprehends the symbolism of Ophelia's fate and the wisdom of the wood sprite Silenus: nausea invades him.

Then, in this supreme jeopardy of the will, art, that sorceress expert in healing, approaches him; only she can turn his fits of nausea into imaginations with which it is possible to live. These are on the one hand the spirit of the *sublime*, which subjugates terror by means of art; on the other hand the *comic* spirit, which releases us, through art, from the tedium of absurdity. The satyr chorus of the dithyramb was the salvation of Greek art; the threatening paroxysms I have mentioned were contained by the intermediary of those Dionysiac attendants.

*

The satyr and the idyllic shepherd of later times have both been products of a desire for naturalness and simplicity. But how firmly the Greek shaped his wood sprite, and how self-consciously and mawkishly the modern dallies with his tender, fluting shepherd! For the Greek the satyr expressed nature in a rude, uncultivated state: he did not, for that reason, confound him with the monkey. Quite the contrary, the satyr was man's true prototype, an expression of his highest and strongest aspirations. He was an enthusiastic reveller, filled with transport by the approach of the god; a compassionate companion re-enacting the sufferings of the god; a prophet of wisdom born out of nature's womb; a symbol of the sexual omnipotence of nature, which the Greek was accustomed to view with reverent wonder. The satyr was sublime and divine – so he must have looked to the traumatically wounded vision of Dionysiac man. Our tricked-out, contrived shepherd would have offended him, but his eyes rested with sublime satisfaction on the open, undistorted limnings of nature. Here archetypal man was cleansed of the illusion of culture, and what revealed itself was authentic man, the bearded satyr jubilantly greeting his god. Before him cultured man dwindled to a false cartoon. Schiller is also correct as regards these beginnings of the tragic art: the chorus is a living wall against the onset of reality because it depicts reality more truthfully and more completely than does civilized man, who ordinarily considers himself the only reality. Poetry does not lie outside the world as a fantastic impossibility begotten of the poet's brain; it seeks to be the exact opposite, an unvarnished expression of truth, and for this reason must cast away the trumpery garments worn by the supposed reality of civilized man. The contrast between this truth of nature and the pretentious lie of civilization is quite similar to that between the eternal core of things and the entire phenomenal world. Even as tragedy, with its metaphysical solace, points to the eternity of true being surviving every phenomenal change, so does the symbolism of the satyr chorus express analogically the primordial relation between the thing in itself and appearance. The idyllic shepherd of modern man is but a replica of the sum of cultural illusions which he mistakes for nature. The Dionysiac Greek, desiring truth and nature at their highest power, sees himself metamorphosed into the satyr.

Such are the dispositions and insights of the revelling throng of Dionysus; and the power of these dispositions and insights transforms them in their own eyes, until they behold themselves restored to the condition of genii, of satyrs. Later the tragic chorus came to be an aesthetic imitation of that natural phenomenon; which then necessitated a distinction between Dionysiac spectators and votaries actually spellbound by the god. What must be kept in mind in all these investigations is that the audience of Attic tragedy discovered *itself* in the chorus of the orchestra. Audience and chorus were never fundamentally set against each other: all was one grand chorus of dancing, singing satyrs, and of those who let themselves be represented by them. . . .

Enchantment is the precondition of all dramatic art. In this enchantment the Dionysiac reveller sees himself as satyr, and as satyr, in turn, he sees the god. In his transformation he sees a new vision, which is the Apollonian completion of his state. And by the same token this new vision completes the dramatic act.

Thus we have come to interpret Greek tragedy as a Dionysiac chorus which again and again discharges itself in Apollonian images. Those choric portions with which the tragedy is interlaced constitute, as it were, the matrix of the *dialogue*, that is to say, of the entire stage-world of the actual drama. This substratum of tragedy irradiates, in several consecutive discharges, the vision of the drama – a vision on the one hand completely of the nature of Apollonian dream-illusion and therefore epic, but on the other hand, as the objectification of a Dionysiac condition, tending towards the shattering of the individual and his fusion with the original One-ness. Tragedy is an Apollonian embodiment of Dionysiac insights and powers, and for that reason separated by a tremendous gulf from the epic.

On this view the chorus of Greek tragedy, symbol of an entire multitude agitated by Dionysus, can be fully explained. Whereas we who are accustomed to the role of the chorus in modern theatre, especially opera, find it hard to conceive how the chorus of the Greeks should have been older, more central than the dramatic action proper (although we have clear testimony to this effect); and whereas we have never been quite able to reconcile with this position of importance the fact that the chorus was composed of such lowly beings as – originally – goatlike satyrs; and whereas, further, the orchestra in front of the stage has always seemed a riddle to us – we now realize that the stage with its action was originally conceived as pure vision and that the only reality was the chorus, who created that vision out of itself and proclaimed it through the medium of dance, music, and spoken word. Since in this vision, the chorus beholds its lord and master Dionysus, it remains forever an *attending* chorus; it sees how the god suffers and transforms himself, and it has, for that reason, no need to act. But, notwithstanding its subordination to the god, the chorus remains the highest expression of nature, and, like nature, utters in its enthusiasm oracular words of wisdom. Being compassionate as well as wise, it proclaims a truth that issues from the heart of the world. Thus we see how that fantastic and at first sight embarrassing figure arises, the wise and enthusiastic satyr who is at the same time the 'simpleton' as opposed to the god. The satyr is a replica of nature in its strongest tendencies and at the same time a herald of its wisdom and art. He combines in his person the roles of musician, poet, dancer, and visionary. . . .

Everything that rises to the surface in the Apollonian portion of Greek tragedy (in the dialogue) looks simple, transparent, beautiful. In this sense the dialogue is a mirror of the Greek mind, whose nature manifests itself in dance, since in dance the maximum power is only potentially present, betraying itself in the suppleness and opulence of movement. The language of the Sophoclean heroes surprises us by its Apollonian determinacy and lucidity. It seems to us that we can fathom their innermost being, and we are somewhat surprised that we had such a short way to go. However, once we abstract from the character of the hero as it rises to the surface and becomes visible (a character at bottom no more than a luminous shape projected on to a dark wall, that is to say, *appearance* through and through) and instead penetrate into the myth which is projected in these luminous reflections, we suddenly come up against a phenomenon which is the exact opposite of a familiar optical one. After an energetic attempt to focus on the sun, we have, by way of remedy almost, dark spots before our eyes when we turn away. Conversely, the luminous images of the Sophoclean heroes – those Apollonian masks – are the necessary productions of a deep look into the horror of nature; luminous spots, as it were, designed to cure an eye hurt by the ghastly night. Only in this way can we form an adequate notion of the seriousness of Greek 'serenity'; whereas we find that serenity is generally misinterpreted nowadays as a condition of undisturbed complacence.

from sections VII, VIII, and IX of *The Birth of Tragedy*, 1872. Translated by Francis Golffing

---

THIRTY-TWO

The Implications of Tragedy

CLIFFORD LEECH

THE gulf between the learned use and the popular use of the same word is nowhere better illustrated than in 'tragedy'. The term is used from day to day in referring to incidents of a distressful nature, and, in so far as it is popularly used as the name of a literary type, it is applied to any play or story with an unhappy ending. This is unfortunate, for the widespread vague use of the term makes it more difficult for students to clarify their ideas on the significance of *King Lear* and the *Agamemnon*: if our labels are smudged, we are forced to make a continual effort to remind ourselves of the contents of each package. Yet here we cannot blame the journalist for the blurring of the word's meaning, for the vague use of 'tragedy' goes back to medieval times. Moreover, even those who have aimed at using the word precisely have not reached agreement concerning the nature of the literary type to which the word is, by then, applied.

The most famous definition of tragedy in medieval times is given by Chaucer in the Prologue to *The Monk's Tale*:

> Tragedie is to seyn a certeyn storie,
> As olde bokes maken us memorie,
> Of him that stood in greet prosperitie
> And is y-fallen out of heigh degree
> Into miserie, and endeth wrecchedly.

He adds that tragedies are commonly written in hexameters, but that 'many oon' has been written in prose as well as in other metres. Similarly in his translation of Boethius he adds the gloss:

> Tragedie is to seyn, a ditee of a prosperitie for a tyme, that endeth in wrecchednesse.

It is evident that, in Chaucer's view, a tragedy need not be written in dramatic form. This rose out of the break in continuity between the drama of antiquity and the drama of the medieval church, and indeed most medieval references to tragedy similarly make no mention of dramatic representation. But this is not the only omission which strikes us in Chaucer's definition, for he indicates no cause for the fall from high degree. This, however, he had to consider when writing the 'tragedies' of *The Monk's Tale*: he could not pen tales of woe without implying why the woe came about. In the opening lines of *The Monk's Tale* he averred that it was Fortune who was responsible for the change in a man's estate: capriciously she might turn her back, and man should steel himself for these methodless reversals. On the other hand, in some of the Monk's 'tragedies' a totally different idea is put forward: man is there frequently robbed of his prosperity on account of sin: Adam, for example, is turned out of Paradise 'for misgovernaunce'. Chaucer, in fact, hesitates in his conception of tragedy in much the same way as do most people who tell sad tales: at times they believe that misfortunes come because they are merited, at times they feel that there is such a thing as bad luck: they waver between a planned universe of rewards and punishments and a chaotic universe in which chance operates without motive.

Yet if Chaucer's use of the term is the common one, we should recognize that literary theorists have been justified in trying to use the term more precisely. They have felt that certain pieces of dramatic literature are of a special kind, leaving an impression on our minds which is peculiar to themselves, and thus demanding a special label. Aristotle in Chapter 6 of *The Poetics* produced a definition of tragedy which has served as a starting-point for every modern critic who has attempted to describe the effect of plays of this kind; and though the definition is obscure in the crucial point, that of *catharsis*, it provides clear evidence that Aristotle recognized tragic plays as constituting a special *genre*. At the same time Aristotle illustrates how difficult it is to be precise concerning the nature of his *genre*: in Chapter 13 he claims that the tragic hero, 'a man not pre-eminently virtuous and just', should fall from prosperity to misery through a fatal flaw in his character or an error of judgement, and thus he defends the unhappy ending in tragedy; in Chapter 14, however, he gives especial praise to that type of tragedy in which disaster is avoided at the last moment through the revelation of something previously unknown. The contradiction may well be due to the conflicting claims of philosophic theory and dramatic effectiveness. In any event, it may serve as a warning of the difficulty of achieving consistency in a theory of tragedy, and of deciding exactly which plays are to be accepted as tragic.

It is not my purpose here to consider the many explanations of *catharsis* that have been put forward from the time of the Italian Renaissance critics. In all likelihood Aristotle's notion was that tragedy served as a safety-valve, a means of freeing the mind from the pity and the fear that might otherwise enter public or private life, and Mr F. L. Lucas may be right in his belief that Aristotle claimed this cathartic effect for tragedy as a defence against the charges of Plato. But that the emotions of pity and fear are concerned in the tragic effect has not been disputed by any subsequent theorist. Dr I. A. Richards, indeed, has seen these two emotions as opposing forces which tragedy brings into a state of equilibrium. For him the tragic effect is the achievement of a state of repose in the nervous system, a repose without inertia because it is the result of a perpetual opposition (*Principles of Literary Criticism* p. 245):

Pity, the impulse to approach, and terror, the impulse to retreat, are brought in tragedy to a reconciliation which they find nowhere else, and with them who knows what other allied groups of equally discordant impulses. Their union in an ordered single response is the *catharsis* by which tragedy is recognized, whether Aristotle meant anything of this kind or not. This is the explanation of that sense of release, of repose in the midst of stress, of balance and composure, given by tragedy, for there is no other way in which such impulses, once awakened, can be set at rest without suppression.

But the difficulty about this is that Dr Richards does not tell us what it is that we feel an impulse to approach and a simultaneous impulse to retreat from. We feel pity – or perhaps sympathy would be the better word – with reference to the tragic hero and to other characters who are involved in disaster, but we are not terrified by him or them. Even where the tragic hero, like Orestes or Macbeth, causes fear to the other characters, we do not share their feelings. Our fear is aroused by the picture of the universe that the tragic writer presents, we are impelled to retreat from the contemplation of evil, we should like to shut our eyes if we could. If, therefore, the pity and the fear are aroused by different stimuli, it is difficult to see how any balancing of them can be other than fortuitous. Our sympathy with Hamlet is greater than our sympathy with Othello, because most of us find Hamlet the more attractive character: yet it would be a rash assumption that the play of *Hamlet* arouses more terror than the play of *Othello*. Moreover, Dr Richards's view of tragedy is weighted on the therapeutic side. He claims that it makes us feel that 'all is right . . . in the nervous system', but he neglects that part of our experience which is the recognition that the dramatist's view of the universe is terrible as well as strengthening.

Yet the idea that the tragic effect resides in an equilibrium of opposing forces does seem to correspond with our experience. After witnessing a successful performance of one of Shakespeare's four great tragedies, or of Webster's *The Duchess of Malfi*, or of the *Agamemnon*, our state of mind is active, and yet active to no immediate end: we are in a state of unusual stimulation, and yet we are more inclined to contemplate the experience than to plan our future conduct: we have seen a picture of evil, but it has neither palsied our faculties nor aroused us to struggle against it.

It is not surprising, therefore, that Professor Una Ellis-Fermor has also seen a balance of opposing forces in the effect of tragedy. For her the balance is between the view that the world is controlled by an alien and hostile destiny and the view that somehow this apparent evil may be explained in terms of good. She points out that in the *Agamemnon* and the *Choëphoroë* Aeschylus presents the evil of things through the actions and the words of the actors, and through the speeches of the Chorus suggests that outside the human world there is a divine organization of things. In Shakespeare, she suggests, the fact that such characters as Cordelia and Kent can exist must lead to what she calls a 'positive' interpretation – that is, an idea that the universe is under benevolent direction. Feeling, perhaps, that the indications of goodness are in some indubitable tragedies rather too slight, Professor Ellis-Fermor adds that the very principle of order apparent in the formal articulation of tragic plays acts as a counterpoise to the evil chaos that seems to prevail. Her view, in brief, is that the tragic equilibrium consists in the simultaneous holding in the mind of the two conflicting ideas: that the universe is divinely directed and that it is devil-ridden. She implies, however, that this equilibrium is impermanent, that the tragic writer may find his way beyond it to an acceptance of the idea of divine control, and she refers here to Shakespeare's final romances as evidence that Shakespeare escaped from the dark vision of *Othello* and *Lear*.

The difficulty in Professor Ellis-Fermor's position is that the indications of a divinely controlled universe are in many tragedies scarcely sufficient to counterpoise the presentation of evil. It is not enough that in *Othello* we have characters who mean no harm: Othello and Desdemona are well-intentioned enough, but their disaster comes upon them through his credulity and her lack of directness: in view of the magnitude of the suffering that is brought about by these comparatively minor faults, it is difficult to see that their good qualities point to a divinely controlled universe. And the control of art need suggest nothing more than that man has a certain faculty for ordering part of his experience: it does not transform the nature of that experience, and it does not necessarily suggest that either he or a creator can control the totality of experience.

That there is an equilibrium of forces in the tragic effect I think we can admit, but Professor Ellis-Fermor has looked too far in trying to reconcile the tragic and the Christian pictures of life. We need to examine the tragic picture in more detail – to consider, banishing pre-suppositions as far as we can, the view of life offered to us by plays that we will all agree to have a similar effect on us, plays that we will not hesitate to call 'tragic'.

Not only are great evil and suffering presented in such plays but there is no comprehensible scheme of rewards and punishments suggested. Oedipus sins, as Aristotle puts it, through an error of judgement, yet he is led to a state of mind where even the thought of death is no escape from the horror; Othello is induced to murder his innocent wife and then to realize his mistake: only suicide offers itself as a way out; Desdemona and Ophelia are guilty of nothing more than weakness, yet they are destroyed; Lear is hot-tempered and foolish, yet no one will claim that he deserved to endure madness and the storm on the heath; Cordelia refuses to play her father's game, and is hanged for it; Gloucester begets Edmund, and his eyes are plucked out; Webster's Duchess of Malfi loves and marries her steward Antonio, and on that account is slowly tortured to death. Moreover, the plays frequently include a number of minor characters whose sudden and cruel deaths do not arise out of any fault of their own: Lady Macduff and her son, Polonius, Rosencrantz and Guildenstern, the brave servant in *King Lear* who tries to save Gloucester from blindness, the virtuous Marcello in Webster's *The White Devil* – all these can hardly be said to get their deserts. It is true that in some tragedies the final disaster springs from an evil act on the part of the hero – *Macbeth* and the plays of Marlowe come quickly to the mind – but even there we feel no satisfaction in the hero's punishment. Rather, we have a feeling that his initial conduct was hardly within his own control: Macbeth was singularly unfortunate in the joint temptation from the witches and his wife, and the witches' prophecy suggests from the beginning that his crime was predetermined; Marlowe's heroes are felt to act as they do because the world is what it is, a world which presents a perpetual challenge to the man of high courage. Thus we feel no desire to rejoice when the perpetrator of evil is brought to his doom, and at the same time we are aware that many characters in these plays are subjected to an evil for which they are in no way responsible.

Nor is there in great tragedy the suggestion that these things will be put right in another world. It is true that in comparatively minor works like Kyd's *The Spanish Tragedy* we are assured in an epilogue that the hero and his supporters will find their way to the Elysian Fields while their adversaries will know infernal tortures, but in *Othello* and *Lear* and *Macbeth* there is no such emphasis on a compensatory future life. Othello contemplates immortality only with horror:

> O ill-starr'd wench!
> Pale as thy smock! When we shall meet at compt,
> This look of thine will hurl my soul from heaven,
> And fiends will snatch at it.   v. 2. 273

Cleopatra assumes a heavenly encounter with Antony, and fears that Iras will get to him first:

> This proves me base:
> If she first meet the curlèd Antony,
> He'll make demand of her, and spend that kiss
> Which is my heaven to have.   v. 2. 298

Her speech is no consolation to the audience, who are made to feel only the strange limitations of this late tragic figure. In *Hamlet* heavenly joys are on occasion referred to: Horatio's

> Good night, sweet prince,
> And flights of angels sing thee to thy rest!   v. 2. 351

and Laertes's

> I tell thee, churlish priest,
> A minist'ring angel shall my sister be
> When thou liest howling.   v. 1. 239

are, however, pieces of embroidery on the situation of the moment rather than functional utterances in the play. Indeed, *Hamlet* is essentially a play of doubt concerning what happens after death, and we are likely to agree that in no Shakespearian tragedy are we made to think of the characters as emerging from their suffering into the beatific vision: the stresses they encounter are not preparations for a future life but are inescapable conditions of the only world in which they certainly have an existence. What may or may not happen after death is something that the tragic dramatist normally leaves out of consideration: on the rare occasions when he does consider it, as Marlowe does in *Faustus*, it is to see it as part of the evil which his tragic hero must endure.

Because of the apparent absence of a kindly or just disposition of things in the world and because of his disregard of a future life, the tragic dramatist inevitably sees the gods as remote, if not as beings actively hostile to man. Perhaps the remoteness of the gods is given most succinct expression in Webster's *The Duchess of Malfi*, where the Duchess is subjected to intense mental torture before she is finally killed. Hearing false news of the death of her husband and children, she cries out that she could curse the star: Bosola, her enemies' instrument, lets her tongue run on in grief for a few moments and then bids her look heavenward:

> Look you, the stars shine still.   IV. 1

All seventeenth-century English tragedy is, indeed, marked by a feeling that, if there are gods who control the universe, they are far away from men, and indifferent to the individual's fate. Sometimes this sense of remoteness becomes sharpened into a belief that the gods are malicious, enjoying the impotence and the suffering in the world beneath them. Gloucester's cry in his despair:

> As flies to wanton boys are we to th' gods –
> They kill us for their sport.   IV. 2. 37

is almost paralleled by this piece of bitterness from *The Duchess of Malfi*:

> We are merely the stars' tennis-balls, struck and bandied
> Which way please them.   V. 4.

But these are dramatic utterances, mere exclamations of the characters' despair, and are no more to be taken as expressing the totality of the playwright's attitude than are the words of Horatio and Laertes, already quoted, envisaging post-lethal joys. In the tragedies of the Greeks the gods intervene more directly than in Elizabethan tragedy, but there, too, there is no assurance of an even-handed justice in the fates of men, and no suggestion that man can find his compensation in an after-life. When, as in the *Eumenides*, the dramatist tries to humanize the justice of the gods, the play becomes more of a civic pageant than a tragedy: the acquittal of Orestes through the casting-vote of Pallas answers no questions but diverts the spectators' emotions into a new, and non-tragic, direction. But when a play is consistently tragic, the Greek writer does not see a man's problems as solved by a mere appeal to the gods.

Nevertheless, it is noticeable that tragedy does not necessarily or even normally present an indictment of the divine powers. Professor Ellis-Fermor is certainly right in claiming for the choric utterances in the *Agamemnon* an expression of faith in the divine plan: here, indeed, is a passage which simultaneously brings out the remoteness of Zeus and the divine guidance of man through suffering to wisdom:

> Zeus, whoever He is, if this
> Be a name acceptable,
> By this name I will call him.
> There is no one comparable
> When I reckon all of the case
> Excepting Zeus, if ever I am to jettison
> The barren care which clogs my heart.

Not He who formerly was great
With brawling pride and mad for broils
Will even be said to have been.
And He who was next has met
His match and is seen no more,
But Zeus is the name to cry in your triumph-song
And win the prize for wisdom.

Who setting us on the road
Made this a valid law –
'That men must learn by suffering.'
Drop by drop in sleep upon the heart
Falls the laborious memory of pain,
Against one's will comes wisdom;
The grace of the gods is forced on us
Throned inviolably.

Agamemnon (tr. Louis MacNeice) p. 18

Man thus has no certain knowledge even of God's name, and God is without pity in his hard discipline. So, too, it is remarkable that in *King Lear* there are repeated references to divine justice. When Albany hears that Cornwall was killed immediately after he had plucked out Gloucester's eyes, his comment is:

> This shows you are above,
> You justicers, that these our nether crimes
> So speedily can venge.   IV. 2. 78

And the deaths of Goneril and Regan bring from him these words:

> This judgment of the heavens, that makes us tremble,
> Touches us not with pity.   V. 3. 231

Most striking of all is Edgar's comment to his dying brother, Edmund: he sees the misery of their father as springing from the dissolute begetting of Edmund, and pronounces that

> The gods are just, and of our pleasant vices
> Make instruments to plague us.
> The dark and vicious place where thee he got
> Cost him his eyes.   V. 3. 170

This terrible sentence seems as outrageous to our moral sense as the hanging of Cordelia or the torture of Webster's Duchess. What kind of justice, we wonder, is this, which will seize on so small a fault and inflict so terrible a punishment? The 'justice' of the gods, as seen in tragedy, is as terrible as their indifference: in fact, we shall not see tragedy aright unless we recognize that the divine justice mirrored in it is an indifferent justice, a justice which cares no whit for the individual and is not concerned with a nice balance of deserts and rewards.

This justice operates like an avalanche or an echo in an enclosed space. If an evil act is committed, no matter how trifling, it will bring consequences which are far more evil than the original act. Lear, vain and delighting in power and its display, indecently demands a public profession of love from his daughters: that leads to the events of the heath, the hanging of Cordelia, the loss of Gloucester's eyes, civil war, and Lear's own death. Thyestes seduces his brother's wife, and the long train of disasters begins for the house of Atreus. Sometimes, however, it is a neutral act which provides the starting-point: the marriage of Webster's Duchess to her steward Antonio shows only a mild disregard for 'degree', but it releases the evil forces which have been stored up in the minds of her brothers. The justice of the gods consists simply in the natural law that every act must have its consequence and that the consequence will be determined by the act and its context. If the act is in any way evil or if the situation is one with evil potentialities, then a train of evil will be the result. The tragic writer believes in causation, in the doctrine that means determine ends, and in the powerlessness of the human will to interrupt a chain of disasters.

We may therefore easily understand why the revenge-motive is so common in Greek and Elizabethan tragedy: the blood-feud is the most obvious example of the kind of situation in which wrong inevitably succeeds to wrong.

In such a world-picture as the tragic writer presents to us, it may appear difficult to see how an equilibrium of forces can exist. The impact on our minds of such inhuman justice would at first sight appear only terrible and paralysing. Yet it remains true that our experience of tragic drama is not like that. When we think of Shakespeare's tragedies, of Webster's, of Marlowe's, or of modern tragedies like Mr Eugene O'Neill's *Mourning Becomes Electra*, or Mr Sean O'Casey's *Juno and the Paycock*, what we recall is made up of an indifferent universe and certain characters who seem to demand our admiration. Whether the characters are comparatively blameless, like Hamlet or Webster's Duchess, or deeply guilty, like Macbeth, we feel that they have a quality of mind that somehow atones for the nature of the world in which they and we live. They have, in a greater or lesser degree, the power to endure and the power to apprehend: ultimately they are destroyed, but in all their sufferings they show an increasing readiness to endure, an ever greater awareness. As the shadows gather around them, they stand up the more resolutely, they see the human situation with clearer eyes. Webster's Duchess is at the beginning of the play merely an attractive and enterprising woman, but it is when she cries, in the midst of torment: 'I am Duchess of Malfi still', that we recognize her full stature. Lear develops even more remarkably from a vain, hot-tempered tyrant to a man who sees the omnipresence of social wrong and bodily distress of the poor. So, too, our attitude to Electra and Orestes and Oedipus is inevitably one of growing admiration. Because, moreover, the dramatist has made it clear that his tragic hero is human, a man with weaknesses like our own, we feel not merely admiration but pride: we are proud of our human nature because in such characters it comes to fine flower. In a planned but terrible universe we see man justifying his existence.

Thus the equilibrium of tragedy consists in a balancing of Terror with Pride. On the one hand, we are impelled to withdraw from the spectacle, to try to forget the revelation of evil methodized; on the other, we are roused to withstand destiny, to strive to meet it with the fortitude and the clear eyes of the tragic figure. This feeling of Pride comes into full existence when the hero knows his fate and contemplates it: it is essentially distinct from the *hubris* which he may display, but which we cannot share in, before his eyes are opened.

The tragic picture of the universe postulates a limited free will. Man cannot determine the pattern of events, but he is frequently responsible either for the initiation of an evil chain or for the release of evil forces latent in a situation. Moreover, his thoughts and feelings, his attitude to the enveloping situation, are in his own control: like Orestes, he can see the horror of the matricide he must commit; like Macbeth, he can recognize his own weakness and ultimately his own insignificance in the universal scheme. Some degree of free will is, indeed, essential in tragedy, for we could hardly feel proud of an automaton.

Because of its closer approximation to the everyday appearance of things, there seems to be a greater degree of free will in Elizabethan than in Greek tragedy: it seems as if Hamlet could deflect the course of the action at almost any point if he wished, while clearly Orestes and Oedipus are bound to an established pattern. But Shakespeare and his contemporaries have gone out of their way to make us realize that the pattern is pre-ordained for their characters too: in some plays Shakespeare uses supernatural devices to indicate the course of future events – for example in *Macbeth, Julius Caesar,* and *Antony and Cleopatra* – and always he draws his characters in such a way that there is clearly only one line of conduct possible for them in the particular situation in which they find themselves: for them it is the doom-in-the-character rather than the doom-on-the-house. Hamlet must be killed because Hamlet in his particular situation can have no other end: his fate is as inevitable as that of a man lost in the heart of a desert.

Dr E. M. W. Tillyard has put forward an idea of tragedy that must be considered. This has, indeed, often been suggested by writers who have tried to dilute the element of Terror in tragic plays, asserting that in tragedy, as in real life, we see how man can learn and be redeemed through suffering. Dr Tillyard's presentation of this idea is linked up with his view of the *Oresteia* and of Shakespeare's final romances. He sees tragedy as a picture of life disturbed by the intrusion of a disruptive evil force, the apparent triumph of that force, and then the reassertion of a normality which has been strengthened through trial. He points to Othello's last speech, to Lear's wider sympathy near the close of his drama, to Shakespeare's own passage through the despondency of *Timon* to the serenity of *The Tempest.* Certainly our pride in Lear grows as the play proceeds, he emerges as a great figure through the increasing darkness of the situation, but this is not to say that normality resumes her reign, all the better for the testing-time. Lear dies, defeated: that is the essential reason for our Terror; our Pride comes from his acceptance and full knowledge of the situation. The potentialities of evil and suffering are as strong as ever, the gods as ruthless, man's will as powerless. At the end of a Shakespearian tragedy, as at the end of Marlowe's *Faustus* or of *Oedipus at Colonus*, we have a quiet close: words of peace are spoken, and we are conscious that the evil situation no longer exists: the forces of evil have worked themselves out: Hamlet and all his kin are dead. There is nothing reassuring in the new situation, no promise that a new chain of evil will not quickly ensue, no lesson that men or the gods have learned. No message of hope for the future has been brought. The tragic situation, it is implied, is recurrent in human life: that is why we feel Terror; because we have seen men like ourselves yet stronger than we could expect to be, we feel also Pride.

Thus the tragic picture is incompatible with the Christian faith. It is equally incompatible with any form of religious belief that assumes the existence of a personal and kindly God. For that reason we should not be surprised at the rarity of tragedy. Chaucer's view of it as a story of a fall from prosperity to wretchedness, either at the bidding of Fortune or through divine retribution, is a mixture of unconscious paganism with Christian tradition: we cannot expect to find true tragedy anywhere in the Middle Ages, except here and there in early times when literature was not thoroughly Christianized. We can indeed recognize something of the tragic spirit of English poetry before the Conquest, from *Beowulf* to *The Battle of Maldon*. But we should not look for tragedy in the drama of seventeenth-century Spain, for always there the spirit of religion burned brightly: Calderón and Lope de Vega might show evil in their plays, but it was an evil which attended on divine forgiveness or on an acceptable retribution; they might show suffering, but with them indeed it was the suffering of purgatorial fire. Nor should we look for tragedy in the classical drama of India: the gods there are seen as close to man, as his friends and teachers, ready to test human beings but ultimately to reward virtue wherever it should show itself. We can, however, find tragedy in those European countries which were brought most fully under Renaissance influences, with a weakening of medieval faith and some return to stoicism. In the atmosphere of comparative toleration under Elizabeth and James, English tragedy was especially free to develop. In seventeenth-century France, Racine could write tragically, though the form of his plays makes them appear almost like careful exercises in imitation of the classics: there is a lack of immediacy, of direct relation to the life around him, which perhaps made both the author and his audience feel safer: there was no compulsion for them to take too seriously the tragic view of things there presented. But from the seventeenth century until comparatively recent years the tragic form has been exceedingly rare, not because of a revival of religious faith, but because in these years men have not often combined a sharp sense of evil, a faith in man, and a sense of the impersonality of divine justice. In later days it is the faith in man that has been most difficult to come by, though tragedy has made an occasional appearance in modern European and American drama, and the tragic spirit has not infrequently found non-dramatic expression in the modern novel.

But whenever tragedy has come into being, its customary and right dress has been poetry. The equilibrium of Pride and Terror is, as we have seen, an opposition of persistent forces, and consequently the tragic play is characterized by strong tension. An appearance of casualness in the play will weaken the tension, and contradict the implication of a pre-ordained pattern of event. Moreover, in order that the spectator's mind may more fully respond to the vision of evil and of human strength in defeat, the language must be finely turned. The medium of tragedy must be poetry, or at least a kind of prose which in its formal properties is clearly distinguished from the prose of the everyday, haphazard situation – not because the beauty of the words will atone for the presentation of evil, soothing our nerves and dulling our perceptions, but because only by a co-ordination of our faculties can we reach a full realization of any complex picture of the world. Tragedy offers us a view of things which aims at comprehensiveness, and thus in its scope resembles the great religions of east and west. Like them, therefore, it needs all the resources of language for communications with men.

from *Shakespeare's Tragedies*, 1950

THIRTY-THREE

The Elizabethan View of Tragedy

EVANTHIUS

The Elizabethan answer to the question What is tragedy? was very different from ours. Perhaps the most convenient statement of it is this passage, written in late Roman times, perhaps by one Evanthius, and found in a commentary on Terence by Donatus. As far as we can judge from their writings, all Elizabethan critics would have agreed with it.

What must strike any modern reader is how different it is from our definitions – from *any* of the conflicting definitions that dispute the concept nowadays. The second last point ('fugienda vita') probably has the nearest to a modern ring. But the sad ending? This seems incidental to us, a consequence, not a part, of the tragic effect. And the differences of social level between tragic and comic characters? The Elizabethans must have believed this, their tragic heroes were kings and princes. There were a few attempts at domestic tragedy, but they never caught on. And why need a comic story be more fictitious than a tragic one?

We can say that the Elizabethans *did* have a different conception of tragedy from ours: but then we must wonder if we are deceiving ourselves when we respond to their plays. Or we can say that they could write the tragedies and respond to them, but that the ability to articulate that response is a recent one: that we can see, better than they could, what they were really doing. Some historically-minded critics reject this theory indignantly, because it seems to patronize the past. If we accept it, we must wonder if our conception of tragedy will look equally naïve to a future age that may still appreciate our plays. Or we can say that Elizabethan (and ancient) criticism is not as naïve as it looks; that we do not understand the full implications of what it says; and that when the intellectuals repaired from the Globe theatre to the Mermaid tavern to argue about *King Lear* they made, in their awkward critical vocabulary, many of the points that we make today. This is such an attractive theory that it's a pity there isn't more evidence for it.

*

AMONG the many differences between tragedy and comedy, the

following is the principal one: that in comedy the characters are of moderate estate, the passions and dangers are mild, the outcome of the action is happy; but exactly the opposite is true of tragedy: the characters are great, the dangers severe, the conclusion sad. Furthermore, in comedy things are upset at the beginning and peaceful at the close, in tragedy things take place in the reverse order. Tragedies express the view that life should be rejected, comedies that it should be embraced. Finally, the events of comedy are always fictitious, those of tragedy are often true and taken from history.

THIRTY-FOUR

Shakespeare and the Stoicism of Seneca

T. S. ELIOT

THE last few years have witnessed a number of recrudescences of Shakespeare. There is the fatigued Shakespeare, a retired Anglo-Indian, presented by Mr Lytton Strachey; there is the messianic Shakespeare, bringing a new philosophy and a new system of yoga, presented by Mr Middleton Murry; and there is the ferocious Shakespeare, a furious Samson, presented by Mr Wyndham Lewis in his interesting book, *The Lion and the Fox*. On the whole, we may all agree that these manifestations are beneficial. In any case, in so important a case as that of Shakespeare, it is good that we should from time to time change our minds. The last conventional Shakespeare is banished from the scene, and a variety of unconventional Shakespeares take his place. About anyone so great as Shakespeare, it is probable that we can never be right; and if we can never be right, it is better that we should from time to time change our way of being wrong. Whether Truth ultimately prevails is doubtful and has never been proved; but it is certain that nothing is more effective in driving out error than a new error. Whether Mr Strachey, or Mr Murry, or Mr Lewis, is any nearer to the truth of Shakespeare than Rymer, or Morgann, or Webster, or Johnson, is uncertain; they are all certainly more sympathetic in this year 1927 than Coleridge, or Swinburne, or Dowden. If they do not give us the real Shakespeare – if there is one – they at least give us several up-to-date Shakespeares. If the only way to prove that Shakespeare did not feel and think exactly as people felt and thought in 1815, or in 1860, or in 1880, is to show that he felt and thought as we felt and thought in 1927, then we must accept gratefully that alternative.

But these recent interpreters of Shakespeare suggest a number of reflections on literary criticism and its limits, on general aesthetics, and on the limitations of the human understanding.

There are, of course, a number of other current interpretations of

Shakespeare: that is, of the *conscious opinions* of Shakespeare: interpretations of category, so to speak: which make him either a Tory journalist, or a Liberal journalist, or a Socialist journalist (though Mr Shaw has done something to warn off his co-religionists from claiming Shakespeare, or from finding anything uplifting in his work); we have also a Protestant Shakespeare, and a sceptical Shakespeare, and some case may be made out for an Anglo-Catholic, or even a Papist Shakespeare. My own frivolous opinion is that Shakespeare may have held in private life very different views from what we extract from his extremely varied published works; that there is no clue in his writings to the way in which he would have voted in the last or would vote in the next election; and that we are completely in the dark as to his attitude about prayer-book revision. I admit that my own experience, as a minor poet, may have jaundiced my outlook; that I am used to having cosmic significances, which I never suspected, extracted from my work (such as it is) by enthusiastic persons at a distance; and to being informed that something which I meant seriously is *vers de société*; and to having my personal biography reconstructed from passages which I got out of books, or which I invented out of nothing because they sounded well; and to having my biography invariably ignored in what I *did* write from personal experience; so that in consequence I am inclined to believe that people are mistaken about Shakespeare just in proportion to the relative superiority of Shakespeare to myself.

One more personal 'note': I believe that I have as high an estimate of the greatness of Shakespeare as poet and dramatist as anyone living; I certainly believe that there is nothing greater. And I would say that my only qualification for venturing to talk about him is, that I am *not* under the delusion that Shakespeare in the least resembles myself, either as I am or as I should like to imagine myself. It seems to me that one of the chief reasons for questioning Mr Strachey's Shakespeare, and Mr Murry's, and Mr Lewis's, is the remarkable resemblance which they bear to Mr Strachey, and Mr Murry and Mr Lewis respectively. I have not a very clear idea of what Shakespeare was like. But I do not conceive him as very like either Mr Strachey, or Mr Murry, or Mr Wyndham Lewis, or myself.

We have had Shakespeare explained by a variety of influences. He is explained by Montaigne, and by Machiavelli. I imagine that Mr Strachey would explain Shakespeare by Montaigne, though this would also be Mr Strachey's Montaigne (for all of Mr Strachey's favourite figures have a strong Strachey physiognomy) and not Mr Robertson's. I think that Mr Lewis, in the intensely interesting book mentioned, has done a real service in calling attention to the importance of Machiavelli in Elizabethan England, though this Machiavelli be only the Machiavelli of the *Contre-Machiavel*, and not in the least the real Machiavelli, a person whom Elizabethan England was as incapable of understanding as Georgian England, or any England, is. I think, however, that Mr Lewis has gone quite wrong if he thinks (I am not sure what he thinks) that Shakespeare, and Elizabethan England in general, was 'influenced' by the thought of Machiavelli. I think that Shakespeare, and other dramatists, used the popular Machiavellian idea, for stage purposes; but this idea was no more like Machiavelli, who was an Italian and a Roman Christian, than Mr Shaw's idea of Nietzsche – whatever that is – is like the real Nietzsche.

I propose a Shakespeare under the influence of the stoicism of Seneca. But I do not believe that Shakespeare was under the influence of Seneca. I propose it largely because I believe that after the Montaigne Shakespeare (not that Montaigne had any philosophy whatever) and after the Machiavelli Shakespeare, a stoical or Senecan Shakespeare is almost certain to be produced. I wish merely to disinfect the Senecan Shakespeare before he appears. My ambitions would be realized if I could prevent him, in so doing, from appearing at all.

I want to be quite definite in my notion of the possible influence of Seneca on Shakespeare. I think it is quite likely that Shakespeare read some of Seneca's tragedies at school. I think it quite unlikely that Shakespeare knew anything of that extraordinarily dull and uninteresting body of Seneca's prose, which was translated by Lodge and printed in 1612. So far as Shakespeare was influenced by Seneca, it was by his memories of school conning and through the influence of the Senecan tragedy of the day, through Kyd and Peele, but chiefly Kyd. That Shakespeare deliberately took a 'view of life' from Seneca there seems to be no evidence whatever.

Nevertheless, there is, in some of the great tragedies of Shakespeare, a new attitude. It is not the attitude of Seneca, but is derived from Seneca; it is slightly different from anything that can be found in French tragedy, in Corneille or in Racine; it is modern, and it culminates, if there is ever any culmination, in the attitude of Nietzsche. I cannot say that it is Shakespeare's 'philosophy'. Yet many people have lived by it; though it may only have been Shakespeare's instinctive recognition of something of theatrical utility. It is the attitude of self-dramatization assumed by some of Shakespeare's heroes at moments of tragic intensity. It is not peculiar to Shakespeare; it is conspicuous in Chapman: Bussy, Clermont and Biron all die in this way. Marston – one of the most interesting and least explored of all the Elizabethans – uses it; and Marston and Chapman were particularly Senecan. But Shakespeare, of course, does it very much better than any of the others, and makes it somehow more integral with the human nature of his characters. It is less verbal, more real. I have always felt that I have never read a more terrible exposure of human weakness – of universal human weakness – than the last great speech of Othello. (I am ignorant whether anyone else has ever adopted this view, and it may appear subjective and fantastic in the extreme.) It is usually taken at its face value, as expressing the greatness in defeat of a noble but erring nature.

> Soft you; a word or two before you go.
> I have done the state some service, and they know't –
> No more of that. I pray you, in your letters,
> When you shall these unlucky deeds relate,
> Speak of me as I am, nothing extenuate,
> Nor set down aught in malice. Then must you speak
> Of one that lov'd not wisely, but too well;
> Of one not easily jealous, but, being wrought,
> Perplexed in the extreme; of one whose hand,
> Like the base Indian, threw a pearl away
> Richer than all his tribe; of one whose subdu'd eyes,
> Albeit unused to the melting mood,
> Drop tears as fast as the Arabian trees
> Their med'cinable gum. Set you down this:
> And say besides that in Aleppo once,
> Where a malignant and a turbaned Turk

> Beat a Venetian and traduced the state,
> I took by th' throat the circumcised dog
> And smote him – thus.   V. 2. 341

What Othello seems to me to be doing in making this speech is *cheering himself up*. He is endeavouring to escape reality, he has ceased to think about Desdemona, and is thinking about himself. Humility is the most difficult of all virtues to achieve; nothing dies harder than the desire to think well of oneself. Othello succeeds in turning himself into a pathetic figure, by adopting an *aesthetic* rather than a moral attitude, dramatizing himself against his environment. He takes in the spectator, but the human motive is primarily to take in himself. I do not believe that any writer has ever exposed this *bovarysme*, the human will to see things as they are not, more clearly than Shakespeare.

If you compare the deaths of several of Shakespeare's heroes – I do not say *all*, for there are very few generalizations that can be applied to the whole of Shakespeare's work – but notably Othello, Coriolanus, and Antony – with the deaths of heroes of dramatists such as Marston and Chapman, consciously under Senecan influence, you will find a strong similarity – except only that Shakespeare does it both more poetically and more lifelike.

You may say that Shakespeare is merely illustrating, consciously or unconsciously, human nature, not Seneca. But I am not so much concerned with the influence of Seneca on Shakespeare as with Shakespeare's illustration of Senecan and stoical principles. Much of Chapman's Senecanism has lately been shown by Professor Schoell to be directly borrowed from Erasmus and other sources. I am concerned with the fact that Seneca is the *literary* representative of Roman Stoicism, and that Roman stoicism is an important ingredient in Elizabethan drama. It was natural that in a time like that of Elizabeth stoicism should appear. The original stoicism, and especially the Roman stoicism, was of course a philosophy suited to slaves: hence its absorption into early Christianity.

> A man to join himself with the Universe
> In his main sway, and make in all things fit –

A man does not join himself with the Universe so long as he has anything else to join himself with; men who could take part in the life of a thriving Greek city-state had something better to join themselves to; and Christians have had something better. Stoicism is the refuge for the individual in an indifferent or hostile world too big for him; it is the permanent substratum of a number of versions of cheering oneself up. Nietzsche is the most conspicuous modern instance of cheering oneself up. The stoical attitude is the reverse of Christian humility.

In Elizabethan England we have conditions apparently utterly different from those of imperial Rome. But it was a period of dissolution and chaos; and in such a period any emotional attitude which seems to give a man something firm, even if it be only the attitude of 'I am myself alone', is eagerly taken up. I hardly need – and it is beyond my present scope – to point out how readily, in a period like the Elizabethan, the Senecan attitude of Pride, the Montaigne attitude of Scepticism, and the Machiavellian attitude of Cynicism, arrived at a kind of fusion in the Elizabethan individualism.

This individualism, this vice of Pride, was, of course, exploited largely because of its dramatic possibilities. But other drama had before existed without depending on this human failing. You do not find it in *Polyeucte*, or in *Phèdre* either. But even Hamlet, who made a pretty considerable mess of things, and occasioned the death of at least three innocent people, and two more insignificant ones, dies fairly well pleased with himself –

> Horatio, I am dead;
> Thou livest; report me and my cause aright
> To the unsatisfied. . . .
> O God, Horatio, what a wounded name,
> Things standing thus unknown, shall live behind me!
>
> v. 2. 330

Antony says, 'I am Antony still', and the Duchess, 'I am Duchess of Malfi still'; would either of them have said that unless Medea had said *Medea superest*?

I do not wish to appear to maintain that the Elizabethan hero and the Senecan hero are identical. The influence of Seneca is much more apparent in the Elizabethan drama than it is in the plays of Seneca. The influence of any man is a different thing from himself. The Elizabethan hero is much more stoical and Senecan, in this way, than the Senecan hero. For Seneca was following the Greek tradition, which was not stoical; he developed familiar themes and imitated great models; so that the vast differences between his emotional attitude and that of the Greeks is rather latent in his work, and more apparent in the work of the Renaissance. And the Elizabethan hero, the hero of Shakespeare, was not invariable even in Elizabethan England. A notable exception is Faustus. Marlowe – not excepting Shakespeare or Chapman, the most *thoughtful* and philosophic mind, though immature, among the Elizabethan dramatists – could conceive the proud hero, as Tamburlaine, but also the hero who has reached that point of horror at which even pride is abandoned. In a recent book on Marlowe, Miss Ellis-Fermor has put very well this peculiarity of Faustus, from another point of view than mine, but in words from which I take support:

> Marlowe follows Faustus further across the borderline between consciousness and dissolution than do any of his contemporaries. With Shakespeare, with Webster, death is a sudden severing of life; their men die, conscious to the last of some part at least of their surroundings, influenced, even upheld, by that consciousness and preserving the personality and characteristics they have possessed through life. . . . In Marlowe's Faustus alone all this is set aside. He penetrates deeply into the experience of a mind isolated from the past, absorbed in the realization of its own destruction.

But Marlowe, the most thoughtful, the most blasphemous (and therefore, probably, the most Christian) of his contemporaries, is always an exception. Shakespeare is exceptional primarily by his immense superiority.

Of all of Shakespeare's plays, *King Lear* is often taken as the most Senecan in spirit. Cunliffe finds it to be imbued with a Senecan fatalism. Here, again, we must distinguish between a man and his influence. The differences between the fatalism of Greek tragedy, and the fatalism of Seneca's tragedies, and the fatalism of the Elizabethans, proceed by delicate shades; there is a continuity, and there is also a violent contrast, when we look at them from far off. In Seneca, the Greek ethics is visible underneath the Roman stoicism. In the Elizabethans, the Roman stoicism is visible beneath the Renaissance anarchism. In *King Lear* there are several significant phrases, such as those which caught the attention of Professor

Cunliffe, and there is a tone of Senecan fatalism: *fatis agimur*. But there is much less and much more. And this is the point at which I must part company with Mr Wyndham Lewis. Mr Lewis proposes a Shakespeare who is a *positive* nihilist, an intellectual force *willing* destruction. I cannot see in Shakespeare either a deliberate scepticism, as of Montaigne, or a deliberate cynicism, as of Machiavelli, or a deliberate resignation, as of Seneca. I can see that he *used* all of these things, for dramatic ends: you get perhaps more Montaigne in *Hamlet*, and more Machiavelli in *Othello*, and more Seneca in *Lear*. But I cannot agree with the following paragraph:

> With the exception of Chapman, Shakespeare is the only thinker we meet with among the Elizabethan dramatists. By this is meant, of course that his work contained, apart from poetry, phantasy, rhetoric, or observation of manners, a body of matter representing explicit processes of the intellect which would have furnished a moral philosopher like Montaigne with the natural material for his essays. But the quality of this thinking – as it can be surprised springing naturally in the midst of the consummate movements of his art – is, as must be the case with such a man, of startling force sometimes. And if it is not systematic, at least a recognizable physiognomy is there.

It is this general notion of 'thinking' that I would challenge. One has the difficulty of having to use the same words for different things. We say, in a vague way, that Shakespeare, or Dante, or Lucretius, is a poet who thinks, and that Swinburne is a poet who does not think, even that Tennyson is a poet who does not think. But what we really mean is not a difference in quality of thought, but a difference in quality of emotion. The poet who 'thinks' is merely the poet who can express the emotional equivalent of thought. But he is not necessarily interested in the thought itself. We talk as if thought was precise and emotion was vague. In reality there is precise emotion and there is vague emotion. To express precise emotion requires as great intellectual power as to express precise thought. But by 'thinking' I mean something very different from anything that I find in Shakespeare. Mr Lewis, and other champions of Shakespeare as a great philosopher, have a great deal to say about Shakespeare's power of thought, but they fail to show that he thought to any purpose; that he had any coherent view of life, or that he recommended any procedure to follow. 'We possess a great deal of evidence,' says Mr Lewis, 'as to what Shakespeare thought of military glory and martial events.' Do we? Or rather, did Shakespeare think anything at all? He was occupied with turning human actions into poetry.

I would suggest that none of the plays of Shakespeare has a 'meaning', although it would be equally false to say that a play of Shakespeare is meaningless. All great poetry gives the illusion of a view of life. When we enter into the world of Homer, or Sophocles, or Virgil, or Dante, or Shakespeare, we incline to believe that we are apprehending something that can be expressed intellectually; for every precise emotion tends towards intellectual formulation.

We are apt to be deluded by the example of Dante. Here, we think, is a poem which represents an exact intellectual system; Dante has a 'philosophy', therefore every poet as great as Dante has a philosophy too. Dante had behind him the system of St Thomas, to which his poem corresponds point to point. Therefore Shakespeare had behind him Seneca, or Montaigne, or Machiavelli; and if his work does not correspond point to point with any or a composition of these, then it must be that he did a little quiet thinking on his own, and was better than any of these people at their own job. I can see no reason for believing that either Dante or Shakespeare did any thinking on his own. The people who think that Shakespeare thought, are always people who are not engaged in writing poetry, but who are engaged in thinking, and we all like to think that great men were like ourselves. The difference between Shakespeare and Dante is that Dante had one coherent system of thought behind him; but that was just his luck, and from the point of view of poetry is an irrelevant accident. It happened that at Dante's time thought was orderly and strong and beautiful, and that it was concentrated in one man of the greatest genius; Dante's poetry receives a boost which in a sense it does not merit, from the fact that the thought behind it is the thought of a man as great and lovely as Dante himself: St Thomas. The thought behind Shakespeare is of men far inferior to Shakespeare himself: hence the alternative errors, first, that as Shakespeare was as great a poet as Dante, he must have supplied, out of his own thinking, the

difference in quality between a St Thomas and a Montaigne or a
Machiavelli or a Seneca, or second, that Shakespeare is inferior to
Dante. In truth neither Shakespeare nor Dante did any real thinking
– that was not their job; and the relative value of the thought current at their time, the material enforced upon each to use as the
vehicle of his feeling, is of no importance. It does not make Dante a
greater poet, or mean that we can learn more from Dante than from
Shakespeare. We can certainly learn more from Aquinas than from
Seneca, but that is quite a different matter. When Dante says

> la sua voluntade e nostra pace

it is great poetry, and there is a great philosophy behind it. When
Shakespeare says

> As flies to wanton boys are we to th' gods;
> They kill us for their sport. *King Lear* IV. I. 37

It is *equally* great poetry, though the philosophy behind it is not
great. But the essential is that each expresses, in perfect language,
some permanent human impulse. Emotionally, the latter is just as
strong, just as true, and just as informative – just as useful and
beneficial in the sense in which poetry is useful and beneficial, as
the former.

What every poet starts from is his own emotions. And when we
get down to these, there is not much to choose between Shakespeare
and Dante. Dante's railings, his personal spleen – sometimes thinly
disguised under Old Testament prophetic denunciations – his
nostalgia, his bitter regrets for past happiness – or for what seems
happiness when it is past – and his brave attempts to fabricate something permanent and holy out of his personal animal feelings – as in
the *Vita Nuova* – can all be matched out of Shakespeare. Shakespeare, too, was occupied with the struggle – which alone consti-
tutes life for a poet – to transmute his personal and private agonies
into something rich and strange, something universal and impersonal. The rage of Dante against Florence, or Pistoia, or what not,
the deep surge of Shakespeare's general cynicism and disillusionment, are merely gigantic attempts to metamorphose private
failures and disappointments. The great poet, in writing himself,
writes his time. Thus Dante, hardly knowing it, became the voice

of the thirteenth century; Shakespeare, hardly knowing it, became the representative of the end of the sixteenth century, of a turning point in history. But you can hardly say that Dante believed, or did not believe, the Thomist philosophy; you can hardly say that Shakespeare believed, or did not believe, the mixed and muddled scepticism of the Renaissance. If Shakespeare had written according to a better philosophy, he would have written worse poetry; it was his business to express the greatest emotional intensity of his time, based on whatever his time happened to think. Poetry is not a substitute for philosophy or theology or religion, as Mr Lewis and Mr Murry sometimes seem to think; it has its own function. But as this function is not intellectual but emotional, it cannot be defined adequately in intellectual terms. We can say that it provides 'consolation': strange consolation, which is provided equally by writers so different as Dante and Shakespeare.

What I have said could be expressed more exactly, but at much greater length, in philosophical language: it would enter into the department of philosophy which might be called the Theory of Belief (which is not psychology but philosophy, or phenomenology proper) – the department in which Meinong and Husserl have made some pioneer investigation; the different meanings which belief has in different minds according to the activity for which they are oriented. I doubt whether belief proper enters into the activity of a great poet, *qua* poet. That is, Dante, *qua* poet, did not believe or disbelieve the Thomist cosmology or theory of the soul: he merely made use of it, or a fusion took place between his initial emotional impulses and a theory, for the purpose of making poetry. The poet makes poetry, the metaphysician makes metaphysics, the bee makes honey, the spider secretes a filament; you can hardly say that any of these agents believes: he merely does.

The problem of belief is very complicated and probably quite insoluble. We must make allowance for differences in the emotional quality of believing not only between persons of different occupation, such as the philosopher and the poet, but between different periods of time. The end of the sixteenth century is an epoch when it is particularly difficult to associate poetry with systems of thought or reasoned views of life. In making some very commonplace investigations of the 'thought' of Donne, I found it quite impossible to come to the conclusion that Donne believed anything. It seemed as if, at that time, the world was filled with broken fragments of systems, and that a man like Donne merely picked up, like a magpie, various shining fragments of ideas as they struck his eye, and stuck them about here and there in his verse. Miss Ramsay, in her learned and exhaustive study of Donne's sources, came to the conclusion that he was a 'mediaeval thinker'; I could not find either any 'mediaevalism' or any thinking, but only a vast jumble of incoherent erudition on which he drew for purely poetic effects. The recent work of Professor Schoell on the sources of Chapman seems to show Chapman engaged in the same task; and suggests that the 'profundity' and 'obscurity' of Chapman's dark thinking are largely due to his lifting long passages from the works of writers like Ficino and incorporating them in his poems completely out of their context.

I do not for a moment suggest that the method of Shakespeare was anything like this. Shakespeare was a much finer instrument for transformations than any of his contemporaries, finer perhaps even than Dante. He also needed less contact in order to be able to absorb all that he required. The element of Seneca is the most completely absorbed and transmogrified, because it was already the most diffused throughout Shakespeare's world. The element of Machiavelli is probably the most indirect, the element of Montaigne the most immediate. It has been said that Shakespeare lacks unity; it might, I think, be said equally well that it is Shakespeare chiefly that *is* the unity, that unifies so far as they could be unified all the tendencies of a time that certainly lacked unity. Unity, in Shakespeare, but not universality; no one can be universal: Shakespeare would not have found much in common with his contemporary St Theresa. What influence the work of Seneca and Machiavelli and Montaigne seems to me to exert in common on that time, and most conspicuously through Shakespeare, is an influence towards a kind of self-consciousness that is new; the self-consciousness and self-dramatization of the Shakespearian hero, of whom Hamlet is only one. It seems to mark a stage, even if not a very agreeable one, in human history, or progress, or deterioration, or change. Roman stoicism was in its own time a development in self-consciousness; taken up into Christianity, it broke loose again in the dissolution of the Renaissance. Nietzsche, as I suggested, is a late variant: his attitude is a kind of stoicism upside-down: for there is not much difference between identifying oneself with the Universe and identifying the Universe with oneself. The influence of Seneca on Elizabethan drama has been exhaustively studied in its formal aspect, and in the borrowing and adaptation of phrases and situations; the penetration of Senecan sensibility would be much more difficult to trace.

from *Selected Essays,* 1927

THIRTY-FIVE

Gold Morning, Sweet Prince

DELMORE SCHWARTZ

WHAT the sad and passionate gay player of Avon avowed
With vivid exactness, eloquent variety is, as immense
As the sea is. The sea which neither the humble nor the proud
Can dam, control, or master. No matter what our sense
Of existence, or whence we come or where we hope and seek
He knew us all before we were, he knew the strong, the weak,
The silly, the reticent, the pious, the powerful, the experience
Of fortune, sudden fame, extremes reversed, inevitable loss
Whether on land or sea. He knew mortality's immortality
And essential uncertainty, as he knew the land and sea.

He knew the reality of nobility.
He saw the cowering, towering power of treachery.
He hated the flakes and butterflies of lechery.
And he believed, at times, in truth, hope, loyalty, and charity.

See: he saw what was and what is and what has yet to come to be:
A gentle monarch murdered in helpless sleep.
A girl by Regent Hypocrisy seduced.
A child by Archduke Ambition stabbed and killed.
A loving loyal wife by a husband loyal and brave,
Falsely suspected, by a handkerchief accused,
Stabbed by his love, his innocence, his trust
In the glib cleverness of a self-hating knave.

Look: Ophelia lolls and babbles in the river named Forever,
Never Never Never Never Never.
Cordelia is out of breath and Lear
Has learned at last that flattery is clever
That words are free, sentiment inexpensive, vows
And declarations worthless and priceless: at last he knows
How true love is sometimes speechless, always sincere.
He knows — and knows too late — that love was very near and dear.

Are all hearts and all girls betrayed?
Is love never beyond lust, disgust, and distrust?
See: it is clear: Duncan is in his grave,
While Desdemona weeps beneath the willow tree,
Having been granted little time to weep, pray, or rave:
Is this the truth, the truth which is one, eternal and whole?
Surely the noble, the innocent, the gifted, and the brave
Sometimes – surely, at times – prevail. Yet if one living soul
Is caught by cruelty and killed by trust
Whence is our consolation above or before the grave?

Ripeness is all: the rest is silence. Love
Is all; we are such stuff as love has made us
And our little life, green, ripe, or rotten, is what it is
Because of love accepted, rejected, refused and jilted, faded, raided,
    neglected, or betrayed.
Some are defeated, some are mistreated, some are fulfilled, some
    come to flower and succeed
In knowing the patience of energy from the dark root to the
    rounding fruit.
And if this were not true, if love were not kind and cruel,
Generous and unjust, heartless and irresistible, painful to the
    savant and gentle to the fool,
Fecund and various, wasteful and precarious, lavish, savage, greedy
    and tender, begetting the lion and the lamb,
The peacock, the spaniel, the tiger, the lizard, the chicken hawk
    and the dove,
All would be nothing much, all would be trivial, nothing would be
    enough, love would not be love.
For, as there is no game and no victory when no one loses
So there is no choice but the choice of love, unless one chooses
Never to love, seeking immunity, discovering nothingness.

This is the only sanctuary, this is the one asylum unless
We hide in a dark ark, and deny, refuse to believe in hope's con-
    sciousness,
Deny hope's reality, until hope descends, in the unknown, hidden
    and ultimate love,

ON TRAGEDY: AND ON SHAKESPEARIAN TRAGEDY

Crying forever with all the others who are damned and hopeless
that *love is not love*.

Gold morning, sweet prince, black night has always descended and
has always ended,
Gold morning, prince of Avon, sovereign and king
Of reality, hope, and speech, may all the angels sing
With all the sweetness and all the truth with which you sang of
anything and everything.

from *Summer Knowledge: New and Selected Poems* 1938–1958

Suggestions for Further Reading

To keep this list from getting either too arbitrary, or too far out of control it includes only works that are concerned with Shakespeare.

S. L. BETHELL: *Shakespeare and the Popular Dramatic Tradition.* Relates the anti-realistic conventions of the Elizabethan stage to popular tradition; and traces these in Shakespeare's plays.

PATRICK CRUTTWELL: *The Shakespearian Moment.* Though not, except in passing, concerned with tragedy, this book is full of illumination for the reader of Shakespeare. It relates the qualities of seventeenth-century poetry to tensions in the social and intellectual background.

W. H. CLEMEN: *The Development of Shakespeare's Imagery.*

JOHN HOLLOWAY: *The Story of the Night.* Studies of the great tragedies, followed by a tentative attempt to suggest parallels from anthropology.

WALTER KAUFMANN: 'Goethe v. Shakespeare: Some Changes in Dramatic Sensibility' (in *Partisan Review,* 1952, and reprinted in *The New Partisan Reader,* 1945–53). Shakespeare's plays are not 'primarily psychological', but still mythological, still with some of the numinous quality of Greek tragedy; and 'the hero belongs to a world of which the other characters have no inkling'.

G. WILSON KNIGHT: *Principles of Shakespearian Production.* More balanced and coherent, and in its way quite as penetrating as the author's more famous books of Shakespeare criticism.

LAURENCE LERNER: 'Racine and the Elizabethans' (*Essays in Criticism,* October 1962).

A. SEWELL: *Character and Society in Shakespeare.*

FOR THE BEST IN PAPERBACKS, LOOK FOR THE

In every corner of the world, on every subject under the sun, Penguin represents quality and variety – the very best in publishing today.

For complete information about books available from Penguin – including Puffins, Penguin Classics and Arkana – and how to order them, write to us at the appropriate address below. Please note that for copyright reasons the selection of books varies from country to country.

In the United Kingdom: Please write to *Dept JC, Penguin Books Ltd, FREEPOST, West Drayton, Middlesex, UB7 0BR.*

If you have any difficulty in obtaining a title, please send your order with the correct money, plus ten per cent for postage and packaging, to *PO Box No 11, West Drayton, Middlesex*

In the United States: Please write to *Dept BA, Penguin, 299 Murray Hill Parkway, East Rutherford, New Jersey 07073*

In Canada: Please write to *Penguin Books Canada Ltd, 2801 John Street, Markham, Ontario L3R 1B4*

In Australia: Please write to the *Marketing Department, Penguin Books Australia Ltd, P.O. Box 257, Ringwood, Victoria 3134*

In New Zealand: Please write to the *Marketing Department, Penguin Books (NZ) Ltd, Private Bag, Takapuna, Auckland 9*

In India: Please write to *Penguin Overseas Ltd, 706 Eros Apartments, 56 Nehru Place, New Delhi, 110019*

In the Netherlands: Please write to *Penguin Books Netherlands B.V., Postbus 3507, NL–1001 AH, Amsterdam*

In West Germany: Please write to *Penguin Books Ltd, Friedrichstrasse 10–12, D–6000 Frankfurt/Main 1*

In Spain: Please write to *Alhambra Longman S.A., Fernandez de la Hoz 9, E–28010 Madrid*

In Italy: Please write to *Penguin Italia s.r.l., Via Como 4, I-20096 Pioltello (Milano)*

In France: Please write to *Penguin France S.A., 17 rue Lejeune, F-31000 Toulouse*

In Japan: Please write to *Longman Penguin Japan Co Ltd, Yamaguchi Building, 2–12–9 Kanda Jimbocho, Chiyoda-Ku, Tokyo 101*

NEW PENGUIN SHAKESPEARE

General Editor: T. J. B. Spencer

All's Well That Ends Well   Barbara Everett
Antony and Cleopatra   Emrys Jones
As You Like It   H. J. Oliver
The Comedy of Errors   Stanley Wells
Coriolanus   G. R. Hibbard
Hamlet   T. J. B. Spencer
Henry IV, Part 1   P. H. Davison
Henry IV, Part 2   P. H. Davison
Henry V   A. R. Humphreys
Henry VI, Part 1   Norman Sanders
Henry VI, Part 2   Norman Sanders
Henry VI, Part 3   Norman Sanders
Henry VIII   A. R. Humphreys
Julius Caesar   Norman Sanders
King John   R. L. Smallwood
King Lear   G. K. Hunter
Love's Labour's Lost   John Kerrigan
Macbeth   G. K. Hunter
Measure for Measure   J. M. Nosworthy
The Merchant of Venice   W. Moelwyn Merchant
The Merry Wives of Windsor   G. R. Hibbard
A Midsummer Night's Dream   Stanley Wells
Much Ado About Nothing   R. A. Foakes
Othello   Kenneth Muir
Pericles   Philip Edwards
The Rape of Lucrece   J. W. Lever
Richard II   Stanley Wells
Richard III   E. A. J. Honigmann
Romeo and Juliet   T. J. B. Spencer
The Sonnets and *A Lover's Complaint*   John Kerrigan
The Taming of the Shrew   G. R. Hibbard
The Tempest   Anne Righter (Anne Barton)
Timon of Athens   G. R. Hibbard
Troilus and Cressida   R. A. Foakes
Twelfth Night   M. M. Mahood
The Two Gentlemen of Verona   Norman Sanders
The Two Noble Kinsmen   N. W. Bawcutt
The Winter's Tale   Ernest Schanzer